Tessa

Peter & Susan

Gameelah

Maureen

Jennie & Bridget

Eele

Connie

Fiona

the HAIRY BIKERS'

Complete Mums know best!
xXx

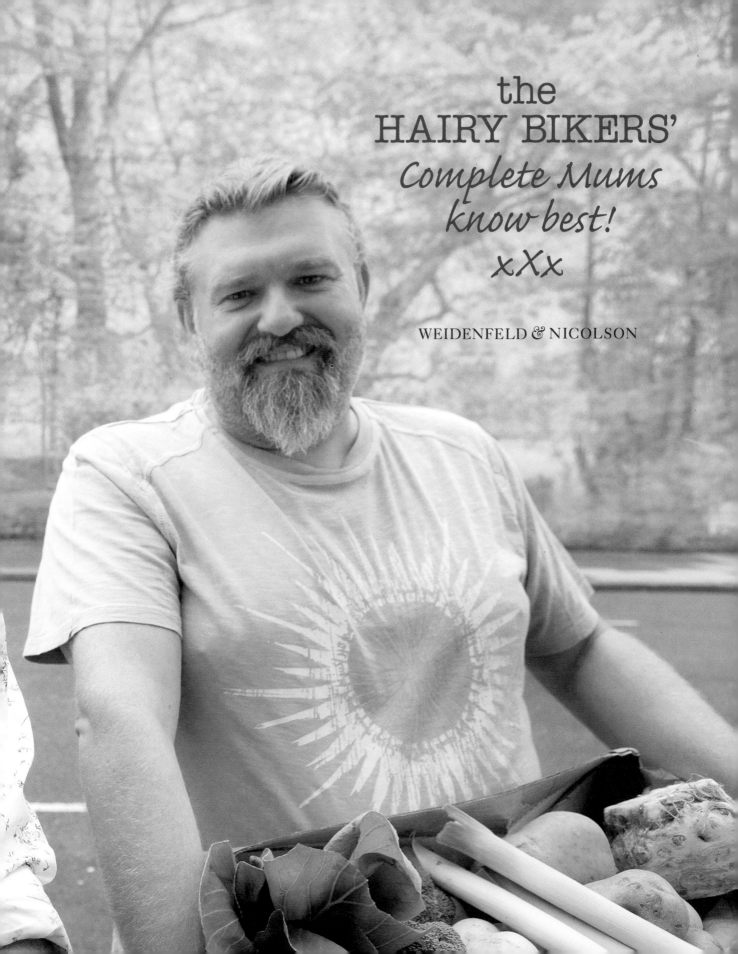

the
HAIRY BIKERS'
*Complete Mums
know best!*
xXx

WEIDENFELD & NICOLSON

We dedicate this book to our mams, **Stella** & **Margaret**, without whom it would not have been possible. And to mums everywhere – the world can't exist without you.

First published in hardback in Great Britain in 2010 and 2011 as *The Hairy Bikers' Family Cookbook: Mums Know Best* and *The Hairy Bikers' Best-Loved Recipes: Mums Still Know Best* by Weidenfeld & Nicolson as an imprint of the Orion Publishing Group Ltd
Orion House, 5 Upper St Martin's Lane, London WC2H 9EA
an Hachette UK Company

1 3 5 7 9 10 8 6 4 2

Photography by Cristian Barnett
Food styling by Sammy-Jo Squire (*The Hairy Bikers' Best-Loved Recipes: Mums Still Know Best*)
Designed by Kate Barr
Edited by Jinny Johnson
Index by Vicki Robinson

Printed in China

The Orion Publishing Group's policy is to use papers that are natural, renewable and recyclable and made from wood grown in sustainable forests. The logging and manufacturing processes are expected to conform to the environmental regulations of the country of origin.

www.orionbooks.co.uk

There's nothing better than sitting round the table with your nearest and dearest and enjoying a good meal.

Cooking is a huge part of family life and in every family, who knows best? Mum, of course! We learned lots of our favourite recipes from our own mums and we still cook and enjoy these dishes with our families today. All our favourites are included here – roast beef, fishcakes, blackberry and apple pie and other classics, as well as our own twists on new family treats, such as samosas and chicken Maryland.

Looking at our family recipes got us thinking and made us want to find out what secrets and treasures the nation's mums have hidden in their family recipe books and apron pockets. We invited everyone to tell us about their favourites and the response was fantastic. We've met so many great mums who've shared their family dishes with us and told us about their cooking traditions from many different heritages that have been handed down through generations. The best are in this book – fantastic feasts like Texas cornbread, Caribbean curried mutton, an Estonian pudding and a wealth of wonderful Indian curries.

We also organised some Recipe Fairs up and down the country and invited everyone and anyone to come along with family recipes, cooked dishes, favourite cooking tools and tips. We couldn't believe how many people turned up and shared their family favourites, including community groups such as the Bradford Curry Project, the WI and even some soldiers from a Gurkha regiment! We all had a cracking time and learned a lot about what families in Britain today like to eat.

All the recipes in this book are served up with a huge ladleful of love. They are dishes that we will cook time and time again and we hope you will too.

love Si & Dave

Family
favourites

BEER-BATTERED FISH

To make good battered fish, you need really fresh fish and oil at the perfect temperature to cook the batter. If the oil temperature is right, the fish will steam inside, forcing the fat out, and the batter will be super-light and crispy.

SERVES 4

1½ –2 litres sunflower oil,
for deep frying
4 tbsp plain flour
½ tsp fine sea salt
4 x 200g thick white fish fillets,
such as haddock or cod

BATTER

75g cornflour
200g plain flour
1 tsp fine sea salt
330ml bottle of real ale
2 tbsp white wine vinegar

First make the batter. Mix the cornflour, plain flour and salt together in a large bowl. Make a well in the centre and stir in the ale and vinegar. Beat with a large metal whisk to make a smooth batter. It should have the consistency of double cream.

Half fill a large deep saucepan with sunflower oil and heat the oil to 180°C. It's important to use a cooking thermometer and check the temperature regularly. Do not allow the oil to overheat and never leave the hot oil unattended. (Alternatively, use an electric deep-fat fryer heated to 180°C.)

Put the flour in a large plastic food bag and season with the salt. Add the fish fillets, one at a time, and shake to coat them in the seasoned flour.

When the oil has reached the right temperature, stir the batter well. Take one floured fish fillet and dip it in the batter until it is thoroughly coated. Lift it out with some tongs and gently drop it into the hot oil. Watch out for splashes as the oil will be extremely hot.

Do the same with a second fish fillet and cook it with the first for 5–6 minutes, depending on the thickness of the fillet, or until golden and crisp. Make sure the batter doesn't brown too quickly leaving the fish uncooked. Transfer the fish to a plate lined with kitchen paper to absorb any excess oil. Reheat the oil and cook the next two pieces of fish in exactly the same way. Serve with freshly cooked chips.

In fact, you can cook the fish in the same oil as the chips. Cook the fish after giving the chips their first fry, then keep the fish warm while you finish the chips.

THE BEST CHIPS EVER

The secret of good chips is to cook them twice at two different temperatures,
so you will need a deep pan and a thermometer for this recipe.

SERVES 4

4 large floury potatoes
2 litres sunflower oil, for deep frying
sea salt
malt vinegar

*For the best chips,
always use floury potatoes
with a good fibre content –
that is, more potato and
less water. Yukon Gold,
Nadine and Maris Piper
are all great, or try Cyprus
if you're feeling flush.*

Peel the potatoes and cut them into slices roughly 1cm thick.
Cut each slice into fairly thick chips and rinse them in a
colander under plenty of cold water to remove excess starch.
(If you have time, it's worth letting the chips soak in a bowl
of cold water for several hours or overnight.) Blot them dry
on kitchen paper.

Half fill a large deep saucepan with sunflower oil and heat to
130°C. It's important to use a cooking thermometer and check
the temperature regularly. Do not allow the oil to overheat and
never leave hot oil unattended. (We've learned that the fire
brigade are dead against this method of deep frying so if
possible, get yourself an electric deep-fat fryer.)

Gently drop half the chips into the hot oil and stir carefully
with a large metal spoon. Leave to fry for 10 minutes until
cooked through but not browned. Remove the chips with a
slotted spoon and drain on plenty of kitchen paper. Follow
the same method with the rest of the chips and drain well.
(The chips can be left for several hours at this stage.)

When ready to serve, reheat the oil to 190°C. Lower all the
chips gently into the pan and cook for 4–5 minutes until
crisp and golden brown. Lift them out with a slotted spoon
and drain on kitchen paper. Tip into a serving dish and
sprinkle with salt and vinegar to serve.

MINCED MEAT PLATE PIE

We have wonderful memories of this sort of pie, which both our mothers used to make – Dave's mam used to crimp the edges of the pastry with her false teeth! This really is a cut-and-come-again pie. You think you'll just have one more bit and suddenly there isn't enough left to feed a sparrow.

MAKES A PIE FOR A LARGE DINNER PLATE

FILLING
750g good-quality minced beef
2 onions, diced
1 beef stock cube
400ml boiling water
salt and pepper to taste, (heavy on the pepper)
butter, for greasing the plate
1 egg, beaten, for sealing the edge and glazing the top crust

SHORTCRUST PASTRY
450g plain flour
2 tsp baking powder
½ tsp salt
60g unsalted butter, diced
60g lard, diced
1 egg yolk

First make the pastry. Briefly mix the flour, baking powder and salt in a food processor. Add the butter, lard and egg yolk and process until the mixture forms crumbs. Gradually add up to 120ml of cold water until a ball of pastry miraculously appears. Alternatively, struggle on with a basin, your fingers and a spoon. Wrap the pastry in clingfilm and leave it to chill in the fridge for an hour so it's easier to roll out.

Meanwhile, make the filling. This is Si's mam's method and it worked for several decades, so give it a go. Preheat the oven to 180°C/Gas 4. Mix the mince with the onions in a casserole dish. Dissolve the beef stock cube in the water and pour this over the meat. Season well, going heavy on the pepper. Put the lid on the casserole dish and cook in the preheated oven for 30 minutes.

Then, take the lid off and leave the meat to cook until most of the liquid has evaporated and the flavour has developed. This will take about another 30 minutes. Remove from the oven and leave to cool.

Preheat the oven to 180°C/Gas 4. Grease the dinner plate with a splodge of butter. Roll out half the pastry and line the plate, then add the meat filling, leaving a good rim of pastry. Brush the edges of the pastry with the beaten egg. Roll out the rest of the pastry to make the lid and cover the meat, sealing the edges together well. Cut a couple of slashes in the pastry lid to let out the steam, brush with beaten egg and bake for about 30 minutes until the pastry is golden.

CHEESE PIE

Maureen Kirkland lives outside Glasgow. She learned to cook from her mum, taught her own children and now loves to cook with her grandchildren. This cheesy mash was a dish she always made when her children were poorly – it's real comfort food and a proper family tradition.

SERVES 6

700g potatoes
butter and milk
white pepper
550g mature white cheese, grated
55g fresh breadcrumbs

Peel the potatoes, cut them into chunks and boil in slightly salted water until soft. Drain well and mash with a large knob of butter and a little milk. Season with ground white pepper – white tastes better in mash than black. Add about one-third of the grated cheese and mix it in well. Preheat the oven to 180°C/Gas 4.

Now you need an ovenproof dish, about 5–7.5cm deep. Add half the mashed potato and top with half the remaining cheese. Season with more pepper and add the rest of the potato. Mix the rest of the cheese with the breadcrumbs and sprinkle over the top of the potato. Bake in the oven for 25–30 minutes until crisp and golden on top. Serve with some seasonal vegetables.

One variation is to soften a finely chopped onion in a small amount of olive oil and add this to the potato/cheese mixture. Or, 10 minutes before the end of the cooking time, top with a couple of sliced tomatoes.

CHILLI CON CARNE

When Maureen's children were little she used to cook a dish they always called beany mince – basically a way of eking out a bit of meat, but they loved it. As the children grew up and their tastes changed, the recipe got spicier and spicier until it evolved into a full-on chilli and now they all cook their own versions. This is the recipe Barry, Maureen's son, makes. And below is the beany mince where it all started.

SERVES 2

1 tbsp vegetable oil
250g minced beef
1 large onion, peeled and finely chopped
1 green and 1 red pepper, seeded and chopped
dash of Worcestershire sauce
2 small bird's eye chillies, chopped
couple of splashes of Tabasco sauce
1 x 400g can of chopped tomatoes
2 tbsp tomato purée
1 beef stock cube
2 limes
1–2 tbsp ground cumin
handful of fresh coriander, chopped
1 x 400g can of red kidney beans

Heat the oil in a large pan with a lid. Brown the beef, then add the onion, peppers, Worcestershire sauce, chillies, Tabasco, tomatoes and tomato purée. Crumble in the stock cube and add the juice of 1 lime and some ground cumin – start with one spoonful, taste and add another if you like. Season with salt and pepper and add a little of the chopped coriander.

Cover and simmer until the meat is ready – it will take about 45 minutes to an hour. Stir in the kidney beans and cook until they are warmed through, then add lots more chopped coriander. Garnish with extra chillies if you like. Wipe the serving dish with the juice of half a lime and serve with some lime slices. Dish up with rice or on top of lightly salted tortilla chips, open a cold beer and book a fire engine!

BEANY MINCE

And this is the junior version. Maureen serves it with pasta, rice, mash or wraps and some more veg – whatever's in the cupboard.

SERVES 3–4

1 tsp vegetable oil
225g minced beef
1 onion, peeled and finely chopped
110g carrots, finely chopped or grated
30–60g turnip or swede, peeled and finely chopped
1 generous tbsp tomato purée
1 x 415g can of baked beans

Heat the oil in a large pan with a lid. Brown the mince, then add the chopped onion and continue cooking until it has softened. Add the carrots and turnip or swede with up to 150ml boiling water. Don't add it all at once, as too much water makes the final dish sloppy. You can always add more if you need it.

Cover the pan and cook until the meat and veggies are done, then add the tomato purée and baked beans (including the liquid). Continue to cook until everything is heated through. Season lightly before serving.

RUMPY-PUMPY SOUP

Maureen used to make this red lentil soup for her children as a way of getting them to eat more veg without any fuss – she'd liquidise the soup so that they didn't know what was in it. Now, though, she prefers to leave the vegetables in chunks or she mashes them down with a potato masher. And in case you're wondering, in Maureen's family, rumpy-pumpy doesn't mean what you think it does. Her dad named the soup because of the well-known effects of lentils – they make you trump!

SERVES 6

about 2 litres ham stock
450g carrots, peeled and chopped
225g turnip or swede peeled and chopped
340g onions, finely chopped
any other 'secret' veggies, such as sprouts, leeks, finely chopped cabbage, even a can of chopped tomatoes
225g red lentils
salt and pepper

Best to make the stock the night before with a ham bone or hock so the flavour can develop.

Cook the vegetables in the ham stock until soft, then add the lentils. Stir frequently at this stage, as lentils can burn quite easily. If you have made the stock with a ham hock, remove any meat, chop it and add to the soup. Season to taste.

Maureen sometimes adds chunks of potato to cook in the soup to make it more filling, or stirs in 1–2 teaspoons of ground cumin to give it a curry flavour.

YELLOW SPLIT PEA & HAM SOUP

And here's our version. Make a big pan of this and let it moulder on for days.
It will taste better and better.

SERVES 6

2 tbsp vegetable oil
2 onions, peeled and diced
1 ham knuckle
500g yellow split peas
2 bay leaves
chopped parsley
salt and pepper

Heat the oil in a big pan. Add the onions and sweat until translucent, then add the ham knuckle, split peas, bay leaves, lots of pepper and a little salt. Go easy with the salt until the end because the knuckle will give out a lot of salt. Pour in about 2 litres of water and bring everything to the boil.

Simmer gently, skimming the scum off as necessary, for about 2 hours. By this time, the peas will have 'dropped' – that is, gone all mushy. Remove the knuckle and as soon as it is cool enough, shred off the meat and add it to the soup.

When you have stripped the meat from the bone, put the bone back in the soup to steep and enrich the flavours.

Put the bone back in too, reheat the soup and check the seasoning. Serve with crusty bread and parsley sprinkles if the vicar is coming for his tea.

TANDOORI CHICKEN SAMOSAS

This is a fantastic recipe we got off a fella we met on a train in Goa.
He swore blind that his mother used to make it all the time. It might look like a lot of work
but you can make the filling in advance and then fill and cook the samosas when you're ready.
Dead easy really and well worth it. Give it a go and spice up your life.

MAKES 10–12

FILLING

1 tbsp tandoori paste
1 tbsp yoghurt
2 chicken breasts
2 medium potatoes, peeled
2 tbsp vegetable oil
1 small onion, very finely diced
½ tsp ground turmeric
2 tsp garam masala
1 tsp mustard seeds
½ tsp ground black pepper
1 tsp salt
4 cloves garlic, crushed
1 green chilli (or half if you don't like things too hot!)
10 curry leaves
75g frozen peas
1 tsp lemon juice
handful of coriander leaves, chopped
more vegetable oil, for deep frying

Mix the tandoori paste with the yoghurt. Put the chicken breasts in a bowl, cover them with the yoghurt mixture and leave in the fridge to marinate for an hour.

Meanwhile, make the pastry. Place the flour in a bowl and stir in the salt. Work in the oil and the egg yolk until the mixture has a crumb-like texture. (Keep the egg white for later when you assemble the samosas.)

Gradually mix in the warm (blood-temperature) water to form a stiff elastic dough, adding more or less water to get a workable texture. Wrap the dough in clingfilm and put it in the fridge to chill while you make the filling.

Preheat the oven to 190°C/Gas 5. Put the marinated chicken in a baking dish and bake in the oven for about 20 minutes or until just cooked through. Leave to cool, then chop into tiny chunks. All of this can be done ahead of time if you like.

Boil the potatoes whole for about 15 minutes or until tender. Drain and set them aside to cool, then dice finely.

Heat the 2 tablespoons of oil in a frying pan and sweat the onion until soft but not brown. Add the turmeric, garam masala, mustard seeds, black pepper and salt and cook for a minute. Then add the garlic and chilli and sauté for another 2 minutes. Add the curry leaves to the pan and cook for a further minute.

PASTRY
250g plain flour
1 tsp salt
1 dsrtsp vegetable oil
1 egg, separated
9 tbsp warm water

Add the diced potato and mix well, but gently, into the spices and cook over a low heat for another 10 minutes to release all the flavours into the potatoes. Add the peas and cook gently for 2–3 minutes. Finally, fold in the chicken, add the lemon juice and chopped coriander and check the seasoning. Set the filling aside to get cold.

ASSEMBLING THE SAMOSAS
Roll out the pastry to about 3mm – not too thin, but not too thick. Take a side plate and press it onto the pastry to make an impression. Cut round the impression with a knife to make a circle, then cut this in half. Take one half and make a cone. Make sure the edges of the cone overlap, then use your fingers to squash the edges gently together to seal them.

Spoon the filling into the cone until it is about three-quarters full – do not overfill. Brush the top edge with egg white and, using your fingers, pinch the edges together to seal in the filling. Repeat until you have used up all the filling.

Heat the oil to a gentle rumble and deep fry the samosas for about 5 minutes until they are golden and crunchy. Serve with some chutney and raita.

TRADITIONAL SAMOSAS

Gameelah Ghafoor from Dundee cooked us some amazing food. Her dad is from Yemen and her mother is Scottish, so she grew up eating food from both traditions. Dad's specialities were curries and samosas, while mum showed her how to make stovies and stews. Gameelah has brought both cultures together to create family favourites in her own special style. Her dad has a neat trick with samosas. Instead of making pastry, he uses tortillas to wrap the filling and this is the way Gameelah cooked them for us.

2 tbsp vegetable oil, such as sunflower
1 onion, peeled and finely chopped
½ tsp chopped garlic
½ tsp grated root ginger
1 tsp cumin seeds
1 tsp coriander seeds
1 rounded tbsp curry paste (any kind)
1 tsp garam masala
500g minced beef
1 potato, peeled and diced small
16 tortillas
1 egg, beaten, to seal the tortilla

Heat the oil in a large frying pan and add the chopped onion. Once the onion is soft, add the garlic and ginger. Grind the cumin and coriander seeds and add them to the pan with the curry paste and garam masala. Fry this mixture for 2 minutes, then add the mince. Once the mince is browned, add the diced potato and pour in a little boiling water to allow the potato to cook. Let everything simmer until the potato is soft and the water has reduced.

Cut the tortillas in half, then cut each half into long strips the width of four fat fingers. Put the smaller side of the tortilla next to you and place your finger in the middle of the bottom side. Keeping your finger in place, diagonally fold over the bottom right side to the top to make a kite shape. Do the same with the other side. Brush egg onto the folds of the tortilla to help the sides stick together. Lift up the tortilla and make a cone shape, then add some filling.

Lay the filled tortilla down, brush the flap at the top with beaten egg and fold it over to make a triangle. Turn it flap-side down on the work surface and gently press to seal. Pinch the points of the tortilla to make sure the filling does not come out. Continue filling tortillas in the same way until all the mixture is used up.

Heat some oil in a large pan or deep-fat fryer to about 160°C if the filling is cold and to 180°C if the filling is already hot. Fry the samosas for a couple of minutes, turning them once, until they are golden brown on each side. Don't overcrowd the pan – just cook 3 or 4 at a time. Eat and enjoy!

VEGGIE SAMOSAS

This is a favourite variation in Gameelah's household.

1 tbsp sunflower oil
½ onion, peeled and finely diced
½ tsp chopped garlic
¼ tsp turmeric
¼ tsp chilli flakes
100g mushrooms, chopped
100g peeled prawns
100g petit pois
1 red pepper, finely diced
100g rice
soy sauce, to taste

Heat the oil in a saucepan and fry the onion and garlic until softened. Stir in the turmeric and chilli flakes and fry for another 2 minutes. Then add the mushrooms, prawns, peas and red pepper and continue to cook for 2 minutes.

Stir in the rice. Add about 250ml of hot water, bring to the boil and cover the pan. Simmer over a low heat until the rice is done. Splash on some soy sauce and use this mixture to fill the samosas as before.

OTHER FILLINGS TO TRY

Haggis

Mushroom risotto

Prawn, spinach, onion, garlic, ginger and chilli

Chickpea, spinach, onion, garlic, chilli, cumin, coriander

Black pudding

MINCE & DUMPLINGS

**This is something we both loved as kids – and still do. If you want
your dumplings golden, take the lid off the pan 10 minutes before the end
of the cooking time so that they crisp up, or finish them off under the grill**

SERVES 6

2 tbsp sunflower oil
1 large onion, halved and thinly sliced
2 garlic cloves, peeled
and finely chopped
2 celery sticks, stringed
and finely sliced
2 medium carrots, peeled and diced
500g lean minced beef
1 x 400g can of chopped tomatoes
2 tbsp tomato purée
350ml beef stock (fresh or from a cube)
150ml red wine
pinch of caster sugar
1 bay leaf
salt and freshly ground black pepper

DUMPLINGS
250g self-raising flour
125g shredded beef suet
½ tsp fine sea salt
2 tbsp finely chopped fresh parsley

Heat the oil in a large saucepan or flameproof casserole
dish. Cook the onion, garlic, celery and carrots for
15 minutes, stirring occasionally, until they begin to
soften and lightly colour. Add the beef and cook with
the vegetables for another 5 minutes until the mince
is no longer pink. Stir regularly to break up the meat.

Add the tomatoes, tomato puree, beef stock, red wine,
sugar and bay leaf. Season with a good pinch of salt and
plenty of black pepper. Bring to the boil, then reduce the
heat and simmer gently for 20 minutes, stirring occasionally.

To make the dumplings, put the flour in a bowl and stir
in the suet, salt and parsley. Make a well in the centre and
add enough cold water – you'll need about 200ml – to make
a soft, spongy dough. Lightly flour your hands and roll the
dumpling mixture into 12 small balls.

Stir the mince well and remove it from the heat. Drop
the dumplings carefully on top of the mince. Cover with
a tight-fitting lid and return to a medium heat. Cook for
18–20 minutes or until the dumplings are well risen
and light.

BOILED LEEK & ONION PUDDING
WITH COLD CUTS & GRAVY

This is Si's mam's recipe for a mid-week family filler. Fantastic with cold cuts and leftover gravy.

SERVES 6

25g butter, plus extra for greasing
1 tbsp sunflower oil
1 medium onion, finely chopped
2 slender leeks, trimmed
and finely sliced
150g fresh white breadcrumbs
200g self-raising flour, plus
extra for dusting
115g shredded beef suet
1 heaped tsp fine sea salt
freshly ground black pepper
1 large free-range egg
75ml whole milk
cold roast meat and hot gravy, to serve

Melt the butter with the oil in a large frying pan. Gently fry the onion and leeks for 5 minutes or until well softened, stirring regularly. Remove from the heat and set them aside to cool for a few minutes.

Mix the breadcrumbs, flour, suet, salt and plenty of freshly ground black pepper in a large bowl. Stir in the onion and leeks. Beat together the egg and milk. Stir into the dry ingredients until well combined – the dough should feel light and spongy. Turn the dough out onto a floured board, knead very lightly and form into a large ball.

Half fill a large saucepan with water and bring to the boil. Sprinkle flour liberally over a large piece of clean sheeting, or a thin drying-up cloth. (An old pillow case can also be cut to size for this job.) Place the pudding on the sheet and gather up the sides. Leave room for expansion, then tie tightly with kitchen string to seal the parcel.

Lower the pudding gently and carefully into the boiling water, cover with a lid and boil for 1 hour. By this time, the pudding should be well risen and light. Check the water level now and then while it's boiling and top up if necessary. (Alternatively, put the pudding in a 1.5-litre basin lined with buttered baking parchment. Cover with pleated parchment and foil and tie it tightly with string. Steam the pudding on a trivet in a deep saucepan half filled with boiling water for about 2 hours.)

Turn off the heat and lift the pudding carefully from the water using tongs. Take great care as the water will be very hot. Put the pudding on a board and leave it to cool for a few minutes before snipping off the string and transferring the pud to a serving dish. Serve in wedges with cold roast meat and a jug of steaming hot gravy.

STEAK & KIDNEY PUDDING

We agree that a proper steak and kidney pudding is one of life's great pleasures –
a real family treat. Just make sure you trim the meat carefully and core and trim
the kidneys so you don't have any nasty chewy bits spoiling your fun.

SERVES 6

700g braising steak, well marbled
with fat
3 very fresh lambs' kidneys
3 tbsp plain flour
4–5 tbsp sunflower oil
1 medium onion, chopped
200ml red wine
4–5 sprigs of fresh thyme
1 bay leaf
500ml good beef stock
1 tbsp tomato purée
fine sea salt and black pepper

SUET PASTRY

350g self-raising flour
175g shredded suet
½ tsp fine sea salt
butter, for greasing

Trim the beef of any thick fat or tough bits of gristle and cut
into cubes of about 2.5cm. Rinse the kidneys and pat them
dry with kitchen paper. Snip out the white cores and cut the
kidneys into 1.5cm chunks. Put the steak and kidneys in
a large, strong plastic bag. Add the flour, salt and plenty of
black pepper. Knot the top of the bag and shake until the
meat is well coated in the seasoned flour. Preheat the oven
to 170°C/Gas 3.

Heat 2 tablespoons of the oil in a large non-stick frying pan
and fry the steak and kidneys over a medium heat until well
browned all over. You'll need to do this in a few batches so
you don't overcrowd the pan, so add an extra tablespoon or
two of oil if the pan gets dry. Transfer the meat to a flameproof
casserole dish as it is browned. Return the pan to the heat and
add the remaining oil, then the onion. Cook over a low heat
for 5 minutes or until softened, stirring often. Stir the onion
into the casserole dish with the steak and kidneys.

Deglaze the frying pan with the wine, bringing it to the boil
while stirring hard to lift all the sediment from the bottom
of the pan. Pour immediately over the meat and onions. Strip
the thyme leaves from the stalks and add them to the casserole
dish. Stir in the bay leaf, beef stock and tomato purée. Bring
everything to the boil, then cover and cook in the oven for
1½–2 hours or until the meat is tender. Give it a stir halfway
through the cooking time. Take out 3 ladlefuls of the sauce
and set aside to use for gravy later – once cool, this can be
kept in the fridge until needed.

When the meat is done, take the dish out of the oven and
place it on the hob. Simmer, uncovered, for 2–3 minutes or
until the sauce is thick enough to coat the beef generously.
The sauce needs to be thick enough not to run out over
the plate when the pudding is cut, but not too thick or the
pudding will taste dry. Take off the heat and leave to cool.

To make the suet pastry, put the flour in a large bowl and stir in the suet and salt. Stir in enough water to make soft, spongy dough – you'll probably need about 300ml. Turn the dough out onto a floured surface and bring it together to form a ball. Knead lightly, then remove a generous quarter of the dough to make a lid for the pudding and roll the rest into a circle measuring about 25cm (the size of an average dinner plate). It should be about 1cm thick.

Use this to line a well-buttered 1.5-litre pudding basin with the pastry level resting at about 1cm below the top edge of the dish. Press well against the sides of the basin and trim neatly, then pile in the cooled steak and kidney mixture. Brush the top edge of the pastry with water. Roll the remaining pastry into a round just large enough to sit on top of the pastry edge and place over the filling. Trim into place and press the edges together to seal.

Cover the dish with a large circle of baking parchment, with a pleat in the middle to allow for expansion. Cover the parchment with a circle of foil, again with a pleat. Tie both tightly in place with string. Create a carrying handle by tying the excess string across the top of the basin – this will help you lift the pudding once it's cooked.

Place on an upturned saucer or a small trivet in a large deep saucepan and add enough just-boiled water to come halfway up the sides of the basin. (Alternatively, cook in a hob-top steamer.) Cover the pan with a tight-fitting lid and place over a medium heat. Allow to steam in simmering water for 2½ hours, adding more hot water when necessary.

When the pudding is done, turn off the heat and carefully lift the basin from the water. Leave it to stand for 5 minutes. Take the sauce that you set aside earlier and heat it in a small pan until bubbling – keep stirring it so it doesn't stick and burn. Strain it through a small sieve into a warmed jug.

Cut the string, foil and paper off the basin. Loosen the sides of the pudding with a blunt-ended knife and turn the pudding out onto a deep plate. What a sight! Serve in generous wedges with hot gravy for pouring.

A nice touch is to mix 2 teaspoons of dried mixed herbs into the suet pastry. As the pud steams, they will give the suet crust a lovely herby flavour.

Take great care when taking the pudding out of the pan and removing the covers. The bowl will be scalding hot!

CRUMPETS

Home-made crumpets are a million miles away from the rubbery packet versions.
They're as easy to make as they look, so make a big batch and toast as required.

MAKES 12

350ml whole milk
225g strong white flour
125g plain flour
7g sachet fast-action dried yeast
½ tsp fine sea salt
1 tsp caster sugar
1 level tsp bicarbonate of soda
150ml warm water
softened butter, for greasing the rings

Put the milk in a saucepan and warm it very gently until tepid. Sift the flours into a large bowl and stir in the yeast, salt and sugar. Make a well in the centre and stir in the warm milk. Beat well with a wooden spoon for 3–4 minutes until the batter is thick and elastic. Cover with clingfilm and leave to rise in a warm place for an hour or until doubled in size.

Mix the bicarbonate of soda with the warm water. Beat this into the batter for a couple of minutes and leave to rest in a warm place for a further 30 minutes. By this time, the batter should look risen and be covered with tiny bubbles. Heat a flat griddle pan or large heavy-based non-stick frying pan over a medium-high heat.

Generously butter the insides of 4 crumpet rings or 9cm chef's rings and place them on the griddle or in the frying pan. Warm for a minute or two. Using a dessertspoon, drop 3 large spoonfuls of the crumpet batter into each ring. It should come about 1.5cm up the sides of each ring, but no more. Cook for 9–12 minutes or until lots of tiny bubbles have risen to the surface and burst and the tops look dry and set. Carefully lift off the rings – this shouldn't be too difficult as the crumpets will ease back from the sides when they are ready. (Use an oven cloth and take care as they will be hot.)

Flip the crumpets over with a spatula and cook on the other side for 2 minutes or until golden brown. You can keep these crumpets warm while the remaining batter is prepared, or serve immediately spread with lots of butter. Cook the rest of the crumpets in exactly the same way as the first, washing and buttering the rings well before using each time. (The crumpets can also be cooled and then toasted.)

When you make the last few crumpets, you may find that the batter has thickened and the bubbles take longer to burst. If this happens, prick each one lightly with a cocktail stick.

LEMON DRIZZLE CAKE

This is dead easy to make and really tasty. It's the one cake that the soggier it is, the better.

SERVES 10

2 small unwaxed lemons, well scrubbed
275g granulated sugar
175g unsalted butter, softened, plus
extra for greasing the tin
200g self-raising flour
½ tsp baking powder
3 large free-range eggs

Preheat the oven to 180°C/Gas 4. Line the base of a 900g (2lb) non-stick loaf tin with baking parchment and butter the tin well. Finely grate the zest of the lemons. Put 175g of the sugar in a food processor with the butter, flour, baking powder, eggs and lemon zest and blend on the pulse setting until the mixture is just combined and has a thick, smooth texture.

Spoon the cake batter into the prepared tin and level the surface. Bake for 35 minutes or until well risen and pale golden brown. Remove from the oven and cool in the tin for 5 minutes. Squeeze one of the lemons to get about 3 tablespoons of juice and mix this with the remaining 100g of granulated sugar.

Turn the cake out onto a wire rack set above a tray or plate. Remove the baking parchment and gently turn the cake the right way up. Make about 50 deep holes in the top of the cake with a skewer.

Slowly and gradually, spoon over half the lemon sugar, allowing it to thoroughly coat the top of the cake and drizzle down the sides. Leave the cake to stand for 5 minutes, then do the same with the remaining lemon sugar. Leave to set for at least an hour or until the sugar and lemon has crystallised. Serve the cake in thick slices with a nice cup of tea.

BUTTERFLY CAKES

Aida Grier and her daughter Victoria are amazingly talented bakers. We visited them
at their home in Perthshire and they put on an incredible spread for us. They're both
passionate about cooking and everything was really scrumptious – we had the best time.
Their recipes are brilliant, and things like the empire biscuits are dead easy for kids to make.

MAKES 12

110g baking margarine
110g caster sugar
110g beaten egg
110g self-raising flour

TOPPING
110g butter, room temperature
110g icing sugar, plus extra for dusting
grated zest of 1 orange
1 jar of orange curd

You will need a 12-hole bun tin, lined with paper cake cases.
Preheat the oven to 190°C/Gas 5.

Cream the margarine and sugar until light in colour, then
gradually add the beaten egg. Gently fold in the flour. Spoon
the mixture into the cake cases and bake for 12–15 minutes.
Turn the cakes out onto a wire rack and leave them to cool.

Cut the top off each cake and set aside. To make the butter
icing, mix the butter with the icing sugar and zest. Put half a
teaspoon of orange curd on each cake and top with a teaspoon
of butter icing. Cut the tops in half to make butterfly wing
shapes and add them to each cake. Dust with icing sugar.
For birthdays and parties, sprinkle with a little edible glitter.

You can use lemon curd instead of orange and add lemon zest
to the butter icing.

MRS MILLER'S EMPIRE BISCUITS

Mrs Miller is a lifelong friend of Aida's and a baking inspiration. Her cakes are legendary in the area.

MAKES 12

170g plain flour, plus extra for
sprinkling the baking tray
170g butter, room temperature
55g icing sugar
55g cornflour
1 pot of seedless raspberry jam
icing (optional)
glacé cherries (optional)

Preheat the oven to 190°C/Gas 5. Sprinkle a large baking tray
with flour. Mix all the ingredients together with your hands
until the mixture forms a soft dough. Roll it out to about 1cm
thick and cut into circles with a scone cutter. Place the biscuits
on the baking tray and bake for 10–12 minutes. The secret of
getting these biscuits perfect is to watch them carefully while
they are in the oven and remove them as soon as they are firm
to the touch but still pale. Leave them to cool on a wire rack.

When they are cool, sandwich the biscuits together with
raspberry jam and top with icing and a cherry if you like.

BRAN LOAF

Aida says that this works equally well with oat or wheat bran. The fat content can be lessened by using low-fat milk, making it a great low-cholesterol treat.

MAKES 1 LOAF

1 mug of bran
1 mug of soft brown sugar
1 mug of sultanas or other dried fruit
1 mug of full-fat milk
1 mug of self-raising flour

Mix the bran, sugar, sultanas and milk together in a bowl with a wooden spoon and leave to soak overnight. The next day, grease and line a small (450g) loaf tin and preheat the oven to 180°C/Gas 4. Stir the flour into the bran mixture, then place the dough in the loaf tin and bake for 45–50 minutes until firm to the touch. This loaf keeps well in a tin for a week to 10 days, ideal if baking for one!

ROCKY ROAD

This is so easy to make and tastes wonderful. Aida says she uses large fluffy marshmallows and leaves them whole – more of a boulder road really!

3 Mars bars
100g butter
5 shortbread fingers
140g marshmallows
50g Rice Krispies

Chop up the Mars bars and place them in a small pan with the butter. Melt over a gentle heat. Break the shortbread into chunks and stir into the mixture with the marshmallows and Rice Krispies. Press the mixture into a lightly oiled 15cm-square tin and leave to set in the fridge. When set, cut into squares, turn them out upside down and serve.

MILLIONAIRE'S SHORTBREAD

This is a truly decadent treat so don't skimp on the chocolate. Enjoy!

BASE
125g butter, room temperature
50g caster sugar
175g plain flour

TOPPING
400g condensed milk
50g butter
50g soft brown sugar
150g of your favourite chocolate

Mix the butter, sugar and flour to form a dough. Press this into a greased 23cm-square cake tin and bake at 190°C/Gas 5 for 20 minutes. Leave to cool.

Meanwhile, make the topping. Pour the milk into a heavy-bottomed pan and add the butter and sugar. Bring to the boil and then boil gently for 5 minutes, stirring continuously so the mixture doesn't stick. Pour the topping over the shortbread and place in the fridge to set. Once the topping has set, melt the chocolate in a bowl over a pan of simmering water and pour it over the topping. Leave to set again and cut into squares.

FOUGASSE À L'ANCHOIS

François Gandolfi, one of our directors, gave us this recipe. This is what he told us about it: 'This is a version of a popular Provençal snack called anchoïade, which is a paste made of anchovies, onion or garlic and olive oil into which you dip raw vegetables. Then someone decided that the paste would be nice spread on bread and to make this more child-friendly my mum transformed it into a kind of garlic bread with a twist. Rachel, my wife, loves it but she has changed the recipe a little. Here are both versions – frankly, I prefer my wife's, but don't tell my mum! The dough is the same in both – it's a traditional focaccia dough, but you can use a pizza-type dough instead. For both recipes, use anchovies in olive oil rather than those in salt or brine.'

SERVES 6

DOUGH
2 tbsp olive oil
450g strong white flour
1 tsp salt
7g dried yeast
275ml water

MUM'S ANCHOÏADE
12 anchovies in oil
1 onion, peeled and roughly chopped
4 tbsp olive oil

RACHEL'S ANCHOÏADE
1 x 60g jar of anchovies in oil
2 large garlic cloves, peeled
10 green olives
2 tbsp olive oil
(use the oil from the jar of anchovies)

Mix all the dough ingredients in a large bowl to make a smooth but sticky dough. Leave it to rise for 30 minutes and knead again for about 10 minutes. Alternatively, put everything in a bread machine and let that do the work for you!

Roll the dough out into 2 large ovals and cut several slashes in each one with a knife – these make it easier to tear the fougasse apart. Leave the dough to rest again for at least 45 minutes while you make the anchoïade. Preheat the oven to 200°/Gas 6.

For mum's anchoïade, use a pestle and mortar to mash all the ingredients into a paste. For Rachel's recipe, use a hand-held blender to mix everything into a smooth paste. Spread the paste over the dough. It will be a thin layer, but the taste is strong so you don't need much. Place the fougasse on a baking tray and bake for 15–20 minutes – take care that they don't dry out too much.

Drizzle a little olive oil on top and enjoy with a glass of cold rosé wine. Best eaten as a snack with drinks or with a simple soup, as the strong anchovy flavour overpowers most other tastes.

CHEESE NIBBLES

Duncan Barnes, our other director, sent us this recipe and the one below from his mum. She describes them as simple but great to nibble with coffee and a chat, and says she must have made thousands over the years.

MAKES ABOUT 30

170g self-raising flour
110g soft margarine
½ tsp mustard or horseradish (optional)
170g strong cheese, such as mature Cheddar, grated

Preheat the oven to 190°C/Gas 5. Put the flour, margarine and mustard or horseradish (if using) into a bowl and mix until it has the texture of breadcrumbs. Add the cheese and mix again with your hands.

Take a large teaspoon of the mixture, make it into a little ball with your fingers and place on a large baking tray. Continue until all the mixture is used up, taking care to leave space between each one. Bake in the oven for 10–12 minutes until golden. Remove from the oven and immediately take the nibbles off the baking tray with a fish slice or palette knife or they will stick. Place them on a wire rack and eat warm or cold. If you like, you can put an olive, date or peanut into each one before baking as a little surprise for the eater.

COFFEE KISSES

Tasty nuggets of coffee cookies – just right with a cup of tea in the afternoon.

MAKES ABOUT 24

170g self-raising flour
85g butter or margarine
55g white sugar
1 egg yolk or very small whole egg
1 large tsp liquid coffee (or dissolve 1 tsp instant coffee in boiling water)

In a large bowl, mix the flour, butter and sugar until the mixture has a breadcrumb-like texture. Add the egg and coffee and mix again to make a firm dough.

Preheat the oven to 190°C/Gas 5. Take teaspoons of the mixture and roll into small balls with your hands. Place the balls on a baking sheet, leaving space between each one as they will spread, and bake for 15 minutes. Remove and place on a wire rack to cool.

ICING

55g very soft butter
120g icing sugar, more if needed
few drops of vanilla essence
icing sugar (optional)

Meanwhile, make the butter icing. Put the soft butter in a bowl and beat in enough icing sugar to make a thick butter cream icing. Add the vanilla essence. When the cookies are cold, spread half of them with butter cream and top with the rest to make sandwiches. Dust with icing sugar if you like.

WOMEN'S INSTITUTE

The WI movement began in Canada in 1897. The first British Women's Institute was formed in 1915 with two main aims: to provide education and to improve the quality of rural life, and it led to women playing a major part in the First World War. Since then, the aims have broadened and it is now the largest women's organisation in the UK. In 2005, the British WI celebrated its 90th anniversary and there are currently 205,000 members in 6,500 WIs. Members from the North Yorkshire West Federation visited the Mums Know Best recipe fair and provided these recipes.

LEMON, GINGER & BLUEBERRY FLAN

This simple but delicious pudding takes a while to set, so make it the night before serving if possible.

SERVES 6–8

150g ginger biscuits
50g butter, melted
500ml double cream
150g caster sugar
juice and grated zest of 2 lemons
150g blueberries
fresh mint leaves and icing sugar for garnish

Put the ginger biscuits in a plastic bag and crush them into crumbs with a rolling pin. Add the melted butter, mix well and use the mixture to line a loose-bottomed 20cm flan tin. Press it down firmly. Pour the cream into a small saucepan and add the sugar and the lemon zest. Bring to the boil and continue to boil for 3–4 minutes, watching carefully.

Remove from the heat and stir in the lemon juice. Strain the mixture through a fine sieve to remove the lemon zest and leave to cool for a few minutes. Spread the blueberries over the prepared flan base, reserving some for decoration, and pour in the cream mixture. Allow to set in the fridge. Before serving, decorate the top with blueberries, mint leaves and a dusting of icing sugar.

A NEW LOOK
AT SCONES

If the WI doesn't know how to make a good scone, no one does. Here's a great
recipe for the perfect tea time treat – the yoghurt helps the scones to rise.

MAKES 12–14

340g self-raising flour
pinch of salt
85g butter, plus extra for greasing
55g caster sugar
125ml milk
4 tbsp natural yoghurt

Preheat the oven to 220°C/Gas 7 and lightly grease a baking
sheet. Sift together the flour and salt into a bowl and rub
in the butter until the mixture resembles fine breadcrumbs.
Stir in the sugar and add the milk and yoghurt. Work the
mixture together until a soft dough is formed.

Turn the dough out onto a floured surface and knead lightly,
then flatten it out to an even thickness of about 2cm. Using a
5cm cutter, cut out the scones and place them on the baking
tray. Gather the trimmings and cut out more scones.

Bake for 12–15 minutes until brown. Remove the scones from
the oven and leave them to cool on a wire rack.

To make savoury scones, replace the caster sugar with 55g
of grated Cheddar cheese and half a teaspoon of mustard
powder. Prepare and bake the scones in the same way.

Show-off food

CHICKEN IN BRANDY

Muriel Bell is a lovely lady who lives in Tenbury Wells in Worcestershire. Her mum
was in service in a big house and Muriel still has her book of recipes, all hand-written.
Muriel's chicken is a super-rich treat – good for entertaining and a real show-off dish.

SERVES 6

splash of olive oil
30g butter
6 chicken breasts
1 red onion, finely diced
100ml good brandy
170g white button mushrooms, wiped
and trimmed
100ml double cream
sea salt and black pepper

Preheat the oven to 150°C/Gas 2. Heat the olive oil and butter
in a large frying pan. Add the chicken breasts and cook briefly
to seal in the juices. Add the diced onion and cook until
translucent but not coloured.

Remove the pan from the heat. Warm the brandy, pour it into
the pan and ignite, then wait for the flames to die down. Add
the mushrooms, pour over the cream and season well.

Transfer everything to an ovenproof dish and cover with foil.
Bake in the preheated oven for about an hour. Serve with some
rich mustard mash.

MUSTARD MASH

SERVES 6

1kg potatoes, peeled and quartered
75ml single cream
50g butter
2 tbsp grain mustard
sea salt and black pepper

Put the potatoes into a pan of salted water, bring to the boil
and poach them for about 20 minutes until soft – poaching
the potatoes rather than boiling them makes a fluffier mash.
Warm the cream in a separate pan.

When the potatoes are cooked, drain them well and return
them to the pan to drive off any excess moisture, then mash.
Add the warm cream, butter and mustard and mix well.
Season to taste.

LEMON SOUFFLÉ

This is one of Muriel's mum's recipes. Princess Margaret used to visit the house where she worked and this was one of the princess's favourite dishes, which she'd ask to be made specially. In fact, this is not really a soufflé, despite the name. It's a set pudding and more like a mousse.

SERVES 4–6

14g sachet of gelatine
2 medium eggs, separated
200g caster sugar
juice and grated zest of 2 large lemons
300ml double cream, plus extra for garnish
100g hazelnuts or mixed nuts, chopped
100g green grapes, halved

Lightly grease a soufflé dish. Take a piece of greaseproof paper and tie it around the dish to make a collar standing about 5cm above the rim. Make sure it's tied really tightly.

To prepare the gelatine, pour 4 tablespoons of very hot water into a bowl and sprinkle in the gelatine. Place the bowl over a pan of hot water until the gelatine has dissolved. Leave to cool slightly.

Whisk the egg yolks and sugar together until thick and creamy and add the lemon zest and juice. Pour in the cooled gelatine mixture and mix gently but thoroughly.

Whisk the cream to the 'floppy' stage. In a separate bowl, whisk the egg whites until they form stiff peaks. Fold the cream into the yolk and gelatine mixture, then fold in the egg whites.

Pour the mixture into the soufflé dish – it should fill to above the rim but be held by the greaseproof collar. Leave the pudding to set in the fridge for about 2 hours. When ready to serve, remove the collar and decorate with chopped nuts, gently pressing them onto the sides above the dish. Finish the top with whipped cream and halved grapes.

For an extra-special touch, add some crystallised lemon zest as shown in the picture opposite. Remove some fine strips of lemon zest with a zester and blanch them briefly in boiling water. Drain well and leave to dry. Put them in a bowl with a few tablespoons of caster sugar and toss well. Leave overnight.

PROPER PRAWN COCKTAIL

This is a culinary old faithful and an absolute must as a starter in the King household on Christmas Day. Make your own mayonnaise, get great seafood and tuck in. Use whatever sort of prawns you like, even frozen ones, in individual cocktails or make one big posh lobster cocktail (as pictured opposite) for a really spectacular effect. It might all look a bit camp, but it tastes wonderful.

SERVES 4

500g prawns
4 tbsp home-made mayonnaise
2 tsp tomato ketchup
1 tsp tomato purée
dash of Tabasco sauce
1 tsp salad cream
1 tsp lemon juice
4 little gem lettuces, shredded
75g tom berries or cherry tomatoes
lemon slices
paprika to garnish

If the prawns are raw, simply cook them in boiling water for a minute or two until they are cooked through. Set them aside to cool. Shell the prawns, but keep some whole ones to garnish the cocktails. In a bowl, mix the mayonnaise, ketchup, tomato purée, Tabasco sauce, salad cream and lemon juice. Mix the shredded lettuce with the tom berries or halved cherry tomatoes.

Fill each sundae glass two-thirds full with salad. Mix the prawns with the sauce and spoon onto the salad. Garnish with a whole prawn hanging over the edge of the glass with a slice of lemon for company and add a sprinkling of paprika. To make one big cocktail, prepare everything in the same way, but use some lobster meat and garnish with a whole lobster or two!

FOOLPROOF MAYONNAISE

We use a food processor for this, but you can make it almost as easily with a whisk or fork.

SERVES 4

2 egg yolks
1 whole egg
1 tbsp French mustard
juice of ½ lemon
½ tsp salt
½ tsp black pepper
½ tsp caster sugar
400ml vegetable oil

Place everything, except the oil, in a food processor. Blitz for 10 seconds to combine, then drizzle in the oil. When the oil is all in, blitz for another 10 seconds and there you have it – perfect mayonnaise. You'll never buy another jar again.

You can play around with this recipe and add lemon or lime zest for a citrus mayo or garlic to make a garlic mayo as strong or subtle as you like.

SÜLT

Eele Prints-De Tisi gave us this recipe. Eele is from Estonia, but is married to an Englishman and now lives in Bristol. She loves to cook traditional Estonian dishes and this jellied meat dish is one of her favourites. Unlike brawn, which can be a bit of mystery, it's clear what's in this and it looks great. You can use any herbs you like and make the sült in one big mould or a number of smaller ones.

SERVES 10–12

2 pig's trotters, chopped in half
1 pork hock
6–7 tbsp salt
2 tsp black peppercorns
2 bay leaves
1–2 tsp ground black pepper
1 tbsp gelatine (optional)
1 carrot, peeled and cooked

Wash the trotters and hock and put them in a stock pot. Cover with plenty of cold water and add a generous tablespoon of salt. Bring to the boil and boil rapidly for 5 minutes. Pour the water away, wash the meat and rinse the pot. Return the meat to the pot.

Now, add just enough cold water to cover the meat. Add the peppercorns, bay leaves and 2 generous tablespoons of salt. Boil over a low heat for 2–3 hours, until the meat is falling off the bones – it's important to keep the water boiling gently, otherwise the jelly will form a haze.

When the meat is cooked, lift it out and set it aside to cool slightly. Pour the liquid through a fine sieve to remove any small pieces of bone and take out any particles from the pot. Pour the liquid back into the pot and keep it warm.

Remove all the meat from the bones and dice into 1cm cubes. Add these to the liquid. Add the ground pepper and 3–4 tablespoons of salt. It's important to make the liquid taste strong – too salty – because the taste weakens as the dish cools. Bring everything to the boil and if you are not sure the jelly will set, add some gelatine.

Slice the carrot and cut it into decorative shapes. Place a piece of carrot at the bottom of each mould and ladle hot meat and liquid on top. Set aside to cool and put into the fridge when cold. To serve, ease the sült out of the mould and serve with hot boiled potatoes with vinegar, mustard or horseradish sauce.

KRINGEL

Every Estonian family has a recipe for kringel and this is Eele's version. It's a pretzel-shaped yeast bread with raisins and chocolate sauce and makes a great party cake. We tried a savoury version with grated cheese, too.

MAKES 1 LOAF

DOUGH
40g fresh yeast
1 tbsp sugar
250ml milk, lukewarm
2 egg yolks
400g plain flour
50g butter, melted

FILLING
100g butter, softened
3 handfuls of raisins
10 tsp sugar

TOPPING
150g dark chocolate
(at least 50% cocoa solids)
75g butter

Mix the yeast and sugar in a bowl. Add the lukewarm milk and egg yolks, then mix in the flour and melted butter and knead well. Shape the dough into a ball, cover the bowl with a kitchen towel and leave to rise in a warm place for 30 minutes.

Preheat the oven to 200°C/Gas 6. Dust your work surface with flour. Take the dough out of the bowl, knock it back and roll out to a thickness of about 1cm. Spread the soft butter evenly over the rolled sheet of pastry, then sprinkle with raisins and finally sugar.

Roll the dough up like a Swiss roll and cut it in half with a sharp knife. Starting from the uncut end, plait the dough, lifting each half over the other in turn. Finally, shape the plaited bread into a B-shape and transfer to a buttered baking tray. Bake for about 25 minutes or until golden.

In the meantime, prepare the chocolate topping by melting the chocolate and butter in a bowl over some boiling water. Once out of the oven, let the bread cool down a bit, place on a serving plate and drizzle on the chocolate sauce.

CHEESE KRINGEL
To make this savoury version, leave out the raisins and sugar and sprinkle the kringel with grated cheddar instead. Add more grated cheese on top instead of chocolate sauce.

ROOSA-MANNA

This is one of Eele's favourite recipes from her childhood – it was made by her grandma, her mum and now by her. It's a way of making semolina attractive by infusing it with fruit juice and a little bit of magic happens when the milk is poured on.

SERVES 4

300ml redcurrant juice
150g sugar
75g semolina
redcurrants for garnish (optional)

Pour the juice into a saucepan and add 300ml of water and the sugar. The mixture should taste strongly of both juice and sugar as the whipping will dilute the flavour.

Bring the liquid to boil. Sprinkle in the semolina while stirring continuously. The semolina cooks quickly and should take just a few minutes.

Once ready, cool the mixture for 5–10 minutes by placing the pan in a sink filled with cold water. Whip with a hand whisk until light and fluffy and pour straight into dessert bowls or glasses. Serve with cold milk poured over the top and garnish with some redcurrants if you like.

WHOLE POACHED SALMON

As seen at wedding receptions, christenings and so on all round the country, a beautifully decorated poached salmon, complete with cucumber scales, makes a perfect centrepiece. It looks impressive but it's simple to make and just takes patience and care. Follow our method below to get perfectly cooked salmon every time.

SERVES 8–10

1 x 2–3kg salmon, gutted and scaled
1 lemon, halved
1 dsrtsp black peppercorns
2 bay leaves
2 cucumbers
mayonnaise (see page 57)
fresh herbs and extra lemon slices
for garnish

Place the salmon in a large roasting tin or fish kettle and cover with cold water. Squeeze the juice from the lemon halves into the water and chuck in the rinds. Add the peppercorns and bay leaves.

Place the pan on the stove and bring to the boil. As soon as the water has boiled, remove the pan from the heat and leave the salmon to cool in the liquid. This way, the salmon will be perfectly cooked and still juicy. Be warned – there is nothing worse than dry poached salmon. Better to be underdone than cremated.

Remove the fish very carefully and place it on your presentation platter. Starting from just behind the gills, remove the skin from the presentation side. Now prepare to enjoy yourself. Cut the cucumbers into thin slices and, with the artistry of Rolf Harris, apply them to the salmon to look like scales. Pipe mayonnaise on and around the salmon as you like and garnish with herbs.

Gorgeous.

CORONATION CHICKEN

This dish became famous when it was served at the coronation luncheon of Elizabeth II in 1953. It's been through many variations – Dave's mam used to make it with a handful of sultanas, mayonnaise, a teaspoon of mild curry powder and some cold roast chicken. This is our modern version, which is fit for the best of occasions.

SERVES 4

2 free-range chicken breasts, boned and skinned
1 tbsp olive oil
zest of 1 lemon, finely chopped
knob of butter
1 shallot, finely chopped
1 red chilli, seeded and finely chopped
2 tsp Madras curry powder
2 tbsp tomato paste
100ml dry white wine
1 tbsp apricot jam
100ml chicken stock
150ml mayonnaise (see page 57)
75ml crème fraîche
1 large mango, peeled and diced
4 spring onions, trimmed and finely chopped
juice of 1 lemon
2 tbsp chopped fresh coriander
dash of Tabasco sauce
sea salt flakes and ground black pepper to taste
green salad to serve
50g flaked almonds (optional)

First rub the chicken with olive oil. Scatter on the lemon zest and season with salt and black pepper. Place the chicken in a steamer – the Chinese bamboo ones work well for this – and steam for about 20 minutes or until the chicken is cooked through. Set aside to cool. The chicken will be fragrant and juicy.

Melt the butter in a frying pan, add the shallot and chilli and sweat gently for about 5 minutes. Stir in the curry powder and cook for a few minutes more, then stir in the tomato paste and cook for a further minute. Add the wine and cook hard until the liquid is reduced by half. Add the jam and stock, then continue to simmer until again reduced by half. Set this mixture aside to cool.

Mix the mayonnaise and crème fraîche in a bowl. Stir in the cooled curry mixture, then add the mango, spring onions, lemon juice and coriander. Fold in the chicken, cut into bite-sized pieces, then add Tabasco and seasoning to taste. Serve with green salad. You can also toast some flaked almonds in a dry frying pan and scatter these over the chicken just before serving if you wish.

BAKED ALASKA

Tessa Johnstone gave us this recipe. She lives in Chippenham, Wiltshire, and has loved cooking since she was a child. Her dad was a yacht designer and her mum used to host dinner parties to entertain clients. Baked Alaska was her dad's party piece – he would finish it off by browning the meringue with a blowtorch at the table. This certainly provides the proper wow factor – but watch the curtains.

SERVES 6

225g fresh raspberries
2 tbsp Cointreau
or similar orange liqueur
20cm sponge flan base
4 egg whites
170g caster sugar
1 litre good vanilla ice cream

Put the raspberries in a bowl and pour on the Cointreau. Leave to macerate for 2 hours.

Preheat the oven to 230°C/Gas 8. Place the sponge base on a baking tray and spoon on most of the soaked raspberries and juice.

Whisk the egg whites until stiff and then gradually whisk in the sugar. Fill a piping bag with this meringue mix.

Scoop the ice cream onto the raspberries and add the rest of the raspberries on top. Immediately pipe the meringue over and around the ice cream – no gaps! Put the Alaska straight into the preheated oven for about 4 minutes until browned.

Serve at once – it won't wait.

Instead of browning the meringue in the oven, you can use a blowtorch like Tessa's dad used to do. Take great care, though, and as soon as a patch of meringue turns golden, move the torch to the next bit or it will burn.

HONEY & MARMALADE ROASTED GAMMON

This is a fusion of tips from both our mams. Si's mam says, 'Using half orange juice and half water to simmer the ham makes it sweet and tasty.' Dave's mam says, 'Use marmalade for a lovely sticky glaze.' We serve it with an apple compote and pickled red cabbage and it's great for a buffet.

SERVES 20 PLUS

1 x 6kg gammon joint
fresh orange juice
2 onions
lots of cloves
4 large bay leaves

GLAZE

120g soft brown sugar
zest of 3 oranges
juice of 1 orange
3 tbsp runny honey
3 heaped tbsp orange marmalade
3 tbsp wholegrain mustard

Place the gammon joint in a large saucepan. Cover with water, bring to the boil and discard the water. This gets rid of any excess salt in the gammon very quickly – a top tip.

Pour the orange juice into the pan until it reaches halfway up the gammon and top up with cold water to cover. Cut the onions in half and put 2 cloves in each half. Add the onions to the pan with the bay leaves, then cover and simmer for about 3 hours. Keep an eye on the level of liquid and top up with boiling water as needed.

At the end of the cooking time, remove the gammon from the saucepan and place it in a roasting tin. Remove the skin, but leave a good layer of fat. Using a sharp knife, score the surface of the gammon into diamond shapes. Stud the centre of each diamond with a clove.

Then make the glaze. Mix together the soft brown sugar, orange zest and juice, honey, marmalade and mustard.

Preheat the oven to 180°C/Gas 4. Spoon the glaze over the gammon, place it in the preheated oven and roast for 45 minutes, basting frequently.

Eat the gammon hot in thin slices with mash and juice or serve it cold. Delicious either way.

QUICK DILL PICKLED CABBAGE

Simple to make and a perfect sweet and sour accompaniment to the gammon.

SERVES 6

1 red cabbage
250ml white wine vinegar
100g granulated sugar
4 tsp salt
handful of fresh dill, chopped

Remove the outer leaves of the cabbage and the core and slice the rest finely.

Pour the vinegar into a saucepan and add the sugar, salt and 125ml of water. Bring to the boil, then add the cabbage and stir well. Remove from the heat, cover and leave to cool for an hour. Add the chopped dill and leave to infuse for another hour before serving.

APPLE COMPOTE

Some sort of apple sauce is a must with any kind of pork and this is a good one.

SERVES 6

150g caster sugar
½ tsp ground cinnamon
6 cloves
500g cooking apples

Put the sugar in a saucepan and add 500ml of water. Heat until a syrup forms and add the cinnamon and cloves.

Peel the apples, core them and cut into quarters. Add them to the syrup and simmer until soft. Smash the apples up a bit and serve with the gammon. Keep some to have cold with the ham sarnies, too.

LIL'S PRETZELS

Lil, Dave's missus, is from Romania. During Ceausescu's reign, her father worked in a factory and while he was there he made a metal pretzel cutter for his daughter. When Lil first came to England she had very little, but she did bring her special pretzel cutter, made by her dad with a lot of love. If you don't have one, just use an ordinary biscuit cutter to stamp out the pretzels.

MAKES ABOUT 30

2 eggs
350g plain flour
250g Cheddar cheese, grated, plus extra for the topping
250g butter, margarine, or lard
2 tbsp caraway seeds
pinch of salt

Beat one of the eggs in a bowl and add the flour, cheese, butter, 1 tablespoon of the caraway seeds and a pinch of salt. Mix well to make a dough, then leave to rest for an hour.

Preheat the oven to 180°C/Gas 4. Roll out the dough to a thickness of about 1cm and cut out the pretzels. Place them on a greased baking tray. Beat the other egg and use it to brush the pretzels, then sprinkle with the rest of the caraway seeds and some grated cheese. Bake for 10–15 minutes or until golden. Remove and cool on a wire rack.

WEST AFRICAN GHANAIAN COMMUNITY GROUP

The centre of this community group is The Gold Coast, a family restaurant in south London. The restaurant opened in 2004 and is run by William and Francesca Quagraine, both from Ghana, who were inspired by their love of food and the rich culture of their homeland. The Gold Coast has now become a focal point for the Ghanaian community in London and specialises in cooking West African recipes passed down through generations.

GUINEA FOWL WITH RED CHILLI (AKONFEM)

Guinea fowl can be cooked just like chicken but it has a delicious, slightly gamey flavour. The birds are native to West Africa and feature in many Ghanaian dishes.

SERVES 2
1 x 1.5–2kg guinea fowl without giblets

MARINADE
1 garlic clove
25g root ginger, peeled
½ medium white onion, peeled and chopped
100ml vegetable oil
1 tbsp dried crushed red chillies

To prepare the marinade, place the garlic, fresh ginger, white onion and vegetable oil in a blender. Blend until smooth and thick and then mix in the dried crushed red chillies.

Cut the guinea fowl from the breast down to the stomach and open it out like a book. Brush the guinea fowl with the marinade inside and out and place it flat in an oven dish. Pour any excess marinade on top of the guinea fowl to ensure it is well covered and leave it in the fridge for 2 hours.

Preheat the oven to 180°C/Gas 4. Bake the guinea fowl in its marinade on the middle shelf of the oven for 30 minutes. Take care not to overcook it – you want the meat to stay juicy. Alternatively, barbecue the guinea fowl for about 30 minutes, turning it regularly. Serve with vegetables and yam balls.

YAM BALLS

An ideal accompaniment to the guinea fowl opposite as part of a splendid Ghanaian feast.
Puna or white yams are the most popular variety in Ghana.

SERVES 5 AS AN APPETIZER

1kg puna yams
½ red pepper
½ green pepper
½ yellow pepper
1 spring onion
3 tbsp margarine
2 egg yolks
4 egg whites
breadcrumbs
500ml vegetable oil, for deep frying

Boil the puna yams until cooked through and soft to the touch. Drain, place in a bowl and mash until they form a smooth paste. Finely chop all the peppers and the spring onion and dry them on kitchen paper, squeezing out any excess water. Stir them into the puna yam mash and add the margarine and egg yolks. Mix well.

Place the egg whites in a bowl and the breadcrumbs in a separate bowl. Mould the puna yam mash mixture into small balls, about the size of golf balls.

Dip the balls into the egg white, then the breadcrumbs and repeat this process twice for each ball. Half fill a deep saucepan with oil or use a deep-fat fryer. Heat the oil to 100–120°C and fry the yam balls until golden brown.

Good
simple
suppers

MEAT & POTATO PIE

Fiona Armitage lives in Ilkley, West Yorkshire and we met her with her mum, Sybil. Although Fiona doesn't do that much cooking herself she does love good food and has become more interested since finding a book of her great-aunt's handwritten recipes. These include many from Fiona's grandmother and other members of the family. Fiona made us this pie from her granny's recipe, but her mum made the pastry, which was top-notch – every northerner's dream. Sybil got a special gold star from us. You need to start this pie the day before by making the stock.

STOCK
couple of marrow bones
4 carrots, roughly chopped
2 celery sticks, roughly chopped
2 bay leaves
4 peppercorns
500g beef shin, roughly chopped

PIE
1kg stewing steak
1 tbsp vegetable oil
2 onions, peeled and chopped
2 carrots, peeled and chopped
2 celery sticks, chopped
500g potatoes, peeled and chopped
shortcrust pastry (see page 14)
1 egg, beaten
sea salt and black pepper to taste

First make the stock. Roast the marrow bones in the oven at 180°C/Gas 4 for 45–60 minutes or until well browned. Transfer the roasted bones to a large pot and add the remaining ingredients. Pour in enough cold water to cover, bring to the boil and simmer gently for 4–5 hours. Keep an eye on the pan and top up with boiling water when necessary.

At the end of the cooking time, remove the bones and boil the liquid until reduced by half. Leave to cool, then skim off the fat. Liquidise the vegetables.

Now the pie. Preheat the oven to 150°C/Gas 2. Cut the stewing steak into cubes, roughly 2.5cm square. Heat the oil in a frying pan and brown the meat, then transfer it to a large ovenproof pot. Add the onions, carrots and celery to the frying pan and sweat them gently until soft. Add them to the meat and pour in the stock to cover. Season to taste. Cook in the oven for 3 hours, then add the potatoes and cook for another hour. Remove and leave to cool.

Turn the oven up to 180°C/Gas 4. Pile the filling into a 1.2 litre pie dish and brush the edges of the dish with beaten egg. Roll out the pastry on a well-floured board and place it gently over the filling. Press the edges firmly to seal and trim neatly. Flute the edges or leave them plain, as you prefer. Decorate the top with any excess pastry and brush with beaten egg to glaze. Place the dish on a baking sheet and bake in the centre of the oven for about 30 minutes until golden on top.

PICCALILLI

This is a great piccalilli recipe from Fiona's great-aunt's recipe book. Fiona says that her great-aunt would have soaked and cooked dried kidney beans, but canned ones work just fine.

MAKES 3 JARS

½ vegetable marrow
½ cucumber
1 onion, peeled
225g canned kidney beans or
cauliflower florets
salt
55g sugar
55g flour
1 tbsp English mustard powder
55g turmeric
1 tbsp ground ginger
1.2 litres white wine vinegar

Cut the vegetables into small pieces and put them on a plate with the beans (if using). Sprinkle everything with salt and leave overnight.

Mix the sugar, flour and spices to a paste with a spoonful of the vinegar. Pour the rest of the vinegar into a saucepan and bring to the boil. Add the paste and boil for 5 minutes. Take the pan off the heat and add the vegetables. Ladle the piccalilli into sterilised jars and cover with waxed discs and cellophane or lids.

TOMATO CHUTNEY

And here is Fiona's granny's classic tomato chutney recipe.

MAKES 3 SMALL JARS

450g tomatoes
110g sour apples
225g onions
110g sugar
1 tsp salt
1 tsp ground ginger
good pinch of cayenne pepper
300ml wine vinegar

Pour boiling water over the tomatoes, then slip off the skins. Cut them into slices. Peel and core the apples and chop them finely. Peel and chop the onions.

Put all the ingredients into a large saucepan and bring to the boil. Cook for up to an hour, stirring often, until the chutney has thickened. Pour into sterilised jars and leave to cool. Cover with waxed discs and cellophane or lids.

DAVE'S MAM'S KILLER FISHCAKES
WITH CHEDDAR CHEESE SAUCE

These are lovely, but they nearly were killer fishcakes. As three-year old Dave sat sucking the key to his clockwork monkey, he was distracted by the delicious smell of fishcakes cooking. One gulp and the key lodged in his throat – he had to have an operation to remove it! So no fishcakes for Dave for a while, but he did have lots of ice cream.

SERVES 6

500g hake steaks
250ml milk
1 bay leaf
3 eggs
1 heaped tbsp chopped curly parsley
500g cold buttery mashed potatoes
4 tbsp plain flour
1 packet of golden breadcrumbs – the bright orange ones!
vegetable oil for shallow frying
black pepper and white pepper
sea salt

CHEDDAR CHEESE SAUCE

reserved fish stock
whole milk
50g unsalted butter
2 tbsp plain flour
175g Cheddar cheese, grated
salt and pepper

First, poach the hake. Preheat the oven to 150°C/Gas 2. Put the fish in an ovenproof dish, season with ground black pepper and sea salt, then pour in the milk. Add the bay leaf, cover the dish with foil and bake for about 25 minutes until the fish is just cooked and falls away from the bone. Leave to cool, then carefully flake the fish, removing all the bones, and set aside. Strain the milky fish stock and set it aside for making the cheese sauce.

Beat one of the eggs. Gently fold the fish, beaten egg and chopped parsley into the mashed potatoes. Season to taste with salt and pepper – use white pepper this time as it tastes better in mash for some reason.

Form the mixture into 4 large cakes. Beat the other 2 eggs in a bowl and pour the flour and some breadcrumbs onto separate plates. Roll the fishcakes in flour, dip in beaten egg, then roll in the luminous crumbs.

Heat the oil in a frying pan and fry these monsters gently until warmed through and golden.

TO MAKE THE CHEESE SAUCE
Make the fish stock up to 500ml by adding milk. Melt the butter in a pan, stir in the flour and cook for 3 minutes. Gradually whisk in the milky stock and cook gently until the sauce thickens. Add the cheese and stir it in until it melts. Season to taste and pour this cheesy duvet over a monolith of a fishcake.

SPICY ROASTED CHICKEN
WITH MINTY SAUCE

Harjinder Kaur lives in Manchester. She's a brilliant cook and we think she could make a curry out of anything. Harjinder learned how to cook from her mum and she told us that her knowledge of spicing dishes has been passed down through generations. Her use of spices is just right – everything she cooked was perfectly spiced and tasted great.

SERVES 4–6

1kg chicken thighs, skinned/washed and drained
4cm piece of root ginger, peeled and finely chopped
juice of ½ lemon
1½ tsp salt
1 tsp ground peppercorns and coriander seeds
1 tsp paprika
½ tsp garam masala (see page 90)
1½ tsp whole cumin seeds
oil, for greasing tin

MINTY YOGHURT SAUCE
500ml plain yoghurt
2 dsrtsp ready-made mint sauce

Wash and dry the chicken thighs and make 3 slits in each one with a sharp knife. Place the chicken in a bowl and add the ginger, lemon juice, salt and spices. Mix well and leave to marinate for 10 minutes.

Preheat the oven to 220°C/Gas 7. Oil a roasting tin and add the marinated chicken, spreading it out evenly, and roast for 45 minutes.

To make the minty yoghurt sauce, add the mint sauce to the yoghurt and mix them well. Serve the sauce chilled with the hot chicken.

CURRIED SALMON

Another great recipe from Harjinder and an excellent way of cheering up a bit of farmed salmon.

SERVES 6

1kg salmon steaks or salmon fillet, descaled
5 garlic cloves, finely chopped
4cm piece of root ginger, finely chopped
1 or 2 green chillies, deseeded and chopped (optional)
1 x 400g can of chopped tomatoes
2 fresh tomatoes, sliced
handful of fresh coriander, chopped

SPICE MIX

2½ tsp salt
1 tsp ground peppercorns and coriander seeds
1 tsp paprika
½ tsp garam masala
2 tsp cumin seeds
2 tsp lovage seeds
½ tsp dried red chilli flakes (add more or less according to taste)
2 tsp turmeric

TARKA MIX

3 tbsp vegetable oil
1 tsp lovage seeds
1 tsp cumin seeds
4 garlic cloves, finely chopped

Wash the salmon in salty water, rinse in fresh water and drain well. Cut the salmon into large chunks and place in a bowl. Add all the spice mix and gently toss the fish so it is covered with the spices. Add the chopped garlic, ginger and chillies if using and gently toss again to mix everything together. Set aside for 10 minutes.

Now prepare the tarka mix in which the salmon will be cooked. Heat the vegetable oil in a frying pan. Add the lovage seeds and fry them until they are almost black, then add the cumin seeds and fry for another 5 seconds. Add the 4 cloves of chopped garlic and fry until slightly golden, then add the salmon.

Cook on medium heat, moving the fish around by gently shaking the pan until the oil begins to separate from spices and the salmon is sealed and brown. Add about 225ml of hot water and the canned and fresh tomatoes, bring to the boil and simmer for a few minutes until the fish is cooked through. Sprinkle on the chopped coriander and remove from heat. Serve with boiled rice.

HARJINDER'S PAKORAS

The recipe below includes onion and potato, but Harjinder says you can use any vegetables you like, such as aubergines, cauliflower and broccoli. Most just need to be parboiled and cooled, but potatoes should be boiled in their skins until cooked, then sliced thickly. To prepare Harjinder's garam masala, grind equal amounts of cinnamon sticks, large cardamom pods and cloves until finely ground.

SERVES 6

450g gram (chick pea) flour
2 tsp baking powder
3 onions, peeled and thinly sliced
1 bunch of spring onions, chopped
5cm piece of root ginger, peeled and chopped
handful of fresh coriander, chopped
2 green chillies, deseeded and chopped
(optional)
350g potatoes, boiled in skins, sliced
vegetable oil for deep frying

SPICE MIX
1½ tsp salt
1½ tsp black peppercorns and coriander seeds
2 tsp cumin seeds and 2 tsp lovage seeds
1½ tsp paprika
½ tsp home-made garam masala (see above)

Mix the gram flour with the baking powder and spice mix in a bowl. Slowly add cold water, about 350ml, to make a batter with a dropping consistency.

Add the onions, spring onions, ginger, coriander and chillies, if using, and mix together really well. This is best done with your hands. Then mix in the potatoes, working gently so they don't break up too much.

Heat the oil to moderately hot in a large pan. Carefully put spoonfuls of the mixture into the oil – a few at a time. Cook gently for 7–8 minutes, turning the pakoras in the oil from time to time to make sure they cook evenly.

Drain and serve with mint chutney (below) as a starter or side dish or with rotis for a light lunch or supper.

MINT CHUTNEY

2 onions, peeled and quartered
2 green chillies, deseeded
3 tomatoes, halved
5cm piece of root ginger, peeled
handful of coriander
3 tbsp mint sauce
3 tbsp lemon juice
1½ tsp salt
1½ tsp paprika

Put all the ingredients in a food processor and mix to a smooth consistency. Best to do this in pulses until the mixture is to your liking.

PURIS

1kg atta (chapati flour)
vegetable oil, for frying

Place the flour in a large bowl and make a well in the centre. Slowly add cold water to make a fairly stiff dough and knead well. Leave the dough to rest for about 20 minutes. Make small balls the size of a plum and roll them out in rounds – or use a special puri press to save time. Heat the oil in a heavy pan or a karai. Drop in the puris a few at a time and fry until golden. Drain on kitchen paper and serve warm.

YOGHURT BOONDI

55g ready-made boondi
1 tsp salt and 1 tsp paprika
1 tsp lovage seeds and 1 tsp cumin seeds
handful of fresh coriander, chopped
500ml plain live yoghurt

Soak the boondi (fried droplets of besan batter) in warm water for about 10 minutes. When it is soft, drain, rinse in cold water and drain again. Stir the spices and coriander into the yoghurt, add the boondi and mix well. Chill before serving.

KEDGEREE

**Great served with dishes like the curried salmon (see page 88) for special occasions.
Mung beans can usually be used straight from the packet without being soaked.**

SERVES 6–8

250g green mung beans
1 tsp salt
300g rice, washed well
1 tbsp clarified butter

Place the mung beans in a large saucepan and add enough boiling water to come to about 2.5cm above them. Add the salt, bring to the boil and simmer until the beans are half cooked. Add the rice and clarified butter and stir gently to mix. Top up with boiling water so that the level is again about 2.5cm above the contents. Bring to the boil and leave on a low heat until the rice is cooked and the liquid is absorbed.

Check on the rice by picking out a grain and gently squeezing it between your fingertips. If it still has a white centre, it is not quite cooked and needs a little longer. If all the liquid has already been absorbed, add a small amount to make a little steam to finish cooking the rice without burning. Once the rice is cooked, remove it from the heat. Use the handle of a ladle or palette knife to fluff up the rice – move it gently through the rice and around the sides of the pan. Do this only once.

To clarify butter, dice and slowly heat the butter in a small pan until it separates and the white solids sink to the bottom. Pour the clarified liquid into a dish, leaving the residue in the pan.

CHICKEN CURRY

A great chicken curry recipe from Harjinder. She says this tarka masala sauce is the base for many Punjabi dishes. Harjinder loves to cook dishes like this for her family and has even made videos of how to prepare her recipes for her children.

SERVES 6

1kg boneless chicken breasts, cut into big chunks
1½ tsp salt
1½ tsp ground black peppercorns and coriander seeds
¾ tsp garam masala (see page 90)
1 tsp paprika
1½ tsp turmeric
½ tsp red chilli flakes
2 fresh tomatoes, sliced
handful of fresh coriander, chopped
3 bay leaves

TARKA MASALA SAUCE

3 tbsp sunflower oil, ghee or olive oil
2 tsp cumin seeds
2 medium onions, peeled and chopped
1 head of garlic, cloves peeled and chopped
small tin of chopped tomatoes
5cm piece of root ginger, peeled and chopped
2 whole green chillies

Wash the chicken and drain it well. Start by making the tarka masala sauce. Heat the oil in a large pan until fairly hot, add the cumin seeds and fry for 10 seconds. Add the onions and fry until golden brown, then add the garlic and fry until slightly golden. Drain the tomatoes (keep the juice), and add them to the pan, then add the ginger and chillies and cook until the oil begins to separate.

Put the chicken, salt, spices and chilli flakes into the pan and cook over a fairly high heat. Keep turning the chicken and continue to cook until the meat is sealed and browned and the liquid has evaporated. Add the juice from the can of tomatoes and about 450ml of water, bring to the boil and simmer over a medium heat for about 15 minutes or until the chicken is tender. Add the fresh tomatoes about 3 minutes before the end of the cooking time.

Sprinkle in the fresh coriander and bay leaves and serve the curry with chapatis, boiled rice or puris.

RHODA'S CHICKEN CURRY

This recipe was given to us at one of the food fairs by a lady called Roz. It's a South African chicken curry that her mum Rhoda used to make and it's great. Give it a go.

SERVES 4–6

3 tbsp olive oil

1 large onion, peeled and sliced

6 green cardamom pods

4 cloves

2 large cinnamon sticks

1 tsp black mustard seeds (optional)

3 bay leaves

3 green chillies, seeded and chopped

1 tsp ground turmeric

2 tsp chilli powder

1 tsp ground cumin

1 tsp garam masala

1.5cm piece of root ginger, crushed

3 garlic cloves, crushed

a few curry leaves

750g–1kg chicken, skinned and cut into large chunks

1 level tsp salt

1 x 400g can of tomatoes

2 large potatoes, peeled and quartered

handful of fresh coriander, washed and chopped

Heat the oil in a large non-stick saucepan. Add the onion and fry gently until it is softened and browned. Add the cardamom, cloves, cinnamon, mustard seeds (if using), bay leaves and chillies and continue to fry gently. Take the pan off the heat and stir in the turmeric, chilli powder, cumin, garam masala, root ginger, garlic and curry leaves. Put the saucepan back on the heat, add the chicken and salt and mix together well.

Cover the pan and cook over a low heat to extract all the flavour from the spices. Add the tomatoes and continue to cook, stirring occasionally. Then add the potatoes and cook until the potatoes are done. Sprinkle in the chopped coriander and serve with basmati rice.

PAN HAGGERTY

Although traditionally a dish from the coalfields of northeast England,
this is not just for underground Geordies. It's a great one-pan supper and
just the job for eating in front of the telly when you want a bit of comfort.

SERVES 4–6

1 tbsp vegetable oil
250g streaky bacon rashers
6 medium potatoes, peeled and sliced
into thin rounds
2 onions, peeled and sliced
5 carrots, peeled and sliced
500ml chicken stock
150g Cheddar cheese, grated
salt and pepper to taste

A high-sided frying pan is best for making this. Heat the oil in the pan and fry the bacon until it starts to crisp and colour. Remove the rashers and set aside, leaving the fat and juices in the pan.

Place a layer of potatoes over the bottom of the pan. Add a layer of onion, then a layer of carrot, then a layer of bacon rashers. Season with freshly ground pepper. Repeat the layers, finishing with a layer of potatoes. Season with salt and pepper, but be careful not to add too much salt, as the bacon will be salty and the stock too.

Pour on the chicken stock and cover the pan with a lid if you have one or with foil. Leave it to simmer away for about 20 minutes or until the vegetables are tender.

When everything is cooked, preheat the grill. Uncover the pan, top with the grated cheese and grill until bubbling and golden. Serve straight from the pan into bowls, with some bread to mop up the yummy juices.

GREEN BEAN SOUP
(FEIJAO VERDE SOPA)

Jeni Candeias lives in Merseyside. She is British, but has a Portuguese husband, and she really loves to cook Portuguese dishes. Her family life centres around food and everyone sits down to eat an evening meal together. Jeni learned to cook traditional dishes from her mother-in-law, Maria, and has added her own twist to some. She's also introduced her Portuguese relatives to British favourites, like the Sunday roast. The Portuguese are great soup eaters and this is one of the most popular.

SERVES 8

½ medium onion, peeled and chopped
2–3 garlic cloves, peeled and chopped
400g potatoes, peeled and chopped
4 carrots, 2 roughly chopped, 2 sliced
1.2 litres chicken stock
2 tbsp olive oil
200g green beans, sliced diagonally
100g chorizo, cut into slices 1cm thick
salt and pepper

Put the onion, garlic, potatoes and the roughly chopped carrots in a large pan and add the chicken stock and olive oil.

Bring everything to the boil and cook until the vegetables are tender. Pour into a blender and blitz until smooth. Pour the mixture back into the pan and add the green beans, sliced carrots and chorizo. Season to taste and cook until the beans are tender. Stir regularly as the chorizo may stick to the bottom of the pan.

Serve with crusty bread and freshly ground black pepper.

PORTUGUESE FISH & CHIPS
(BACALHAU A BRAS)

Another recipe from Jeni and this one really convinced us about salt cod, a Portuguese staple. This is a great supper dish and her kids love it – they've grown up with her version of fish and chips. You need to start the day before by soaking the salt cod.

SERVES 5

1.3kg salt cod
1 tbsp olive oil
½ onion, peeled and diced
1–2 garlic cloves, peeled and chopped
3 eggs, beaten
vegetable oil, for deep frying
1.2kg potatoes, cut into matchstick chips
good handful of chopped parsley
black pepper

Rinse the salt cod, place it in a bowl and cover with cold water. Leave it to soak for 24 hours, changing the water at least twice.

The next day, drain the cod well and put it in a large pan. Pour in enough cold water to cover, bring it to the boil and cook for 20 minutes or so or until the fish is tender and flaky. Leave to cool, then separate into flakes and remove any skin and bones.

Heat the olive oil in a large pan and cook the onion and garlic until softened. Add the salt cod and the beaten eggs and stir over a gentle heat until the eggs are cooked. Meanwhile, heat the vegetable oil in a deep-fat fryer or large pan and cook the chips until golden. Add them to the pan with the fish and sprinkle with the chopped parsley. Season with black pepper and serve with a tomato and onion salad.

This can also be eaten cold.

TRADITIONAL RICE PUDDING

We love this – a real comforting taste of childhood. A top tip from Si's mam: soak some sultanas in builders' tea for 10 minutes and add them to the rice pudding for some special little explosions of flavour. On high days and holidays, serve this with a dollop of clotted cream and your favourite jam.

SERVES 6

100g sultanas
hot tea
1.3 litres full-fat milk
300ml double cream
200g pudding rice
100g golden granulated sugar
good sprinkling of freshly ground nutmeg
1 vanilla pod

First, put the sultanas in a bowl and cover them with hot tea. Leave for 10 minutes and then drain the sultanas and discard the tea.

Preheat the oven to 160°C/Gas 2–3. Pour the milk and cream into a big casserole dish or a rice pudding dish. Add the rice, sugar and nutmeg and stir well. Split the vanilla pod and scrape out the seeds, then add the seeds and pod to the dish. Stir in the soaked sultanas.

Cover the dish with a lid or some foil, place in the oven and bake for about an hour and a half. Uncover and bake for another 20 minutes so a golden skin forms… some say that's the best bit.

PORTUGUESE RICE PUDDING

This is a recipe from the Alentejo area, where Jeni's mother-in-law lives.

SERVES 6

250g long-grain rice
25g lard
300ml milk
250g caster sugar
1 cinnamon stick
zest of 1 lemon
3 egg yolks
ground cinnamon

Wash and drain the rice and put it in a pan with about 450ml of salted water and the lard. When the rice has just started to cook, gradually add the milk and the sugar with the stick of cinnamon and lemon zest. Stir continuously.

Once the rice is not crunchy or too mushy, remove the cinnamon stick. Take the pan off the heat and add the egg yolks. Stir them in thoroughly before putting the pan on a low heat so the eggs can cook through. Serve hot or cold with a sprinkling of powdered cinnamon.

BALINESE RICE PUDDING

There are so many kinds of rice pudding – it's something that crops up all over the world. Here is an amazing Balinese recipe with black rice. The ingredients sound exotic but they are available in most Thai shops. Screwpine or pandanus leaves have a sweet flavour and scent and are used in many Southeast Asian rice dishes and desserts. If you can't get the leaves, you can use pandan essence or even vanilla essence.

SERVES 6

300g black glutinous rice
170g palm sugar, grated
2 screwpine leaves or
2 drops of pandan or vanilla essence
450ml coconut milk
pinch of salt
fresh coconut to garnish

Wash the rice and leave it to soak in cold water overnight. Next day, drain the rice and put it in a saucepan with about 1.5 litres of water. Bring it to the boil and cook until the rice is soft. Add the sugar (more or less, according to taste) and a screwpine leaf or drop of essence. Continue to boil until the rice is cooked through, then leave to cool for a while, then garnish with fresh coconut.

Pour the coconut milk into another pan, add the remaining leaf or essence and the salt and cook until thickened. Serve with the rice. This pudding looks spectacular when the white milk is poured over the dark rice.

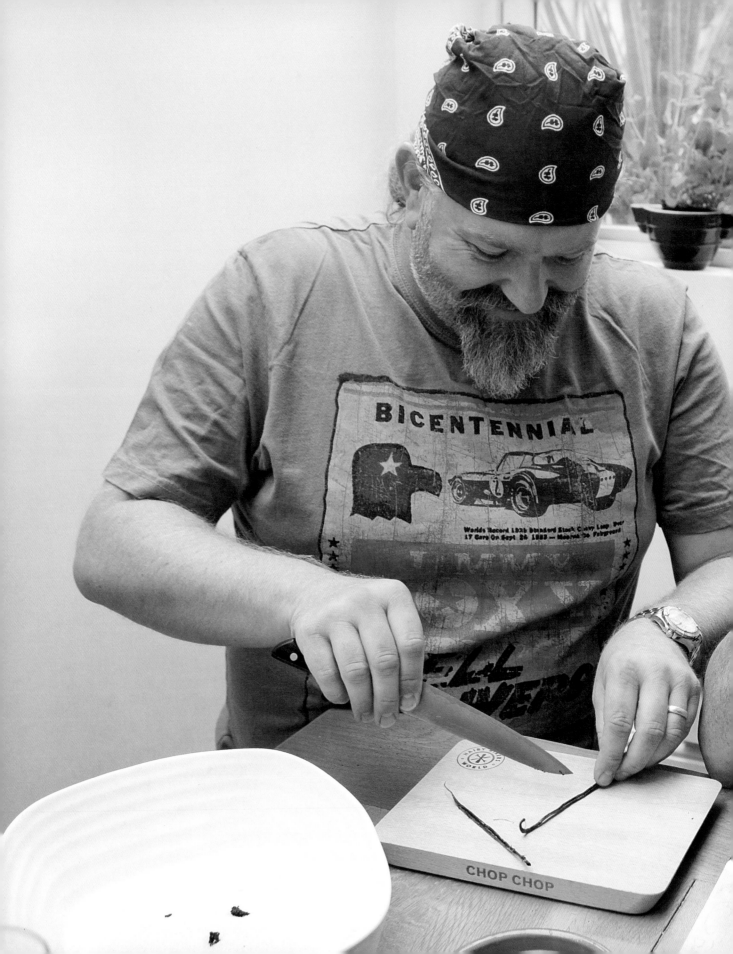

POTTED SHRIMPS

These make Sunday teatime special. You'll need four ramekin dishes.

SERVES 4

200g unsalted butter
splash of lemon juice
zest of ½ lemon
½ tsp mace
pinch of cayenne pepper
200g brown shrimps, peeled
curly parsley, chopped
salt and black pepper

First you need to clarify the butter. Just bring it to the boil in a small pan, then remove it from the heat and skim off the foam. Pour out the clarified butter, leaving the milky residue behind, and mix it with the lemon juice and zest, mace, cayenne and seasoning.

Divide the shrimps between the ramekins and pour a quarter of the spiced butter mixture into each. Add some chopped parsley if you like.

Place the ramekins in the fridge until set solid. Serve with a side salad, lemon wedges and melba toast.

MELBA TOAST

Serve this with potted shrimps or prawn cocktail.

SERVES 4

1 white loaf or
8 slices of white sliced bread

THE PROPER WAY
Preheat the oven to 180°C/Gas 4. Trim the crusts off a good white loaf and cut into wafer-thin slices. Place on a baking tray and bake for about 10 minutes until crispy.

THE QUICK WAY
Take some white sliced bread and pop it into the toaster. Split the slices of toast in two before serving.

SPAGHETTI ALLA CARBONARA

A classic quick supper dish that you will want to make again and again. This is our version and it's a proper carbonara – not the creamy custard effort with bits of tired boiled ham you get in many establishments. You can use Pecorino cheese if you want a slightly more mellow flavour.

SERVES 4

1 tbsp extra virgin olive oil
250g pancetta or very smoky bacon, cut into tiny cubes
100g unsalted butter
150ml dry white wine
4 whole eggs
2 egg yolks
100g Parmesan cheese, grated, plus extra for serving
400g spaghetti
salt and freshly ground black pepper

First, warm the oil in a frying pan and fry the pancetta or bacon slowly until golden. All the lovely smoky flavours will leach into the oil. Add half the butter, then the wine and simmer for a couple of minutes.

In a bowl, beat the whole eggs with the egg yolks and add the cheese. Season, but go easy on the salt because the bacon or pancetta will be salty.

Cook the spaghetti according to the instructions on the packet. Drain the pasta, add to the warm pancetta or bacon mixture and mix until the pasta is nicely coated. Stir in the eggs and cheese – the heat from the pasta will cook the egg.

Stir in the remaining butter, check the seasoning and serve right away with some extra grated cheese and a crunchy salad.

For an even quicker supper dish with a different taste, use cured ham, such as Parma or Serrano, instead of bacon or pancetta. Just cut the ham into small pieces, add it to the pasta with the eggs and warm it through. Serve at once.

THE GURKHAS

The Gurkhas have been part of the British Army for 200 years and are renowned for their bravery in battle. 'Better to die than be a coward', is their motto. The soldiers come from Nepal and northern India and take their name from an eighth-century warrior saint named Guru Gorakhnath. A group from the 2nd Signal Regiment, Imphal Barracks, came to one of our recipe fairs and cooked us some amazing food.

MUTTON CURRY WITH SAUCE
(BHUTEK O DUMBA KO MASU)

This is a great dish that the Gurkhas cooked up for us at the recipe fair.

SERVES 10

1.2kg boneless leg of mutton
250g fresh tomatoes
50g fresh coriander
4 garlic cloves
50g fresh root ginger
250g white onions
75–100ml olive oil
50g garam masala
200g tomato passata
salt to taste

For an extra spicy flavour, add fresh chillies to the mutton.

Cut the mutton into 1.5cm cubes. Blanch the tomatoes, then peel, de-seed and cut them into small dice. Wash the fresh coriander and chop it finely.

Peel the garlic, ginger and onions and chop them very finely until you have a paste – or blitz in a food processor. Heat the oil in a large heavy-based pan until a blue haze appears, then add the ginger, onion and garlic paste and fry for 5 minutes. Add the mutton and fry for a further 5 minutes, then stir in the garam masala, tomato passata, fresh tomatoes and a pinch of salt. Reduce the heat, cover the saucepan and cook for 30–40 minutes.

At the end of this time, check that the mutton is fully cooked and tender and adjust the seasoning. Serve in a heated dish and garnish with the fresh coriander. For a proper feast, serve with basmati rice, dhal (lentils), aludam potatoes, naan bread and Gurkha sesame chutney.

CURRIED POTATOES
(ALUDAM)

Serve this with the mutton curry opposite for a Gurkha-style feast.

SERVES 10

2kg white potatoes, peeled
200g white onions, peeled and sliced
50g fresh green chillies, sliced
4 garlic cloves
50g fresh root ginger
50g fresh coriander
150ml rapeseed oil, for frying
1 tsp ground cumin
1 tsp ground turmeric
1 tsp garam masala
100g tomato passata
salt and pepper

Cut the potatoes into small dice (about 1cm) and blanch them in salted water until partly cooked. Mix the sliced onions with the green chillies. Peel and finely dice the garlic and ginger, then add them to the onion and chilli mix. Wash and finely chop the fresh coriander.

Heat the oil in a large pan until a blue haze appears. Add the onion, garlic and ginger mixture, fry for a few minutes, then add all the remaining spices, tomato passata and a pinch of salt. Fry for a further 5 minutes. Add the potatoes and sauté until all the ingredients have combined and the potato is cooked. Adjust the seasoning to taste and garnish with some fresh coriander.

SESAME CHUTNEY

This is a perfect accompaniment to any lamb or mutton curry.

170g fresh tomatoes
30g sesame seeds
110g cucumber, peeled and diced
170g white onions, peeled and diced
60g green chillies, seeded and diced
juice and zest of 1 medium lemon
55g fresh coriander, washed and finely chopped
½ tsp salt

Blanch the tomatoes, then peel, de-seed and cut them into small dice. Grind the sesame seeds. Mix all the ingredients together, reserving a spoonful of chopped coriander. Add salt to taste, transfer to a chilled bowl to serve and garnish with the rest of the fresh coriander.

Birthday treats

SUMMER BERRY TRIFLE

This fresh fruit trifle may take a little time to make, but it's worth the effort. We like to include the jelly, but if you're short of time, leave it out and the trifle will still be delicious. You can vary the booze to suit the jelly flavour – for example, limoncello with lemon jelly or cassis with blackcurrant.

SERVES 8

1 x 170g jam Swiss roll
5 tbsp cream sherry
75g blueberries
100g raspberries
150g strawberries, hulled and halved
135g packet raspberry or strawberry jelly

CUSTARD

300ml whole milk
300ml double cream
1 vanilla pod, slit lengthways
and seeds removed
2 tbsp cornflour
4 large free-range egg yolks
75g caster sugar

TOPPING

flaked almonds
300ml double cream

Cut the Swiss roll into 12 slices and arrange over the base and a short way up the sides of a glass trifle bowl. Put the remaining slices in the middle. Spoon the sherry over the sponge slices and let it soak in. Scatter the fresh fruit on top of the soaked sponge. Make the jelly according to the instructions on the packet and pour it over the fruit. Cover the dish with clingfilm and leave in the fridge for about 2 hours for the jelly to set.

Meanwhile, make the custard. Pour the milk and cream into a medium saucepan and add the vanilla pod and seeds. Bring to the boil, taking care that it doesn't boil over. Remove from the heat and leave to infuse for 15 minutes. Remove the vanilla pod.

Blend the cornflour with 2 tablespoons of cold water and set aside. Whisk the egg yolks and sugar in a large bowl until pale and thick. Gradually stir in the milk and cream mixture until smooth. Pour the mixture back into the saucepan and return to the heat. Cook over a low heat for 8–10 minutes, stirring constantly, until the custard is thick enough to coat the back of a spoon – it should have the consistency of single cream. Do not overheat or the eggs may scramble!

Give the cornflour mixture a stir, then mix quickly into the custard. Cook for 1–2 minutes longer, until the custard is well thickened and smooth, stirring constantly. Remove from the heat and pour into a bowl placed over another bowl filled with iced water. Cover the surface of the custard with clingfilm to prevent a skin forming and leave until it is cold.

Remove the clingfilm, stir the custard and gently pour it onto the set jelly. Return the trifle dish to the fridge for another 30 minutes or until the custard is lightly set. To prepare the topping, lightly toast the almonds in a dry frying pan over a low heat until golden, turning regularly. Set aside to cool.

Whip the cream until it forms soft peaks. Spoon the whipped cream over the custard, starting at the sides of the bowl before working your way into the middle. Scatter over the almonds, cover and return to the fridge until ready to serve.

Thickening the custard with a little cornflour stops the cream topping from sinking into the custard.

CURRIED MUTTON
WITH RICE & PEAS & FRIED DUMPLINGS

Connie Smith runs an amazing Caribbean takeaway called Connie's Nine Mile in Leicester and she serves up the tastiest food. She learned to cook from her granny and great-granny back in Jamaica and came to Britain in the 1960s. She cooked a dish for us that features at every Caribbean social event, from birthdays and weddings to christenings. It's often referred to as 'big people's food' but is enjoyed by young and old alike. Rice and peas is a great accompaniment – Connie explained to us that it's always called rice and peas, whatever kind of dried pea or bean you use.

SERVES 6

CURRIED MUTTON
900g mutton
1 medium onion, finely chopped
2 garlic cloves, finely chopped
2 spring onions (scallions), roughly chopped
1 Scotch bonnet pepper, finely chopped
2½ tbsp curry powder
1 sprig of fresh thyme
1½ tsp of salt
½ tsp ground black pepper
2 carrots, peeled and roughly chopped
2 celery sticks, roughly chopped
1 tbsp vegetable oil

RICE AND PEAS
225g kidney beans, soaked overnight, or a can of beans
1 fresh coconut or a can of coconut milk
2 whole spring onions (scallions)
1 sprig of fresh thyme
2 tsp salt
900g easy-cook long grain rice
1 Scotch bonnet pepper
1 knob of butter or margarine

Wash the meat and cut it into cubes. Place it in a large dish and season with the onion, garlic, spring onions, Scotch bonnet, curry powder, thyme, salt and pepper, then add the chopped carrots and celery. Leave to marinate for at least 2 hours but ideally overnight.

When the meat has marinated, heat a heavy-based pan with the oil. Remove the meat from the seasoning and brown it in the pan in batches. Set the seasoning aside for later. Then put all the meat in the pan, cover it with boiling water and simmer for 2 hours or until tender.

Add the seasoning and simmer for another 30 minutes, adding more water if necessary. At the end of the cooking time, the mutton mixture should be reduced to a tender stew.

RICE AND PEAS
If using dried beans, soak them overnight in cold water. The next day, drain them, place in a large saucepan and cover with fresh water. Bring to the boil and boil for 10 minutes, then simmer until the beans are tender.

If you want to use fresh coconut instead of canned coconut milk, grate the flesh of the coconut into a bowl. Pour 150ml of boiling water over it, leave to stand for 1 hour, then squeeze through a damp cloth.

Add the coconut milk to the beans, with the spring onions, thyme and salt. Bring to the boil and add the rice and Scotch bonnet (whole, not chopped) and stir. The water should be just covering the rice.

FRIED DUMPLINGS
700g self-raising flour
½ tsp salt
30g butter or margarine
300ml oil, for frying

Reduce to a very low heat and simmer for 30 minutes by which time the rice should be tender and the water absorbed. If the rice is still hard, add a little more water and continue to simmer until cooked.

Remove the whole Scotch bonnet and spring onion. Add a knob of butter, then simmer for a further 5 minutes. Serve hot with curried mutton and dumplings.

FRIED DUMPLINGS
Sieve the flour into a bowl and stir in the salt. Cut the butter into small cubes and add to the flour.

Add water a little at a time and work it into the mixture to make a dough – if the water is added too quickly the mixture may not bind properly. Knead the dough until it is smooth. Divide into small balls about 5cm in diameter, then flatten the balls so that they are about 2cm thick.

Heat the oil over a low heat and fry the dumplings until they are golden brown all over – about 5 minutes. Place them on some kitchen towel to absorb the excess oil and serve hot.

SKY (SEXY) JUICE

Connie says you can make this drink into a light meal by adding some vanilla nourishment powder. Or you can make it with Guinness instead of pineapple juice!

1 x 1 litre carton of pineapple juice
½ can of condensed milk (or to taste)
grated nutmeg
vanilla essence

Whizz up the pineapple juice and the condensed milk – add more or less according to how sweet you like your treats. Add a grating of nutmeg and a few drops of vanilla essence.

SATURDAY SOUP

Another recipe from Connie. This is what she told us about this one: 'When I was growing up in Jamaica, it was a tradition that every Saturday we'd all eat soup made from various meats, an assortment of Caribbean vegetables and soft spinner dumplings. It was the only thing cooked on a Saturday and was made in a huge pot to serve all the members of the family and any friends visiting. This tradition still goes on today, not only in Jamaica but also throughout the Caribbean islands and with many families living in the UK. This is my version of Saturday soup, just like mama used to make.'

SERVES 10–12

1 chicken carcass for stock
750g boned chicken thigh meat
450g pumpkin
1 cho-cho (or squash)
450g soft yam
450g potatoes
225g sweet potatoes
2 sweetcorn (on the cob)
2 spring onions (scallions)
1 Scotch bonnet pepper, finely chopped
2 sprigs of fresh thyme
1 packet of chicken noodle soup
salt and black pepper to taste
cornflour (optional)

SPINNER DUMPLINGS
450g plain flour
½ tsp salt

Half fill a large saucepan with water and bring it to the boil. Add the chicken carcass and cook it for 1 hour. Discard the bones, add the chicken meat, cut into pieces, and cook for another 30 minutes until the chicken is cooked. Skim any froth from the top of the stock.

Wash and peel the vegetables, except the Scotch bonnet, and cut them into bite-size pieces – not too small. Add them to the stock, bring it back to the boil and simmer for another 30 minutes, stirring occasionally.

Meanwhile, sift the flour and salt into a bowl. Add enough cold water to make a soft dough and knead for 5 minutes. Roll the dough in the palm of your hand to make sausage-shaped dumplings about 6cm long and 1.5cm thick.

Add the dumplings, Scotch bonnet, thyme and chicken noodle soup mix to the saucepan and season to taste. Stir and simmer for 15–20 minutes, then serve hot. The soup should be of a medium consistency so add some boiling water if it's too thick. If it's too watery, add some cornflour, stir well and simmer for another 5 minutes.

COTTAGE PIE
WITH CHEESY MASH

We both think that cottage or shepherd's pie is the perfect birthday tea – these were a real treat for us when we were lads. Our special version of shepherd's pie is made just the same way as below, but with two parts minced lamb to one part haggis for a good gamey flavour.

SERVES 4–5

1 tbsp sunflower oil
1 large onion, chopped
2 celery sticks, stringed and diced
2 medium-large carrots, peeled and diced
2 garlic cloves, finely chopped
500g lean minced beef
150ml red wine
2 tbsp plain flour
250ml beef stock (fresh or from a cube)
2 tbsp tomato purée
½ tsp mixed dried herbs
1 bay leaf
splash of Worcestershire sauce
salt and freshly ground black pepper

TOPPING

800g medium potatoes, peeled and cut into even-sized pieces
40g butter, cubed
3 tbsp milk
100g good mature Cheddar cheese, grated
salt and freshly ground black pepper

Heat the sunflower oil in a large deep sauté pan or saucepan and gently fry the onion, celery and carrots for 8 minutes or until the onions are softened and lightly coloured. Add the garlic and cook for 2 minutes more. Stir all the vegetables occasionally to prevent them from becoming too brown.

Tip the mince into the pan and cook with the vegetables for 5 minutes or until no pinkness remains, stirring regularly to break up the meat. Pour the wine into the pan and cook until all the liquid evaporates, then sprinkle over the flour and stir well for a minute or two.

Gradually stir the beef stock into the pan. Add 250ml of cold water, the tomato purée and herbs. Bring to a gentle simmer, cover and cook over a low heat for 25–30 minutes, stirring occasionally, until the mince is tender and the sauce has thickened. If it starts to look too dry, add some more stock or water. Season with Worcestershire sauce and salt and pepper to taste. Remove from the heat and spoon the mince mixture into a 1.5 litre ovenproof dish. Leave to stand while you get the mash ready.

Boil the potatoes until they are very soft. Drain well, then return them to the saucepan and add the butter, milk and cheese. Mash until smooth and creamy and season to taste. Preheat the oven to 200°C/Gas 6.

Spoon the potato over the mince mixture, working around the edge before heading towards the middle. When all the mince is covered, rough up the surface with a fork and place the dish on a baking tray. Bake in the centre of the oven for about 25 minutes or until the potatoes are golden brown and the filling is bubbling. Serve with freshly cooked green beans or shredded Savoy cabbage. And don't forget the ketchup!

STUFFED VINE LEAVES (DOLMADES/KOUBEBIA)

In Birmingham, we met Ira Phedon, whose family is from Cyprus. Ira loves to cook for her large family and admits she spends much of her time cooking for the masses. This is what she says about her version of stuffed vine leaves: 'These are a bit fiddly to make but well worth it, I promise you! It goes without saying that tender, fresh vine leaves are better in flavour and texture than the preserved ones, but I realise that the fresh variety can be difficult to come by. So if you know anyone who has a vine growing in their garden, get friendly! You can wrap the leaves in clingfilm in batches of about 35 and freeze them so that you have fresh leaves all year round. But don't worry if you can only get the preserved leaves. You'll still end up making the tastiest "koubebia" you've ever tasted. If you do use leaves preserved in brine, though, do make sure you wash them really well. These stuffed vine leaves are wonderful eaten with a nice Greek salad (don't forget the dips) and some warm pitta bread. Or serve with roast chicken as an alternative to your usual veg and gravy.'

MAKES ABOUT 30

30–35 vine leaves (about 200g)
500g pork mince
1 large onion, peeled and finely chopped
about 60g fresh flat-leaf parsley, finely chopped
100g long-grain white rice, rinsed and left to drain
1 chicken stock cube
½ x 400g can of good-quality chopped tomatoes
1 very generous tbsp tomato purée
juice of 1 large lemon
120ml extra virgin olive oil
1 tbsp dried mint
½ tsp ground cinnamon
salt and freshly ground black pepper
1 heaped tsp butter

Whether your vine leaves are fresh, frozen or preserved, place them in a wide shallow bowl and pour over enough boiling water to cover them. Leave them to soften and/or thaw for 3–4 minutes. Drain the water and gently squeeze the leaves between your hands to remove as much liquid as possible. Remember that the leaves are quite delicate, so don't squeeze too hard. Wrap them in some kitchen towel to absorb any excess moisture.

The next part is nice and easy. Place all the ingredients, except the butter, vine leaves and 2 tablespoons of the olive oil, into a large mixing bowl. Make sure you crumble the stock cube well between your fingers so that it gets distributed, then start to knead the mixture with your hands until everything is thoroughly combined.

Drizzle the remaining olive oil into the base of a medium-sized saucepan. Gently unravel the vine leaves and use 3 or 4 to line the base of the saucepan so that the stuffed leaves don't stick.

It's best to prepare the vine leaves on a plate rather than a completely flat surface, so that the plate can catch the juices.

Later, when you've finished preparing the dolmades, you can pour any leftover juice from the plate or the mixing bowl over the stuffed vine leaves in the saucepan.

Place a vine leaf (top side down) on the plate. Carefully spoon about a tablespoon of the meat mixture onto the bottom end of the leaf, close to the stem. Now fold the left and right sides of the leaf over the filling and roll it up quite tightly (but not too much so) from the base, into a neat cylinder.

As you stuff the vine leaves, place them into the saucepan, one at a time, working round from the sides of the saucepan to the centre and packing them in quite tightly. Depending on the diameter of the saucepan, you will probably have two layers. Pour over about 75ml of cold water and any juice remaining on your plate or mixing bowl and dot with the butter.

If you are left with any spare leaves, layer them over the top of the dolmades.

Finally, find a plate that fits snugly into the saucepan and place it over the vine leaves to keep them in place. Put the saucepan over a medium heat and when the liquid starts to boil, turn the heat right down, cover the saucepan with a lid and leave to simmer gently for about 45 minutes.

About halfway through the cooking time, remove the lid and partially cover for the rest of the time. When the dolmades are ready, remove the saucepan from the heat and clamp the lid back on.

Always allow at least 45 minutes resting time so the juices are fully absorbed. Then the dolmades are ready to serve.

Obviously, vine leaves can vary quite a lot in size, so reduce or increase the quantity of stuffing to suit your leaves.

BASTICHIO

Another one from Ira and one of her favourite Greek dishes. This is what she says about it: 'Bastichio is the name that I grew up with, but some villages in Cyprus call this dish "macaronia tou fournou", which loosely translated means "baked pasta". There is a lot more to it than that, however! I like to describe it as the Greek version of lasagne and I think it's even nicer if that's possible, but obviously I'm biased. It's also one of those ever-popular dishes that is great for any buffet or celebratory meal. It can be prepared the day before up to the point of baking and refrigerating, so that all of the hard work is out of the way and you can bake it fresh on the day you're going to eat it – great for when you've got friends and family coming round! It goes without saying that a big juicy Greek salad goes really well with this one.' This is how Ira makes bastichio.

SERVES 8 (or 6 Greeks!)

MIDDLE LAYER: MEAT SAUCE

2 tbsp vegetable oil
500g pork mince
5 tbsp olive oil
2 medium onions, peeled and finely chopped
2 fat garlic cloves, peeled and finely chopped
1 heaped tsp ground cinnamon
2 heaped tbsp dried mint
1 chicken stock cube
big handful of fresh flat-leaf parsley, finely chopped
about 500g tomato passata
good sprinkling of paprika
½ tsp sugar
salt and freshly ground black pepper

BOTTOM LAYER: PASTA

1 chicken or vegetable stock cube
350g penne rigate
pinch of grated or ground nutmeg
1 heaped tbsp butter
about 200g Greek halloumi cheese, grated
2 egg whites from large eggs, lightly beaten
8 tbsp béchamel sauce

You will need a rectangular oven dish measuring about 33 x 29cm and 7cm deep.

Even though the meat sauce forms the middle layer of the bastichio, I always prepare it first and leave it to simmer gently while I get on with the rest of it. The way I like to fry mince may be different to what you're used to: basically I like to drain away the fat before adding any of the other ingredients, so that I don't lose any of those gorgeous flavours.

Begin by heating the oil in a large saucepan and then add the mince. Fry the mince over a medium heat for about 5 minutes until it browns, stirring most of the time to break up any lumps and stop it from sticking to the bottom of the saucepan. Now, drain away most of the fat. There's no need to sieve it, just gingerly tilt the pan over the sink and use the lid or a slotted spoon as a barrier to stop the mince from falling out.

Return the pan to the heat, add the olive oil, onions and garlic and fry for a couple of minutes. Add the cinnamon, mint, crumbled stock cube, parsley, passata, paprika, sugar and a seasoning of salt and freshly ground black pepper and give it all a really good stir.

Partly cover with a lid and leave the meat to simmer on a low heat, stirring every now and then, until about 10 minutes before it's time to assemble the bastichio.

Bring a large pan of lightly salted water to the boil and add the stock cube. Add the penne and cook according to the instructions on the packet.

TOP LAYER: BÉCHAMEL

200g butter, melted and cooled
½ tsp grated or ground nutmeg
pinch of ground cinnamon
pinch of salt
2 egg yolks from large eggs
1.2 litres milk
200ml crème fraîche
150g cornflour
about 100g Greek halloumi cheese,
grated

Like a lot of Greek food, bastichio tastes best served lukewarm, rather than piping hot.

While the meat and the pasta are simmering, start on the béchamel sauce. In another saucepan, place the cooled, melted butter, nutmeg, cinnamon, salt and egg yolks and gently whisk until well combined – a balloon whisk is best for this. Add the milk and crème fraîche and whisk again to incorporate. Set aside for a few moments while you attend to the pasta.

When the pasta is ready, drain most of the liquid away reserving about 2 or 3 tablespoons. Pour the pasta with the reserved liquid into the base of your oven dish and while it's hot and steaming, add the nutmeg, butter and the halloumi cheese and mix really well. Set aside for a couple of minutes to cool down slightly and then stir in the egg whites.

Preheat the oven to 180°C/Gas 4. To finish the béchamel, add the cornflour, a tablespoon at a time, whisking as each spoonful goes in. Place the saucepan over a medium heat and start to whisk for England – don't stop until the sauce is completely ready. It will look slightly unattractive and lumpy at the start, but don't panic as it will turn into a beautiful, glossy sauce when it's finished. As the sauce starts to thicken, turn the heat down slightly and stir a bit harder, so that it doesn't catch the bottom of the pan. When the béchamel starts to bubble gently, remove from the heat and stir 8 tablespoons into the pasta.

Take the slightly cooled meat sauce and spread it all over the pasta to cover the meat completely. Finally, spread the lovely béchamel over the meat sauce and sprinkle generously with the grated halloumi cheese.

Place the bastichio in the top third of the oven for about 40 minutes until it's nicely browned. Leave to stand for about an hour before dishing up (or preferably a bit longer if you can resist) as it allows the juices to settle and absorb, and makes it easier to cut into pieces. It's definitely worth the wait.

If you have prepared the bastichio for cooking the next day, pop it in fridge once it is cool. Just remember to take it out a couple of hours before you want to cook it. It will need a longer cooking time – about 1 hour – to make sure it is brown and bubbling and the meat is thoroughly reheated.

VERY SPECIAL
CHOCOLATE MOUSSE TRIO

Chocolate mousse must be one of the most popular of all desserts. We love it – but we are talking mousse with good chocolate, really decadent and luxurious. This recipe is from Si's Auntie Hilda who made it for his mam and dad's silver wedding anniversary and we have tinkered a little to make it super special. Using three different chocolates – dark, milk and white – takes this dish to another dimension, and there's an optional hit of Drambuie in the white chocolate part. Auntie Hilda would be proud. You'll need some nice glasses for serving the mousse.

SERVES 6–8

750ml whipping cream
200g dark chocolate, broken into pieces
200g milk chocolate, broken into pieces
200g white chocolate, broken into pieces
150g unsalted butter, divided into
3 x 50g pieces
3 egg yolks
1 big splash of Drambuie
extra dark chocolate for grating on top
(optional)

First whip the cream until it is firm and put it in the fridge to chill while you deal with the chocolate.

Set up 3 bain maries – that's 3 pudding basins over 3 pans of gently boiling water. The mission is to melt the 3 types of chocolate slowly. Place one kind of chocolate in each bowl. Add 50g of butter, cut into cubes, to each bowl. Let the chocolate and butter melt gently on their own – do not stir. Once melted, take the pans off the heat, stir with a fork to mix the butter and chocolate together, then leave to cool.

Once the chocolate and butter mixtures are cool enough, about blood temperature, stir an egg yolk into each bowl. Be patient here. If the chocolate is still too hot the eggs will scramble and we don't want that.

Bring out the whipped cream and divide into three. Into one portion, mix a good splash of Drambuie and fold that into the white chocolate with a spatula. Fold the other portions of cream into the dark chocolate and the milk chocolate.

Now you have 3 different kinds of chocolate mousse. Take the glasses that you are going to use for serving and spoon in some of the milk chocolate mousse. Layer on a spoonful of the Drambuie and white chocolate mousse, then finish with the dark chocolate mixture. Top with some grated dark chocolate if you like.

Refrigerate for at least 2 hours before serving. Pudding doesn't get much more special than this.

SAUSAGE PLAIT

Yvonne Langford from Digby, Lincolnshire, showed us some great recipes. Yvonne's grandma was a cook in a big country house and her grandad cooked for the Australian army so she has a real background in food. She herself trained as a chef and spent 30 years in catering. We are of the firm opinion that no birthday party is complete without a sausage roll, but they are the most abused item in British cooking. Yvonne's version – a sausage plait – is a winner so give it a try.

SERVES 6–8

PASTRY
450g plain flour
2 pinches of salt
140g lard, diced
140g margarine, diced
1 egg, beaten, and a little milk

FILLING
500g good quality sausage meat
2 medium onions, peeled and finely chopped
2 tsp mixed herbs
salt and black pepper

Start by making the pastry. Mix the flour and salt, then add the diced lard and margarine. Stir the fat in with a knife – do not rub in – and add a little cold water to make a stiff dough.

Roll the dough out to a narrow strip on a floured surface. Then fold it into 3 and turn it 90 degrees clockwise so that one of the open ends is towards you. Roll out and turn again. Repeat this 3 times, then cover the pastry and leave it to rest for about 15 minutes. Roll out into a rectangle ready for filling. (In hot weather, chill the pastry in the fridge or a cool place for 20–30 minutes before using.) You can, of course, use a packet of puff pastry if you prefer.

Preheat the oven to 230°C/Gas 8. Mix the sausage meat with the onions and add the mixed herbs and seasoning. Place the rectangle of pastry on a greased non-stick baking tray. Place the sausage mixture down the centre of the pastry, leaving a 5cm border down each side.

Working down each side, cut strips from the mixture to the edge of the pastry at a 45° angle at 2.5cm intervals. Carefully plait these strips across the sausage filling, working alternately left to right, then right to left. When the plaiting is complete, brush the pastry with a mixture of beaten egg and milk. Place in the oven and bake for about 30 minutes or until golden brown. Great hot or cold – just slice as required.

MANCHESTER TART

This used to be a school dinner favourite. We love it and Yvonne's version with banana
is especially good. Yvonne told us that she used to keep her recipes secret, but is now
happy to share them so that they don't disappear.

SERVES 6

PASTRY

450g self-raising flour
pinch of salt
110g lard
110g margarine
55g sugar

FILLING

3 tbsp custard powder
3 tbsp sugar
850ml milk
200g strawberry jam
3 large bananas, sliced
3 tbsp desiccated coconut

To make the pastry, mix the flour and salt in bowl, then rub
in the lard and margarine until the mixture has a crumbly
texture. Mix in the sugar. Using a knife, mix in a little cold
water until a stiff dough is formed. Turn the dough out onto
a floured worktop and roll it out to fit your flan tin. Lay the
pastry over the tin, taking care to push it well into the sides.
Trim off any excess.

Preheat the oven to 190°C/Gas 5. Put a circle of greaseproof
paper over the pastry and pour in some baking beans or rice
to keep it from rising. Bake for 15–20 minutes, then take
the pastry out of the oven and leave it to cool. Remove the
greaseproof paper and baking beans.

Put the custard powder and sugar in a bowl, add 2 tablespoons
of the milk and mix to a smooth paste. Pour the rest of the
milk into a saucepan and heat until nearly boiling, then pour
this onto the custard mix, stirring well. Return the custard to
the saucepan and bring to the boil over a gentle heat. Cook,
stirring continuously, until the mixture thickens. Take off the
heat and leave to cool.

Spread the jam on the base of the baked pastry case and
add the sliced bananas. Pour the custard on top of the
bananas and chill in the fridge overnight. Before serving,
top with toasted coconut. To prepare this, put the desiccated
coconut on a baking tray. Heat up the grill and place the
coconut under the grill to toast. Watch the coconut carefully
as it burns easily. Sprinkle the coconut on top of the custard
and serve the tart with a jug of cream.

SNOW QUEEN

This recipe comes from Si's mother-in-law, Margaret. It's simple to prepare but really wows the taste buds. You'll need one of those jars of stem ginger in sugar syrup, which you can find in the supermarket or a good deli. It's worth hunting one out because it makes all the difference. Enjoy! We have on numerous occasions.

SERVES 4 GENEROUSLY

500ml double cream
2 tbsp brandy
1 tbsp caster sugar
1 tbsp chopped stem ginger, plus extra for garnish
1 tbsp stem ginger syrup (from the jar)
150g meringues
½ tsp groundnut oil
chocolate sauce or grated dark chocolate to serve

Pour the cream into a bowl and whisk until stiff – be careful not to overwhip it though, or it will split. Gently fold in the brandy, sugar, chopped ginger and ginger syrup until evenly distributed through the cream. Check for sweetness and add a touch more sugar or syrup if you want it sweeter. Roughly break up the meringues by hand – you need nice chunks, not dust – and fold them into the cream. This is your snow queen!

Lightly grease a 600ml pudding basin or an ice cream bomb mould with the groundnut oil. Spoon the mixture into the basin or mould and cover with foil, then clingfilm. Place in the freezer for 8 hours.

When you are nearly ready to serve, turn the snow queen out onto a serving plate and place it in the fridge for 15 minutes to soften a little. Sprinkle with extra stem ginger and top with some chocolate sauce or grated dark chocolate.

CHOCOLATE SAUCE

200g dark chocolate, broken into squares
2 tbsp golden syrup
55g butter, diced
small carton of single cream

Place a bowl over a pan of simmering water and add all the ingredients. Keep over a gentle heat until everything has melted, then stir and pour over your queen!

WELSH GRIDDLE CAKES

A friend of ours, whose family has made these griddle cakes for years, gave us this recipe.
In Argentina, we have eaten these topped with dulce de leche. Closer to home in Wales, they
are served with butter and jam or a slice of Caerphilly cheese.

MAKES ABOUT 12

250g plain flour
1 tsp baking powder
¼ tsp freshly grated nutmeg
¼ tsp salt
1 tsp allspice
75g caster sugar
zest of 1 lemon
50g butter, diced
50g lard or vegetable shortening, diced
1 egg
100ml milk
½ tsp vanilla extract
75g currants

Sift the flour, baking powder, grated nutmeg, salt and allspice into a bowl. Add the sugar and lemon zest and stir them into the flour. Using your fingers, work in the butter and lard or shortening until the mixture is the texture of breadcrumbs.

Beat the egg into the milk and add the vanilla. Add the egg mixture to the flour and mix to make a soft dough, then stir in the currents – this will start to look spottier than a Dalmatian with acne.

Cook the cakes on a griddle if you have one or in a heavy frying pan. Grease the pan and heat it to a medium temperature – don't let it get too hot or the outside of the cakes will burn, leaving the middles uncooked. With wet hands, or a wet spoon, take golf-ball sized pieces of the dough and flatten them to form cakes about 1cm thick. Cook for about 5 minutes on each side over a low heat.

Serve warm with butter and jam – maybe with some clotted cream on the side.

THE BRADFORD CURRY PROJECT
MUTTAR PANEER

The stated mission of the Bradford Curry Project is to provide free meals for the homeless, poor and underprivileged people of Bradford. The project was launched 17 years ago by Lashman Singh, who started out serving food from a van, and it became a charity in 1995. It is a multi-faith, multi-cultural charity in which all the major faiths of Bradford work together to serve those in need. Why is it called the Curry Project? Because in Asian communities the word 'curry' is a common denominator for food. But just as a soup kitchen doesn't only hand out soup, the Bradford Curry Project doesn't just make curry.

The Bradford Curry Project gave us this great recipe. Muttar paneer is a fresh, lightly spiced curry made with home-made Indian curd cheese (paneer) and frozen peas. It's good for vegetarians and you can vary the vegetables – for example, use half peas and half spinach. The cheese needs to be made in advance but it's easy and once that's done the curry is quick to assemble and cook. It can be frozen.

SERVES 4–6

PANEER
2 litres whole milk
2–4 tbsp lemon juice

CURRY
3 tbsp vegetable oil, for frying
1½ tsp cumin seeds
1 large onion, peeled and thinly sliced
1½ tbsp chopped garlic (6–8 large cloves)
thumb-sized piece of fresh ginger
(about 15g), chopped
red chilli or 1 tsp chilli flakes
(more if you like hot curry)
2 tsp ground coriander
750g frozen peas
10–12 cherry tomatoes, halved
(optional but they add some colour)
1–2 tsp garam masala
4 tbsp double cream or 6 tbsp milk
1–2 tbsp chopped fresh coriander
1–2 tsp lemon juice
salt to taste

First make the paneer – you will need a sieve, large bowl or saucepan, and a piece of muslin (or other thin material) for draining the cheese. Pour the milk into a heavy-based pan and slowly bring it to the boil. Once the milk starts to boil and rise up, add the lemon juice and stir with a wooden spoon. The milk will begin to curdle and separate into pale yellow liquid and small white solids (the curds). This should happen within a minute or so. If not, add some more lemon juice and keep stirring. Remove the pan from the heat.

Line a large sieve with the muslin and place it over a large bowl or saucepan. Pour the contents of the pan into the lined sieve and run some cold water through it. Tie the cloth and hang it from the tap over the sink to allow the excess water to drain away for 10 minutes. Then, keeping it fairly tightly wrapped, place the paneer on a board and put a heavy weight on top of it – this could be a pan filled with water.

Leave for at least 30–40 minutes until the paneer feels firm. The longer you can leave it, the better, but it can be used after 40 minutes. For this recipe, cut the paneer into cubes. You can fry the cheese gently in some sunflower oil to give it a crispy texture, but this is not essential.

To make the curry, heat the oil in a heavy-based pan. Add the cumin seeds and sizzle until you can smell the cumin. Add the thinly sliced onions and sauté gently until they have softened and coloured, without burning, for about 10 minutes.

Be patient, it will happen. Add the garlic, ginger and chilli and cook for about a minute. Add the coriander and salt.

Stir in the peas and the tomatoes (if using), then add a splash of water and bring to a gentle boil for about 3 minutes. Add the paneer, garam masala, cream or milk and cook for a few more minutes until everything is combined. Sprinkle on the fresh coriander and the lemon juice. Serve with Indian breads or rice.

Sunday dinners

MUSHROOM RISOTTO

Peter Polledri came along with his mum, Susan, and cooked a risotto for us. His mum is English, but Peter's family on his father's side came to London from Italy before the Second World War and started a chain of Italian cafés. Peter loves cooking and makes a mixture of Italian classics and hearty British dishes that he's learned from his mum. Peter cooks his risotto with home-made chicken broth, then uses the chicken cooked in the broth to make a chicken pie.

SERVES 4

30g dried porcini mushrooms
1 litre chicken or vegetable stock
2 tbsp olive oil
4 shallots, peeled and finely chopped
350g risotto rice
1 glass of dry white wine
2 tbsp butter
200g chestnut mushrooms, washed and sliced
2 tbsp crème fraîche or sour cream
50g Parmesan cheese, grated
salt and black pepper

Put the dried porcini mushrooms in a bowl, cover with warm water and leave them to soak for 20 minutes. Drain and chop the porcini and set aside. You can add the soaking water to the stock, but make sure you strain it well to remove any grit.

Bring the stock to the boil and keep it simmering on the hob. Heat a tablespoon of the olive oil in a high-sided pan and sweat the shallots until they are softened and translucent. Add the rice, stir well and cook for a minute or so, then pour in the wine. Stir as this sizzles and bubbles. Once the wine has evaporated, start adding the simmering stock a ladleful at a time. Wait until each ladleful has been absorbed by the rice before adding another and keep stirring. Continue until the rice is cooked – this will probably take about 20 minutes.

Meanwhile, heat a tablespoon of butter and the rest of the oil in a frying pan and sauté the chestnut mushrooms and the porcini. When the rice is ready, take the pan off the heat and stir in the mushrooms and add the cream, Parmesan and the rest of the butter. Season to taste, but take care with the salt as the stock may be quite salty. Garnish with some extra shavings of Parmesan if you like.

ROAST BEEF & YORKSHIRE PUDDING

Roast beef – England's finest and we think that the best is the standing rib roast. Fatty meat like this gives you the best flavour and beef, like lamb, is always best on the bone – viva la T-bone! Go to a good supplier and buy the best beef you can afford. Always bring the meat to room temperature before roasting and use a meat thermometer so you can get the joint roasted exactly as you want. Leave the meat to rest before carving and tip any juices into your gravy pan. Serve with roast potatoes and creamed horseradish (see page 154) and whatever vegetables are in season.

SERVES 10–12

1 x 5kg standing rib of beef, French trimmed
1 tbsp vegetable oil
1 tbsp English mustard powder
1 tbsp sea salt flakes
1 tbsp cracked black pepper
2 onions, cut in half
2 carrots or other root veg, peeled and cut into chunks
1 glass of red wine
1 dsrtsp cornflour
500ml beef stock, for gravy

Cooking times
Rare: 20 mins per kg
Medium rare: 25 mins per kg
Medium: 30 mins per kg
Well done: 40 mins per kg

Preheat the oven to 220°C/Gas 7. Warm a large frying pan on top of the stove until it is searing hot. Rub the beef with the vegetable oil, place it in the frying pan and brown it all over. Remove it from the pan and set it aside. Mix the mustard with the salt and pepper and rub it into the seared joint.

Put the onions and carrots in a roasting tin and place the seasoned meat on top. Pour some water into the tin to a depth of about 5mm – this will stop the beef from drying out and will also help make lots of lovely juices for the gravy. Put the meat into the preheated oven and cook at 220°C/Gas 7 for the first 30 minutes. Turn the oven down to 160°C/Gas 2–3 for the rest of the cooking time.

We think medium rare is the perfect way to serve a rib roast and to achieve this the core temperature of the meat must be 50°C. To check, use a meat thermometer, placing the spike into the centre of the meat. The meat is ready when the reading is 10 degrees below the desired temperature (see opposite), so for medium-rare meat, take the joint out of the oven when the temperature is 40°C. Then set it aside to rest somewhere warm for 15 minutes. During the resting time, the meat will continue to cook inside so it will reach the required temperature within the 15 minutes.

While the meat is resting, make gravy from the juices. Pour away some of the fat, put the roasting pan on the hob and add a glass of red wine. Let it bubble away for a minute or two to boil off the alcohol. Mix the cornflour with 2 tablespoons of the beef stock to make a paste. Add the rest of the stock to the pan, then stir in the cornflour paste to thicken. Mash in the veg and add any juices from the meat. Strain before serving.

YORKSHIRE PUDDING

This is Dave's mam's recipe. Dave learned to cook this when he was six years old and it always works.
Put the spoon in the bag and take out as much flour as you can load onto a tablespoon.

4 heaped tbsp flour
½ tsp salt
2 eggs, beaten
275ml full-fat milk
2 tbsp vegetable oil, such as sunflower
oil, or a blob of goose fat

Sift the flour with the salt into a bowl. Make a well in the centre and gradually work in the beaten eggs. Then whisk in the milk, until the mixture resembles single cream. Leave the batter to stand for at least an hour.

Meanwhile, put the oil or goose fat in a Yorkshire pudding tin and get it smoking hot in a 200°C/Gas 6 oven. Give the batter a stir, quickly pour into the tin and watch it sizzle – this is a good thing! Bake for about 30 minutes or until it has risen to golden-brown perfection. If you're making individual puddings, cook for 10–15 minutes.

TOAD IN THE HOLE

Dave's mam used to make this with tomato sausages
so you got great red fat trails in the Yorkshire pudding.

4 good pork sausages
Yorkshire pudding batter as above

First of all, part-cook the sausages. Put them in a preheated oven at 180°C/Gas 4 and cook until browned and just cooked through. This can be done in advance.

Preheat the oven to 200°C/Gas 6. Make the Yorkshire batter as above and once you've poured it into the sizzling fat, drop in the sausages, spacing them evenly. Bake for about 30 minutes or until beautifully risen and golden and serve with gravy of any kind.

BEST-EVER ROAST POTATOES

Adding semolina is a tip we learned in Ireland and goose fat is a must for really crispy roasties. These really are the tastiest roast potatoes ever.

SERVES 4–6

1.5kg good spuds
(Maris Pipers are good for roasting)
100g goose fat
2 tbsp semolina
sea salt and black pepper

Peel the potatoes and cut them into chunks – whatever size you fancy, according to how you like your roasties.

Put them in a saucepan of cold, salted water, bring to the boil and boil for about 5 minutes. Drain well and then put the potatoes back in the saucepan and shake them to scuff up the surfaces. This helps to give you lovely crispy potatoes.

Meanwhile, preheat the oven to 200–220°C/Gas 6–7 and melt the goose fat in a roasting tin. Sprinkle the semolina over the potatoes and carefully tip them into the sizzling goose fat. Season liberally and roast until golden – this will take about 45–50 minutes, depending on the size of the potatoes.

HORSERADISH SAUCE

No roast beef dinner is complete without this!

4 tbsp grated horseradish root
1 tbsp white wine vinegar
pinch of English mustard powder
1 teaspoon caster sugar
150ml double cream
salt and black pepper

Mix all the ingredients together, season with salt and pepper to taste and serve with the beef.

APPLE & BLACKBERRY CRUMBLE

Everyone likes a good crumble! Using eating apples and Bramleys gives a lovely depth of flavour.

SERVES 6

FILLING
3 eating apples, peeled,
quartered and cored
2 Bramley cooking apples, peeled,
quartered and cored
2 tsp cinnamon
100g demerara sugar
300g blackberries

CRUMBLE TOPPING
175g plain flour
1 tsp cinnamon
140g soft brown sugar
35g porridge oats
180g cold unsalted butter

Put the quartered apples in a bowl and shuffle them around to mix them up a bit. Mix the cinnamon with the sugar in a separate bowl. Put half the apples in an oven dish and sprinkle with a third of the sugar mixture. Add the blackberries and sprinkle with the second third of sugar mixture. Cover with the remaining apples and add the remaining sugar and cinnamon mixture.

Now make the crumble topping. Put the flour and cinnamon in a bowl and mix well, then stir in the sugar and the oats. Cut the butter into small cubes, add to the mixture and rub it in with your fingertips until the mixture is the texture of breadcrumbs. Lay the crumble mixture on top of the fruit.

Preheat the oven to 170°C/Gas 3 and bake the crumble for about 40 minutes. Keep an eye on the top. If the sugar goes golden it looks great – if it turns black, not so good. Serve with home-made custard.

HOME-MADE CUSTARD

An old-fashioned treat that is definitely worth the effort. Sorry – custard powder can't compete with this.

SERVES 6

600ml whole milk
1 vanilla pod
6 large egg yolks
75g caster sugar

Pour the milk into a saucepan. Slash the vanilla pod and scrape out the seeds. Add the seeds to the cold milk and throw in the pod. Heat the milk up to boiling point, remove from the heat and leave to infuse for 15 minutes. Beat the egg yolks with the sugar until they are a pale golden colour.

Remove the vanilla pod from the milk and place the milk back on the heat. Gradually stir in the egg yolk and sugar mixture and cook until thickened. If it goes lumpy, don't despair – just pour it through a sieve. May be eaten hot or cold.

LEMON MERINGUE PIE

A pudding that everyone loves and everyone eats. Make it and enjoy yourself.

SERVES 6

PASTRY

200g plain flour

½ tsp caster sugar

125g butter, cut into cubes

1 medium free-range egg, beaten

LEMON FILLING

50g cornflour

350ml cold water

200g caster sugar

freshly squeezed juice and finely grated
zest of 4 large lemons

3 medium free-range egg yolks

1 medium free-range egg

MERINGUE TOPPING

3 medium free-range egg whites

175g caster sugar

¼ tsp vanilla extract

To make the pastry, put the flour, sugar and butter in a food processor and pulse until the mixture resembles fine breadcrumbs. With the motor running, gradually add the beaten egg and blend until the mixture forms a ball. Do not over blend or the pastry will be tough. Tip the dough onto a floured board and roll out to about 5mm thick, turning the pastry and flouring the surface regularly. Use the pastry to line a 20cm fluted flan tin. Trim the edges of the pastry neatly and chill for 30 minutes. Preheat the oven to 200°C/Gas 6.

While the pastry is resting, make the filling. Put the cornflour in a bowl and mix with enough of the cold water to make a thin paste. Set aside. Pour the remaining water into a large saucepan and add the sugar, lemon zest and juice – you should have about 225ml of lemon juice. Heat gently until the sugar dissolves, then bring to the boil. Reduce the heat slightly, then stir in the cornflour and the mixture should start to thicken.

Stir over a low heat for 3 minutes until the mixture is thick and glossy. Remove from the heat and cool for 5 minutes. Whisk the egg yolks with the whole egg until smooth, then whisk vigorously into the mixture. Set aside to cool for 25 minutes.

Put the flan tin with the pastry on a sturdy baking sheet and line with baking parchment. Fill with baking beans and bake blind in the preheated oven for 15 minutes. Carefully take it out of the oven and remove the paper and beans. Return the pastry to the oven for another 3–4 minutes until the surface is dry. Remove from the oven and reduce the temperature to 150°C/Gas 2.

To make the meringue, whisk the egg whites in a large bowl until stiff, then gradually whisk in half the sugar. Add the vanilla extract and continue whisking in the remaining sugar until it is all used. Stir the cooled lemon filling well and pour it into the pastry case. Very gently, spoon the meringue onto the top of the pie and swirl into peaks. Bake for 25 minutes at 150°C/Gas 2 or until the meringue is set and very lightly browned. Leave to cool before removing from the tin and devouring!

TEXAS CORNBREAD

Julia Vinson lives in Pakenham, Suffolk. Her mother is English, but her dad is a Texan and she's married to a man from Oklahoma who's of Cherokee descent. Julia cooked us a brilliant Sunday lunch that really made us smile and brought a true touch of Americana to Suffolk. There's a family battle over the cornbread, as both dad and husband Tony say their recipe is the best. We think the Southern cornbread is a great accompaniment, but the Texas version (pictured) is a meal in itself. Julia gets all her ingredients from the American store on the air base near where she lives, but you can buy cornmeal in the UK.

SERVES 6–8

150g yellow cornmeal
½ tsp bicarbonate of soda
1 tsp salt
240ml buttermilk
1 x 400g can of creamed corn
2 large eggs
50g bacon drippings or butter

FILLING
1 tsp vegetable oil
450g minced beef or other meat
2 onions, peeled and chopped
225g hard cheese, grated
50g jalapeño peppers, chopped

Preheat the oven 180°C/Gas 4. In a large bowl, mix the cornmeal with the bicarb and salt. Add the buttermilk, creamed corn and eggs, then beat until the batter is smooth and set aside. Put the bacon drippings or butter into a heavy pan or baking dish and place in the oven to heat up.

To make the filling, heat the oil in a frying pan and lightly brown the minced beef and the chopped onions. Pour half the batter into the hot dish and sprinkle on the browned beef and onion, cheese and jalapeños (add more if you like your food really hot), then top with the remaining batter. Bake for 45–50 minutes.

SOUTHERN CORNBREAD

SERVES 6–8

1½ tbsp melted butter
225g white cornmeal
1 tsp salt
1 tsp bicarbonate of soda
2 eggs, well beaten
480ml buttermilk

Preheat the oven 180°C/Gas 4. Add the melted butter to a heavy pan or baking dish and put the dish in the oven to heat up.

Sift the cornmeal, salt and bicarbonate of soda into a bowl. Mix the eggs with the buttermilk and stir into the cornmeal to make a smooth batter. Take the hot dish out of the oven, stir the hot butter so the sides of the pan are coated, then carefully pour the batter into the dish. Bake for 30 minutes.

PORK BBQ RIBS
& BOSTON BAKED BEANS

More from Julia. If you want to cook spare ribs and beans for a Sunday lunch in the garden, look no further than this recipe. The marinade is fantastic and the ribs are great cooked on the barbecue or in the oven. Sure to tickle a Texan.

SERVES 6

1 rack of pork ribs

3 tomatoes, chopped (plum tomatoes are best for this)

1 red onion, finely chopped

1 tsp Worcestershire sauce

1 garlic clove

1 tsp ground mustard

240ml ketchup

2 tbsp soy sauce

55g sugar

1 tbsp cornflour mixed with 3–4 tbsp of water

salt and pepper

BOSTON BAKED BEANS

400g navy or pinto beans

500g smoked streaky bacon

1 onion, peeled and finely diced

2 garlic cloves, peeled and finely diced

3 tbsp molasses

1 tsp salt

¼ tsp ground black pepper

80ml American mustard

120ml tomato ketchup

1 tbsp Worcestershire sauce

3 tbsp tomato paste

35g brown sugar

Clean the ribs and pat them dry. Slice to separate and place in a pan of boiling water for 3–5 minutes. Leave to cool.

To make the marinade, mix all the remaining ingredients, except the cornflour, in a pan and bring to boil. Once boiling, slowly stir in the cornflour mixture until the marinade has thickened, then pour it into a bowl. Add the ribs and leave them to marinate for at least 1 hour, preferably 2.

When you're ready to cook, transfer the ribs to a shallow pan and cook them in a preheated oven at 150°C/Gas 2 for 1 hour or wrap the ribs in foil and cook them on the barbecue. Timing will depend on the temperature of the grill so keep a close eye on the ribs.

BOSTON BAKED BEANS

Soak the beans overnight in cold water. The next day, bring them to the boil in the same water and simmer for 1–2 hours until tender. Drain and reserve the liquid.

Preheat the oven to 170°C/Gas 3. Chop two-thirds of the bacon into strips about 5cm long. Pour the beans into a large 2-litre pot or casserole dish and mix in the bacon strips, diced onion and garlic. Mix all the remaining ingredients in a saucepan and bring to the boil. Add some of the bean water to the mixture to give it a pouring consistency and then pour it over the beans.

Lay the remaining rashers of bacon on top of the beans and cover the dish with a lid or a piece of foil. Bake for 2 hours in the preheated oven. Check about halfway through cooking and add more liquid if the beans are getting too dry. Take off the lid 15 minutes before the end of cooking to crisp the bacon.

BUTTERMILK PIE

An American classic, this pie made a perfect end to our Sunday lunch with Julia.
It's a family favourite and Julia told us that at one time her mum wouldn't eat any American
food – except for this buttermilk pie, which her great-aunt used to make for her!

SERVES 6–8

1 unbaked pastry case or a packet of
shortcrust pastry
110g butter
150g sugar
5 eggs
240ml buttermilk
1 tsp vanilla extract
2 tbsp plain flour
juice and grated zest of ½ lemon

If you've made your own pastry or you are using a packet of bought pastry instead of a prepared pastry case, put the dough onto a floured board and roll it out to around 5mm thick, turning the pastry and flouring the surface regularly. Use it to a line a 20cm fluted flan tin. Trim the edges neatly, prick the base lightly with a fork and chill the pastry for 30 minutes. Preheat the oven to 230°C/Gas 8.

Cream the butter and sugar together until light and fluffy, then beat in the eggs one at a time. Add the remaining ingredients and pour the mixture into the unbaked pastry shell. Bake at 230°C/Gas 8 for 10 minutes, then reduce the heat to 180°C/Gas 4 and bake for a further 40 minutes until the filling is firm.

Serve with cream, ice cream or fresh fruit.

KEY LIME PIE

This is usually made in a deep pastry or biscuit crust case but can be made in a wider shallow one if you prefer. Fresh berries are often served with this traditional American dessert – blueberries are particularly good. Lots of lightly whipped cream is good too, but miss this out if you prefer.

SERVES 8

BISCUIT CRUST
175g digestive biscuits or half digestives and half Oreo cookies
80g butter
50g sugar

FILLING
3 large free-range/organic eggs, separated
finely grated zest of 2 limes
125ml lime juice
1 x 210ml can of condensed milk
½ tsp vanilla extract
½ tsp cream of tartar
pinch of salt
80g caster sugar

Crush the biscuits with a rolling pin or in a food processor. Melt the butter in a saucepan and add the biscuit crumbs and sugar. Mix everything together well, then spread over the base of a 23cm flan tin or ceramic dish. Mould some of the mixture up the sides of the dish.

Preheat the oven to 180°C/Gas 4. Whisk the egg yolks until pale and fluffy. Beat the lime zest, juice and condensed milk together until thick and smooth, then mix with the beaten egg yolks. Spoon the filling into the biscuit case.

Whisk the egg whites until they form soft peaks. Fold in the vanilla extract, cream of tartar and salt. Then whisk in the caster sugar, a little at a time, and whisk until firm and glossy. Spoon the meringue over the filling. Use a fork to lift the surface into peaks, then bake the pie in the preheated oven for 15–20 minutes until light golden brown.

Leave to cool, then chill in the fridge before serving with blueberries and cream as desired.

BREAD & BUTTER PUDDING

A great Sunday dinner treat. Dave's mam also had another version –
she used to spread each slice of bread with some marmalade. Delicious.

SERVES 6

8 thick slices of white bread, ideally
taken from an unsliced sandwich loaf
75g butter, softened,
plus extra for greasing
freshly grated nutmeg
150g caster sugar,
plus 4 tbsp for sprinkling
4 large free-range egg yolks
2 large free-range eggs
300ml double cream
300ml whole milk
1 tsp vanilla extract
100g mixed dried fruit

Cut the crusts off the bread. Put the bread on a tray, cover
with a clean tea towel and leave for 3–4 hours until slightly
dried. (Partly drying the bread helps it absorb the custard.)

Spread one side of each slice of bread with softened butter
and sprinkle with a generous grating of nutmeg. Keep 4 slices
of bread whole and cut the remaining 4 into triangles. To
make the custard, whisk the sugar, egg yolks and whole eggs
together in a large bowl until smooth. Whisk in the cream,
milk and vanilla extract.

Butter a 1.75 litre ovenproof dish – a lasagne dish is ideal.
Line the dish with the whole slices of bread in one layer,
butter side up, and scatter over three-quarters of the mixed
dried fruit. Arrange the triangles on top, butter-side up and
almost standing vertically. Sprinkle the remaining fruit
between the triangles as you go.

Give the custard a stir, then pour it slowly over the bread.
The bread will float, so press it down gently for a few seconds
to help it absorb the custard. Leave to stand for 30 minutes.
Preheat the oven to 180°C/Gas 4.

Place the dish in a roasting tin. Pour in enough just-boiled
water to come halfway up the sides of the dish. Bake for
30 minutes or until the custard is just set and the bread is
golden brown and crisp on top. Carefully remove the tin
from the oven and lift out the pudding. Serve hot with cream
or good vanilla ice cream.

SMOKED EEL & PANCETTA SALAD

Susan Burningham and her daughter Leonie Stockdale cooked us some amazing food, including this salad. Susan's mum was a cook at a stately home and she has great memories of her mother's skills. Leonie also loves cooking and is enjoying learning to make some of her mother's and grandmother's recipes. The celeriac part of this salad also goes well with smoked trout or smoked salmon, but do try the eel. It is expensive but a little goes a long way.

SERVES 12

24 paper-thin slices of pancetta or smoked back bacon
1 smoked eel
1 medium celeriac
1 white onion
1 bunch of flat-leaf parsley
125ml single cream (or crème fraîche)
4 unwaxed lemons
walnut oil
4 bunches of fresh watercress (not pre-packed)
freshly ground black pepper
sea salt

Preheat the oven to 200°C/Gas 6. Put the pancetta or back bacon on a roasting tray and bake on a high shelf in the oven until the bacon is crisp. Remove and place on kitchen paper to cool and drain. Set aside.

Cut the eel into slices measuring about 7.5 x 2.5cm and set aside in a cool place. Peel and grate the celeriac and the onion. Finely chop the parsley. Mix the grated vegetables with the cream and parsley, then season with black pepper and sea salt. Spoon the vegetable and cream mixture onto plates and arrange the pieces of eel and bacon on top.

Grate the zest of 2 of the lemons and squeeze the juice of one. Make a light vinaigrette with the lemon juice and walnut oil. Before serving, lightly drizzle some vinaigrette over each serving and scatter on grated lemon zest. Wash the watercress carefully and use it to garnish the plates. Add the remaining lemons cut into slices.

TURBOT
WITH SHRIMP SAUCE

Another recipe from Susan and Leonie. Turbot is the king of fish and this dish is fit for a king. Turbot can weigh up to 12kg and be a metre long, but the smaller variety is known as chicken turbot.

SERVES 12

2 chicken turbot, cleaned
about 1.2 litres milk, plus enough water
to cover each fish
1 lemon, sliced
2 tbsp chopped flat-leaf parsley

SAUCE
600ml shrimps
2 tsp plain white flour
350g unsalted butter, diced
2 pinches of ground mace
2 pinches of cayenne pepper
salt and white pepper to taste

First prepare the sauce. Peel the shrimps and set them aside. Put the shells in a pan with 900ml of water, cover, bring to the boil and simmer for 20 minutes. Strain the liquid into a measuring jug. You should have about 600ml, but if necessary, add a little water or pour the stock back into the pan and simmer again to reduce. Allow to cool slightly.

Gradually add this stock to the flour in a bowl, stirring to make a smooth sauce – the sauce should have a pouring consistency and not look like glue! Pour the sauce into a clean saucepan and add the diced butter. Stir the sauce over a moderate heat so that it thickens without boiling. Add the mace and cayenne, then season with salt and white pepper to taste. Set aside.

Score the cleaned fish through to the backbone on the dark-skinned side and place them in separate pans on top of the stove. Pour in a mixture of milk and water to cover and add the slices of lemon. Bring to a simmer and cook gently for 10–15 minutes or so. To test whether the fish is cooked, pierce the thickest part with a sharp knife. The fish should be opaque right down to the bone.

Once the fish are cooked, carefully lift them out and place on a large serving dish. Garnish with chopped parsley and a couple of tablespoons of the shrimps. Add the remaining shrimps to the sauce and warm it through gently (do not boil) before serving.

If you are cooking for a smaller number and don't want to use whole fish, you can make this dish with poached or grilled turbot fillets, or other white fish, as pictured.

ROAST SADDLE OF VENISON

A feast of a dish from Susan's mum's country house repertoire. This is a classic way of feeding a crowd and perfect for a New Year's Eve party. The venison really does need to marinate for two days, so don't skip this step.

SERVES 12

1 saddle of venison
8 streaky bacon rashers
bay leaves (optional)
120ml port wine
a knob of kneaded unsalted butter

MARINADE

300ml red wine
300ml red wine vinegar
300ml water
1 sprig of thyme
6 juniper berries, crushed
2 bay leaves, crumbled
1 blade of mace, crumbled, or ½ tsp ground mace
1 x 2.5cm strip of orange peel, white pith removed
2 star anise, crushed
sea salt
freshly ground black pepper

Use a very sharp knife to trim away any hard skin from the venison, taking care not to tear the flesh. Put the meat into a dish that almost encloses it.

Combine all the ingredients for the marinade and pour the mixture over the meat. Add a little more water if necessary in order to cover the saddle. Don't put a lid on the dish, but cover it with a piece of loosely woven cloth, such as muslin, to keep off the flies and dust. Clingfilm will do, but puncture it in a few places to allow the liquid to breathe. Leave the meat in a cool place for 2 days, turning it from time to time.

At the end of the marinating time, drain the joint (reserving the marinade) and pat it dry with kitchen paper. Preheat the oven to 200°C/Gas 6. Lay the bacon rashers across the top of the saddle and tie them in place with string – this stops the rashers curling during cooking. Add some bay leaves if you like. Place the venison saddle in a roasting tin and cover with a sheet of foil. Cook in the preheated oven for 30 minutes to seal the meat.

Add the port wine to the roasting tin and turn the oven down to 180°C/Gas 4. Continue cooking for another 45–60 minutes. Every 15 minutes, lift the foil and baste the meat with the port and some of the marinade to stop the meat drying out.

Ten minutes before the end of the cooking time, remove the foil and bacon rashers – keep the bacon warm for the garnish. Turn the oven up to 200°C/Gas 6 for 10 minutes to brown the meat.

Take the venison out of the oven, remove it from the roasting tin and keep it warm while you make the sauce. Place the roasting tin on the hob and add enough boiling water to the meat juices in the roasting tin to make up about 300ml of liquid. Stir over a high heat and gently thicken with the kneaded butter. The sauce should not be too thick. Carve the venison and garnish with the crispy bacon.

Strain the sauce and serve it separately. Redcurrant jelly and game chips are perfect accompaniments, plus a selection of fresh vegetables.

GAME CHIPS

**These very thinly sliced, deep-fried potatoes are a traditional accompaniment to venison.
You can make parsnip, beetroot and celeriac crisps the same way and they all go well with game.**

SERVES 6

6 large potatoes
vegetable oil, for deep frying
salt and black pepper

Peel the potatoes and slice them as thinly as you can – a mandolin is great for this. Rinse the slices in cold water to remove excess starch, then drain and dry thoroughly on some kitchen paper.

Half fill a large saucepan or deep-fat fryer with oil and heat to 190°C or use an electric deep-fat fryer. Fry the potatoes a handful at time – don't crowd the pan or they won't turn crisp and golden. Season with salt and black pepper and serve as soon as possible.

STEAK & ALE PIE

Beef and beer – a classic combination made even tastier by a topping of good puff pastry.

SERVES 6

4–5 tbsp sunflower oil

200g smoked streaky bacon rashers, cut into 1cm strips

2 medium onions, peeled, halved and sliced

2 garlic cloves, peeled and finely chopped

850g well-marbled braising steak, trimmed of thick fat and gristle

500ml bottle of real ale

500ml good beef stock

1 tbsp tomato purée

3–4 sprigs of fresh thyme, leaves stripped from the stalks

2 bay leaves

250g small chestnut mushrooms, wiped and halved or quartered if large

2 tbsp cornflour

500g ready-made puff pastry

beaten egg, to glaze

sea salt and freshly ground black pepper

Heat 1 tablespoon of the oil in a large non-stick frying pan. Fry the bacon strips with the onions until pale golden brown, stirring regularly. Add the garlic and fry for a minute or two until softened. Using a slotted spoon, transfer the onions, garlic and bacon to a large flame-proof casserole dish.

Cut the steak into rough 2.5cm cubes and season with salt and pepper. Heat 2 tablespoons of oil in the frying pan and fry the meat over a medium heat in 2 or 3 batches until well browned all over. Add extra oil if the pan seems dry. Transfer the beef to the casserole dish as it is browned.

Preheat the oven to 180°C/Gas 4. Deglaze the frying pan with half the ale. Bring it to the boil while stirring hard to lift all the sediment from the bottom of the pan. Pour this over the beef. Add the remaining ale, then the stock, tomato purée and herbs to the dish. Bring everything to the boil, then cover and cook in the oven for 1½–2 hours or until the meat is very tender. Mix the cornflour with 2 tablespoons of cold water until smooth and stir into the casserole. Put the dish back in the oven for a further 5 minutes or until the juices are thick. Adjust the seasoning to taste and leave to cool.

Turn the oven up to 200°C/Gas 6. Place a pastry funnel in the centre of a 1.2 litre pie dish. Heat the remaining oil in a frying pan and fry the mushrooms over a high heat for about 5 minutes until golden, then add them to the meat. Spoon everything into the pie dish around the funnel.

Roll out the puff pastry on a well-floured board. Brush the edge of the dish with beaten egg. Make a small cross in the centre of the pastry for the top of the pie funnel to poke through. Place the pastry gently over the filling and funnel. Press the edges firmly to seal and trim neatly, then flute them or leave plain, as you prefer. Decorate the top with any excess pastry and brush with more beaten egg to glaze. Place the dish on a baking sheet and bake in the centre of the oven for 30–35 minutes until puffed up and golden brown.

PERFECT
CAULIFLOWER CHEESE

Dave's mam's recipe for a really satisfying cauliflower cheese. Serve with meat
or by itself as a great vegetarian supper dish. Good with some crusty bread.

SERVES 4

1 large cauliflower, big as a gorilla's head

2 tbsp olive oil

250g chestnut mushrooms, wiped and finely sliced

25g butter

2 tbsp plain flour

250ml whole milk

½ tsp English mustard powder

200g Gruyère cheese, grated

pinch of nutmeg, freshly grated

50g ciabatta breadcrumbs

50g Parmesan cheese, finely grated

salt and black pepper to taste

Trim the cauliflower and break it into florets. Bring a big saucepan of water to the boil, add the florets and boil for about 10 minutes until just soft. Drain and set aside. While this is happening…

Heat the oil in a frying pan and sauté the mushrooms until they are just starting to take on a bit of colour. Set aside.

Melt the butter in a saucepan and beat in the flour. Add the milk, stirring all the time, to make a thick white sauce. Add the mustard powder and grated Gruyère, while still stirring, and check the seasoning. Fold in the mushrooms.

Preheat the oven to 180°C/Gas 4. Put the cauliflower florets in an oven dish, pour in the cheesy mushroom sauce and add a sprinkling of freshly grated nutmeg. Mix the ciabatta crumbs with the grated Parmesan and spread them over the top. Place in the preheated oven and bake for about 15 minutes until the sauce is bubbling and the crumbs and Parmesan mixture is golden. Yum, yum.

RUM BABAS

Dave's mam used to make these, so did Si's. They're a real treat and well worth the effort. Don't be shy with the rum! The babas will keep for two or three days in the fridge.

SERVES 8–12

75g currants or mixed dried fruit

4 tbsp dark rum

225g plain flour

1 x 7g sachet of easy-blend dried yeast

½ tsp fine sea salt

4 large free-range eggs, beaten

4 tbsp milk

1 tbsp clear honey

115g butter, well softened but not melted, plus extra for greasing

SYRUP

400g caster sugar

4–6 tbsp dark rum

3 tbsp clear honey

Put the currants in a saucepan with the 4 tablespoons of rum and 2 tablespoons of cold water. Place over a medium heat and bring to the boil. Remove from the heat and leave to cool. Generously grease 8–10 metal rum baba moulds set on a baking tray or a deep 12-hole muffin tin.

Sift the flour into a large bowl and stir in the yeast and salt. Beat the eggs with the milk and honey. Beat the egg mixture and the butter into the dry ingredients with a wooden spoon for about 5 minutes or until very smooth and glossy. Drain the currants, reserving the rum, and stir into the batter. Spoon the mixture into the prepared moulds or tin and leave in a warm place to rise for about 30 minutes or until risen by about a quarter. Preheat the oven to 190°C/Gas 5. Bake for 12–15 minutes or until the babas are well risen and golden brown.

While the babas are baking, make the syrup. Put the sugar in a saucepan with 400ml cold water and heat gently, stirring occasionally until the sugar dissolves. Bring to a simmer and add the rum and honey, plus the rum set aside earlier. Let it bubble for a few seconds, then remove from the heat and leave to stand.

Remove the babas from the oven and cool in the moulds for 5 minutes. Loosen the sides with a blunt-ended knife and turn the babas out into a large, shallow ceramic dish. (You may need to put them on their sides, but that's fine.) Taste the syrup, taking care as it will still be hot, and add a little more rum if you like. Pour half the syrup slowly over the babas. Leave to stand for 5 minutes.

Now, carefully turn the babas over in the dish. Pour over the remaining syrup and leave the babas for a further 10 minutes. They'll be very thirsty, so don't be surprised if they soak up nearly all the syrup. Turn once more, then cover and chill in the fridge for at least 2 hours before serving. Serve with lots of double cream.

SPOTTED DICK

Only in Britain… this is a real rib-sticking pud and we love it.
Serve with lots of home-made custard (see page 159).

SERVES 6

150g fresh white breadcrumbs
200g self-raising flour, plus extra for
dusting
100g golden caster sugar
150g currants
115g shredded beef suet
½ tsp ground mixed spice
pinch of fine sea salt
juice and finely grated zest of 1 lemon
1 large free-range egg
75ml whole milk

Mix the breadcrumbs, flour, sugar, currants, suet, mixed spice, salt and lemon zest in a large bowl. Beat together the egg and milk and add the lemon juice. Stir into the dry ingredients until well combined. The dough should feel light and spongy. Turn out onto a floured board, knead very lightly and form into a rectangle roughly the size of a house brick.

Half fill a large saucepan with water and bring to the boil. Sprinkle flour over a large piece of clean sheeting, or a thin tea towel. (An old pillowcase can also be cut to the right size for this job.) Place the spotted dick on top and bring up the ends of the material. Leave room for the pud to expand, then tie tightly with kitchen string to seal the parcel.

Lower the pudding gently and carefully into the boiling water. Cover with a lid and boil for 1 hour, checking the water level from time to time and topping up as needed. The pudding should be well risen and cooked through at the end of the hour. Turn off the heat and lift the pudding carefully from the water using tongs. Take great care, as the water will be very hot. Put the pudding on a board and leave to cool for 3–4 minutes. Snip off the string, unwrap the spotted dick and place it on a serving dish.

Another way of cooking spotted dick is to wrap the pudding in a double thickness of pleated and buttered baking parchment tied with string and then steam it for 2 hours.

CHINESE OLDER PEOPLE'S GROUP
SWEET & SOUR PORK
HONG KONG STYLE

The Chinese Older People's Group is based in Oxford and meets every Monday to enjoy a meal, sing karaoke and keep fit. On Thursdays, the group meets again to learn IT skills, English and Mandarin and the members also take trips to interesting places around the country. Anyone can join – you just have to be over 50.

This is the group's version of one of the best-known Chinese dishes.

SERVES 4

1kg pork (neck fillet or lean belly pork)
1 chicken stock cube
4 tbsp white sugar
1 egg
4 tbsp cornflour
vegetable oil, for frying
3 tbsp tomato ketchup
75ml red wine vinegar
1 x 400g can of pineapple chunks with natural juice

Cut the pork into pieces measuring about 2.5 x 3cm and put them in a bowl. Mix the chicken stock cube with a little water, add 1 tablespoon of the white sugar, then season with salt and pepper. Add this to the pork, mix well and leave to marinate for 30 minutes.

Whisk the egg with 1 tablespoon of the cornflour and mix this with the pork. Heat a wok, add some oil and heat until very hot, then turn down the heat before frying.

Put 2 tablespoons of the cornflour in a bowl and use this to coat the pieces of pork, one at a time, before frying. Don't mix the cornflour with all the pork pieces at once.

1 tbsp Worcestershire sauce
salt and white pepper

Fry the pork for 7–8 minutes until cooked through. Then drain on kitchen paper and put to one side.

Meanwhile, mix the tomato ketchup with the vinegar, pineapple chunks and juice, Worcestershire sauce and the rest of the white sugar. Pour this into a saucepan and cook for 2 minutes. Mix the remaining tablespoon of cornflour with a little cold water and add to the sauce to thicken it.

Fry the pork pieces again for 2 minutes until golden brown and drain on kitchen paper. Mix the pork with the warm sweet and sour sauce and serve with some rice.

Picnics

STICKY GINGER & SOY CHICKEN WINGS

Yasmeen Ismail's family comes from Pakistan and Afghanistan and she now lives in Hall Green, Birmingham. Yasmeen gave us some great family recipes, including a special masala mix from her Auntie Taz, which up until now has been a closely guarded secret! One of her prized possessions is a pestle and mortar passed down from her grandmother. These chicken wings are fantastically tasty and will fly off your picnic blanket.

SERVES 4

4 tbsp dark soy sauce
1 tbsp wholegrain mustard
1 handful of finely chopped root ginger
2 tbsp oil
20 chicken wings

Mix the marinade ingredients in an ovenproof dish and add the chicken. Leave to marinate overnight for best results.

The next day, preheat the oven to 200°C/Gas 6 and roast the wings for 30 minutes until cooked through and wonderfully brown and sticky. Cook them skin down to ensure they are crispy and serve with a sweet chilli sauce.

AUNTIE TAZ'S CHAAT MASALA MIX

The Ismail family's secret recipe.

whole or flaked red chillies
cumin seeds
coriander seeds
pinch of salt
pinch of lovage seeds
pinch of citric acid powder

Put equal quantities of chillies, cumin and coriander into a pan and roast. Leave to cool and then put them into a pestle and mortar or a spice grinder. Add a pinch each of salt, lovage seeds and citric acid and grind everything together until you have a mixture with a fine consistency – the infamous Ismail masala mix is ready!

SPINACH, CARROT & POTATO PAKORAS

Yasmeen's pakoras were some of the best we've ever tasted and that's the truth.

MAKES 16 LARGE PAKORAS

250g spinach, chopped

4 carrots, grated or julienned

4 medium potatoes, thinly sliced

1 onion, peeled and sliced

250g gram (chick pea) flour

1 tsp salt

1 tsp dried red chillies

1 tsp each of cumin and lovage seeds

vegetable oil

Combine all the ingredients together and add lukewarm water to create a paste. The consistency should be firm enough for you to mould – if it's runny, it won't work.

Take a large dessertspoon of the mixture and mould with your hands.

Heat the oil in a large saucepan until very hot and add a few handfuls of the mixture. Once the pakoras are holding together, turn the heat down so they cook inside and deep fry for 4–5 minutes until golden and crispy. Serve with some mint and coriander chutney.

CHANA CHAAT

This is a spicy yoghurt salad, made extra-special by the Ismail family's masala mix (see opposite).

SERVES 4

1 x 500g tub of natural yoghurt

240ml whole milk

1 tsp salt

½ tsp dried red chillies

1 tsp masala mix

2 tomatoes, diced

½ cucumber, diced

1 red onion, peeled and chopped

1 x 400g can of chick peas

1 green chilli, finely chopped (optional)

Whisk the yoghurt and milk together until the mixture is smooth. Add the salt, chillies and masala mix and stir well. Add the tomatoes, cucumber and onions and stir in the chick peas.

For a salad with a bit more of a kick, add a finely chopped green chilli.

SCOTCH EGGS

Good old-fashioned Scotch eggs are perfect for a coach trip or a picnic. You can use this recipe as a base and get creative – how about Scotch eggs with black pudding (opposite) or smoked haddock?

SERVES 6

6 eggs
500g good sausage meat or 250g
sausage meat and 250g black pudding
½ tsp dried thyme
1 tsp dried sage
½ tsp black pepper
pinch of cayenne pepper
2 eggs, beaten
4 tbsp plain flour
125g fresh white breadcrumbs
vegetable oil, for deep frying

For eggs with a slightly runny middle, put them into cold water, bring to the boil and boil for 5 minutes. Leave to cool, then remove the shells. Meanwhile, mix the sausage meat with the thyme, sage, black pepper and cayenne and divide the mixture into 6. Flatten these portions out into thin patties and wrap one around each egg. Smooth the coating so that it is nice and even.

Put the beaten eggs, flour and breadcrumbs into separate bowls. Roll each Scotch egg in flour, dip into the beaten egg and then roll in the fresh breadcrumbs. Dip each one into the beaten egg again and roll in some more breadcrumbs to build up a good coating. Heat the oil in a large pan to about 170°C. Deep fry the Scotch eggs until golden – this will take 4–5 minutes. Drain on kitchen paper and leave to cool.

NARGIS KEBABS

This is an Indian version of Scotch eggs, rolled in a crunchy sesame seed coating.

SERVES 4

250g minced beef or lamb
2 garlic cloves, peeled and crushed
2.5cm piece of root ginger, grated
½ tsp ground coriander
½ tsp ground cumin
½ tsp chilli powder (or more to taste)
¼ tsp ground cloves
1 tbsp cornflour
salt to taste
1 egg yolk
4 hard-boiled eggs, shelled
2 tbsp flour
1 egg, beaten
2 tbsp sesame seeds
vegetable oil, for shallow-frying

Mix the meat, garlic, ginger, spices, cornflour and salt in a bowl. Bind with the egg yolk and divide the mixture into 4 equal parts.

With well-floured hands, flatten each portion into a round. Place a hard-boiled egg in the centre and carefully work the meat round it to cover.

Put the 2 tablespoons of flour, beaten egg and sesame seeds in separate bowls. Roll the nargis kebabs in flour, egg, then sesame seeds until well coated. Heat the oil in a pan and shallow fry the kebabs until brown.

COURGETTE FRITTERS

Heather Lane lives in Crawley and loves to cook from her own notebooks of recipes that she has collected over the years. She's also a keen gardener and likes to make the most of her vegetables. This recipe is a great way to use up a glut of courgettes and brings an Asian twist to a popular classic.

MAKES ABOUT 12

3 courgettes, grated
1 onion, peeled and grated
1 garlic clove, crushed
vegetable oil
100g gram (chick pea) flour
2 eggs, beaten
1 tsp garam masala
160g strong crumbly cheese, such as feta or Lancashire
1 small red or green chilli, seeded and finely chopped
small handful of mint, chopped
small handful of parsley or fresh coriander, chopped
salt and freshly ground black pepper to taste

Place the grated courgettes and onion in a colander and leave for 10–15 minutes to drain. Squeeze out any excess water and add the garlic. Heat a little vegetable oil in a frying pan and fry the courgettes, onion and crushed garlic until they are just starting to brown. Remove from the heat and allow to cool slightly.

Beat the flour with the eggs and garam masala to make a smooth batter – add a little milk if the batter seems too thick. Stir in the crumbled cheese, chilli, mint, parsley or coriander, salt and pepper and then add the cooked courgettes and onions. Stir until everything is thoroughly mixed.

Heat more oil in the frying pan and drop tablespoon-sized dollops of the mixture into the hot pan, a few at a time. Fry gently, then flip over to cook the other side. When the fritters are cooked through and golden and crispy on the outside, remove them from the pan and drain on kitchen paper.

These fritters freeze well and can be reheated in a hot oven from frozen – just make sure they are really piping hot all the way through.

VICTORIA SANDWICH

Heather's great-granny used to run a bakery in Barrow-in-Furness at the end of the 19th century and Heather recently came across a book of her recipes, all handwritten of course. This is great-granny Gawthrop's classic recipe for Victoria sandwich, which is a must for every picnic. It's so simple. You just weigh the eggs and use the same weight of butter, sugar and flour.

SERVES 10–12

For a 7in/18cm cake
weigh 4 eggs

For a 6in/15cm cake
weigh 3 eggs

butter, room temperature
caster sugar
self-raising flour, sifted
few drops of vanilla extract
pinch of baking powder
1 pot strawberry jam
icing sugar

Grease and line 2 sandwich tins. Weigh the eggs and then weigh out the same amount of butter, caster sugar, and self-raising flour. Preheat the oven to 180°C/Gas 4.

Cream the butter and sugar together and beat until light and fluffy. Beat the eggs and add to the butter and sugar a little at a time. Add a small amount of the flour at the same time to stop the mixture curdlng. Add the vanilla extract.

Gently fold in the rest of the sifted flour and baking powder with a metal tablespoon. Be very gentle at this stage. The mixture should be a soft dropping consistency. If it seems a little stiff, add a dash of milk. Divide the mixture between the sandwich tins and bake in the centre of the oven for 25–30 minutes until done. Remove the cakes from the tins and leave to cool on a wire rack. When the cakes are cool, sandwich them together with strawberry jam and sift some icing sugar over the top.

YUMMY BISCUITS

Another of Heather's recipes. You forget how nice home-made biscuits are and these are some of the best.

MAKES ABOUT 18

100g butter, room temperature
100g caster sugar
200g self-raising flour
1 tsp golden syrup

Preheat the oven to 190°C/Gas 5. Cream the butter and sugar together until light and fluffy. Add the flour and syrup and mix to a soft dough. Roll into small balls and place on greased baking trays, giving the biscuits room to spread. Press each one down slightly.

Bake for about 6–10 minutes until golden, then allow the biscuits to cool slightly before transferring them to a wire rack.

GAME PIE

These quantities make enough pastry and filling for a deep pie in a 20cm tin. Use any game you fancy but make sure you trim it all carefully. Ideal for a high-class picnic.

SERVES 4–6

CRUST
450g plain flour
2 tsp baking powder
½ tsp salt
60g cold unsalted butter, diced
60g cold lard, diced
1 egg yolk
about 120ml water
1 packet of puff pastry for the lid

FILLING
4 tbsp vegetable oil
1.5kg mixed game meat, cut into cubes
500g venison steak, cut into cubes
125g streaky bacon, diced into lardons
2 large onions, peeled and sliced
1 celery stick, sliced
250g chestnut mushrooms, wiped clean and sliced
55g plain flour
2 bay leaves
500ml red wine
1 dsrtsp chopped thyme
500ml beef stock
2 tbsp redcurrant jelly
1 egg, beaten
sea salt flakes
ground black pepper

First, make the shortcrust case. Put the flour, baking powder and salt in a food processor, add the butter, lard and egg yolk and process until the mixture forms crumbs. Gradually add the water until a ball of pastry miraculously appears. If you don't have a processor, struggle on with a basin and a spoon. Wrap the pastry in clingfilm and put it in the fridge to chill for an hour while you get on with the filling.

Heat the oil in a large frying pan and brown the game meat and venison in batches. Take care not to put too much in the pan at once – the meat needs to be sealed, not poached. As the meat is browned, remove it and set aside.

Add the bacon and onions to the same pan and cook until the onions are translucent. Add the celery and the mushrooms and cook for a further 3 minutes. Add the flour and cook for 2 minutes. Now add the bay leaves, red wine, thyme, stock and redcurrant jelly. Season well and simmer gently, uncovered, for about 2 hours or until the meat is tender and melting – exact timing depends on the meat. Leave to cool.

While the pie filling is cooling you can blind bake the pastry case. Preheat the oven to 180°C/Gas 4. Roll out the shortcrust pastry and line a well-greased pie tin. Line with baking parchment, then fill with baking beans. Place in the preheated oven for 20 minutes until the pastry is cooked. Remove and leave to cool.

Once the pastry case is cool, fill it with the cooked meat. Pack it in – a well-filled pie is a happy pie! Preheat the oven to 180°C/Gas 4. Roll out the puff pastry. Paint around the edge of the shortcrust case with the beaten egg and place the sheet of puff pastry on the top. Crimp around the edges, trim and cut a couple of holes in the top to let the steam out. Decorate the top with any excess pastry. Brush with egg and bake at 180°C/Gas 4 for about 30 minutes until golden. Leave to cool completely before serving with some pickles and a glass of wine.

HOT CHICKEN SALAD

We met Bridget Woodcock, from Oxford, with her daughter Jennie and granddaughter Georgia. Bridget was the wife of a headmaster and used to entertain a lot – she would make several main courses and five choices of puddings when people came for dinner. This recipe is one that Jennie remembers from her childhood. We weren't sure about it – until we had a taste. It's irresistible and we couldn't stop eating.

SERVES 6–8

1 large onion, chopped
1 green pepper, seeded and chopped
1 red pepper, seeded and chopped
1 yellow pepper, seeded and chopped
1 tbsp vegetable oil
500g cooked chicken, cut into cubes
250g celery, finely chopped
1 x 295g can of concentrated chicken soup
200ml mayonnaise
4 tbsp lemon juice
butter, for greasing dish
120g cheese, grated
2 packets of cheese & onion crisps, crushed
salt and pepper

Preheat the oven to 180°C/Gas 4. Gently fry the chopped onion and peppers in a little oil for a few minutes to soften. Toss them with the chicken, celery, chicken soup, mayonnaise, lemon juice and seasoning and pile into a buttered ovenproof dish.

Mix the grated cheese and crushed crisps and sprinkle over the top of the dish, then bake for 30 minutes until golden and crispy. That's it!

MARYLAND CHICKEN

Bridget used to make classic chicken Maryland, but Jennie now cooks this healthier version, which she devised. Her daughter, Georgia, prepared the bananas for us. Incidentally, Maryland chicken was on the menu of the last lunch served in the first-class dining room on the *Titanic*!

SERVES 4

4 chicken breasts, skin on
2 tbsp honey
2 garlic cloves, peeled and crushed
4 x 2mm slices of root ginger
55ml soy sauce

Start by making the marinade for the chicken. Warm the honey and mix it with the garlic, ginger and soy sauce. Place the chicken in a dish and pour the marinade over it. Make sure it is well coated, turning the pieces repeatedly if necessary. Cover and leave for a couple of hours or overnight in the fridge. Fry the chicken if you like, or preheat the oven to 200°C/Gas 6 and bake the chicken for 40–45 minutes or until cooked.

BACON-WRAPPED BANANAS

4 bananas, peeled
8 streaky bacon rashers

Wrap the bananas with the streaky bacon and grill or bake in a hot oven, 200°C/Gas 6, until the bacon is crispy.

FRITTERS

110g flour
1 egg
150ml milk
1 x 340g can of sweetcorn
vegetable oil, for frying

To make the fritters, beat the flour, egg and milk together to make a thick batter, adding a little water if necessary. Add the drained sweetcorn. Heat a little oil in a frying pan and drop in spoonfuls of the mixture. Fry until golden brown on both sides and serve with the chicken and bananas.

This is our classic version, which goes well with Jennie and Bridget's fritters and bananas. Yee ha!

SERVES 4

1 chicken, skinned and jointed on the bone, breasts cut in 2
150g flour
1 tsp salt
1 tsp paprika
½ tsp black pepper
2 eggs, beaten
500g breadcrumbs
oil, for deep frying

Dry the chicken with kitchen paper. Mix the flour, salt, paprika and pepper and put the mixture into a plastic bag. Add the chicken and toss until the portions are well covered.

Mix the beaten eggs with 1 tablespoon of water in a bowl and put the breadcrumbs in another bowl. Dip the chicken in the beaten egg, then dredge in breadcrumbs. You might need more egg, depending on the size of your chicken.

Heat the oil to about 160°C in a large pan or deep-fat fryer and fry the chicken until the breadcrumbs are golden and the chicken is absolutely cooked through.

STICKY DATE CAKE

This is a slightly bonkers story but true. A lady came up to us in a supermarket, gave us this recipe, told us to try it and said ta ta. It's odd but brilliant, and fabulous for a picnic. Keeps well, too. Wrap it in foil and store it in a tin.

SERVES AT LEAST 12

110g raisins
225g dates, chopped
175g sultanas
110g currants
275g butter, plus extra for greasing the cake tin
1 x 400g tin condensed milk
150g wholemeal flour
150g plain flour
pinch of salt
scant tsp bicarbonate of soda
1 heaped tbsp chunky marmalade
blanched almonds and glacé cherries for the top (optional)

Grease a 20cm square cake tin with a little butter and line with baking parchment.

Put the raisins, dates, sultanas and currents in a saucepan with the butter, then pour in the condensed milk and 275ml of water. Bring this to the boil, stirring frequently so the mixture doesn't stick to the bottom of the pan, and continue to simmer for 3 minutes. Pour the mixture into a large bowl and allow to cool.

Preheat the oven to 170°C/Gas 3. In another bowl, mix the wholemeal and the plain flour with the salt and bicarb. Once the fruit mixture is cool, fold it into the flour and stir in the marmalade. Spoon the mixture into the greased and lined cake tin and decorate with some whole blanched almonds and glacé cherries if you like. Put a double layer of baking parchment over the top to keep it from burning and bake in the preheated oven for 1¾ hours.

At the end of the cooking time, take the cake out of the oven and leave it to cool in the tin for 10 minutes before turning it out onto a cooling rack. Make a nice cup of tea and cut yourself a big slice.

BLACKBERRY & APPLE PIE

This is a plate pie so you can take it to your picnic on the plate and be sure that it will arrive intact. The pastry recipe makes enough for top and bottom crusts on a good-sized dinner plate.

SERVES 6

PASTRY
450g plain flour
2 tsp of baking powder
½ tsp salt
60g cold unsalted butter, plus extra for greasing the plate
60g cold lard
1 egg yolk

FILLING
½ tbsp semolina
3 eating apples, peeled, quartered and cored
2 Bramley cooking apples, peeled, quartered and cored
1 dsrtsp cinnamon
100g demerara sugar
300g blackberries
1 egg, beaten
1 tbsp granulated sugar

Start by making the pastry. Put the flour, baking powder and salt in a food processor. Cut the butter and lard into cubes, add to the flour with the egg yolk and process until the mixture forms crumbs. Gradually add up to 120ml of water until a ball of pastry miraculously appears. You can, of course, do this with a basin, a spoon and your hands. Wrap the pastry in clingfilm and chill it in the fridge for an hour.

Preheat the oven to 180°C/Gas 4. Roll out half the pastry and line a buttered dinner plate. Sprinkle with the semolina to soak up excess moisture and keep the pastry crisp. Put the quartered apples in a bowl and shuffle them around to mix them up a bit. Mix the cinnamon with the sugar in a separate bowl. Put half the apples on the pastry-lined plate and sprinkle with a third of the sugar mixture. Add the blackberries and sprinkle with the second third of sugar mixture. Cover with the remaining apples and add the rest of the sugar and cinnamon.

Brush the rim of the pastry with beaten egg. Roll out the remaining pastry and put a lid on your pie. Crimp the edges, brush with egg and sprinkle with the granulated sugar. Bake in the preheated oven for about 40 minutes until the pie is golden. Serve with home-made custard (see page 159).

TREACLE TART

For those with a sweet tooth, treacle tart is the ultimate fix. It tastes great hot or cold – and it's even more delicious the next day. Serve with vanilla ice cream, custard or lashings of double cream. The name is misleading, though, as it is always made with golden syrup, not treacle.

SERVES 6

FILLING

2 large free-range eggs, beaten
1 x 454g can of golden syrup
finely grated zest of ½ small lemon
(about 1 tsp)
125g white breadcrumbs, made from a
day-old loaf

PASTRY

200g plain flour
125g cold butter, cut into cubes
1 medium free-range egg, beaten

First make the filling. Put the eggs in a large bowl and stir in the syrup – yes, the whole can. Add the lemon zest, followed by the breadcrumbs and set the mixture aside while you make the pastry. This will give the breadcrumbs time to soften and absorb the syrup.

To make the pastry, put the flour and the butter in a food processor and pulse until the mixture resembles fine breadcrumbs. With the motor running, gradually add the beaten egg and blend until the mixture forms a ball. Do not overblend or the pastry will be tough.

Tip the dough onto a floured board and roll it out to around 5mm thick, turning the pastry and flouring the surface regularly. Use it to line a 20cm loose-based cake tin – the kind used for baking a Victoria sandwich. Trim the edges neatly, prick the base lightly with a fork and chill the pastry for 30 minutes. Preheat the oven to 200°C/Gas 6.

Put the pastry case on a sturdy baking sheet and line with crumpled baking parchment. Fill with baking beans. Bake blind for 15 minutes, then carefully take it out of the oven and remove the paper and beans. Return the pastry to the oven for another 3–4 minutes until the surface is dry. Remove from the oven and reduce the temperature to 170°C/Gas 3.

Pour the syrup mixture into the tart case and smooth the surface. Bake for 25–30 minutes or until the filling is pale golden brown and set. Leave in the tin for 15 minutes before removing, then cut into generous wedges to serve.

AFRICAN & AFRICAN CARIBBEAN COMMUNITY GROUPS

Two African and African Caribbean community groups from Oxford came to our recipe fair. There's an over-50s group and a carers group and they meet every week to give each other support and take part in different activities. The over-50s cook wonderful food from African and Caribbean recipes and they run a lunch club for the many people who want to try their cooking.

CHICKEN & VEGETABLE STIR FRY

A quick, healthy meal with lots of vegetables and a great spicy taste.

SERVES 4–6

500g boneless chicken breasts
2 tbsp soy sauce
1 tsp curry powder
juice of 1 lemon
1 tsp olive oil
1 medium onion, peeled and chopped
3 medium carrots, peeled and cut into strips
½ medium-sized head of broccoli or cauliflower, trimmed and cut into small florets
handful of stringless green beans, cut into strips
3 garlic cloves, peeled and crushed
1 red and 1 yellow pepper, cored and diced
1 bag of fresh spinach
handful of fresh basil leaves, chopped
salt and pepper

Cut the chicken breasts into strips and mix them with the soy sauce. Mix the curry powder with the lemon juice to make a paste and season with salt and pepper.

Put the strips of chicken into the paste and turn them until they are well coated.

Heat the oil in a wok and add the onion and chicken and fry until cooked. Add the remaining vegetables, except the spinach, and fry for 1½ minutes.

Add the spinach and turn off the heat – the spinach will wilt down in the heat of the pan. Sprinkle with chopped basil and serve with rice or mashed potatoes.

Comforting
food

CREAM OF TOMATO SOUP
WITH FRIED CHEESE SANDWICHES

Memories from Dave's childhood – Saturday lunch with fried cheese sarnies and tinned tomato soup. This is still one of our favourite meals, but it's so much better with home-made soup.

SERVES 2

1 tbsp sunflower oil
1 large onion, roughly chopped
1 garlic clove, chopped
1 x 400g can of chopped tomatoes
½ tsp mixed dried herbs
2–3 tsp caster sugar
4 tbsp double cream
sea salt flakes
freshly ground black pepper

FRIED CHEESE SANDWICHES

4 slices of white bread
softened butter, for spreading
75g Cheddar cheese, coarsely grated
3 tbsp sunflower oil, for frying

To make the soup, heat the oil in a large saucepan and gently fry the onion and garlic for 5 minutes until they begin to soften. Stir in the tomatoes, then refill the can with water and pour it into the pan. Add the herbs, 2 teaspoons of the sugar, a good pinch of salt and plenty of freshly ground black pepper. Bring to a gentle simmer and cook for 15 minutes, stirring occasionally.

Remove from the heat and blitz the soup with a stick blender until it's as smooth as possible. Alternatively, let the soup cool for a few minutes, then blend it in a food processor and pour it back into the saucepan. Stir in the cream and adjust the seasoning to taste, adding a little more sugar if you think you need it.

To make the fried cheese sandwiches, spread the bread lightly with butter and put the cheese on 2 of the slices in an even layer, leaving a 1cm border around the edge. Top with the remaining slices of bread.

Heat the oil in a large non-stick frying pan over a medium-low heat. Carefully add the sandwiches to the pan and cook them for about 3 minutes on each side until golden brown and crisp. Warm the soup gently, stirring regularly.

When the sandwiches are done, remove them from the pan and cut into fingers or quarters. Ladle the soup into deep bowls and serve with the sandwiches.

For an extra touch of luxury, try mozzarella in carrozza. These are Italian fried cheese sandwiches, made with mozzarella.

ROUILLE & CROUTONS

Traditionally served as a spicy addition to fish soups and stews, this is a more sophisticated accompaniment to the cheese sarnies on the previous page. Rouille is like a butch mayonnaise and is great with the croutons – a grown-up version of the fried cheese sandwiches really! Please note: this recipe contains raw eggs.

SERVES 4

ROUILLE
3 dried chillies, deseeded
1 tsp coarse sea salt
4 garlic cloves, peeled
pinch of saffron
2 egg yolks
100–150ml olive oil
1 tsp lemon juice
pinch of cayenne pepper
chopped parsley or basil, for serving

CROUTONS
1 French stick
2 tbsp olive oil
knob of butter
150g Gruyère cheese, grated
cracked black pepper

First make the rouille. Grind the chillies into a powder in a pestle and mortar. Add the salt, garlic cloves and saffron and grind to a paste, then add the egg yolks. You should have a paste the colour of a jaundiced canary! Transfer this to a bowl.

Finishing the rouille is like making mayo. Very slowly, start to add the olive oil to the paste, a few drops at a time. When you've added half the oil, add the lemon juice and this will loosen the mixture. Continue drizzling in the oil and beat until you have a good consistency. Finish with the cayenne.

Next, make the croutons. Slice the bread. Heat the oil and butter together in a frying pan – the oil stops the butter burning and the butter ensures you end up with golden croutons. Fry the bread, a few slices at a time, until golden and set them on a baking tray.

When the croutons are all cooked, sprinkle them with grated Gruyère and season with black pepper. Put them under a hot grill until the cheese is melted and bubbling – you can melt the cheese with a cook's blowtorch if you prefer.

To serve, drop a crouton into the centre of each bowl of soup. Add a spoonful of rouille to the side and garnish with some chopped parsley or basil.

GREAT SAUSAGE CASSEROLE

A rich-tasting sausage casserole with a hint of spice, this is a great way to turn your favourite sausages into a main event. We like to add a dash of wine to the sauce, but it's very good without it too.

SERVES 6

1–2 tbsp sunflower oil
12 good meaty pork sausages
6 rindless streaky bacon rashers, cut into 2.5cm lengths
2 medium onions, thinly sliced
2 garlic cloves, crushed
½–1 tsp hot chilli powder or smoked paprika
1 x 400g can of chopped tomatoes
300ml chicken stock, made with 1 chicken stock cube
2 tbsp tomato purée
1 tbsp Worcestershire sauce
1 tbsp dark brown muscovado sugar
1 tsp dried mixed herbs
2 bay leaves
3–4 sprigs of fresh thyme
100ml red or white wine (optional)
1 x 400g can of butter beans or mixed beans
sea salt flakes
freshly ground black pepper

Heat a tablespoon of the oil in a large non-stick frying pan and fry the sausages gently for 10 minutes, turning every now and then until nicely browned all over. Transfer to a large saucepan or a flameproof casserole dish and set aside. Next, fry the bacon pieces in the frying pan until they begin to brown and crisp. Add to the sausages.

Put the onions in the frying pan and fry over a medium heat for 5 minutes until they start to soften, stirring often. You should have enough fat in the pan, but if not, add a little more oil. Add the garlic and cook for 2–3 minutes more until the onions turn pale golden brown, stirring frequently. Sprinkle over the chilli powder or smoked paprika and cook together for a few seconds longer.

Stir in the tomatoes, chicken stock, tomato purée, Worcestershire sauce, brown sugar and herbs. Pour over the wine, or some water if you're not using wine, and bring to a simmer. Tip carefully into the pan with the sausages and bacon. Return to a simmer, then reduce the heat, cover the pan loosely with a lid and leave to simmer very gently for 20 minutes, stirring every now and then.

Drain the beans and rinse them in a sieve under running water. Stir the beans into the casserole, and continue to cook for 10 minutes, stirring occasionally until the sauce is thick. Adjust the seasoning to taste. Serve with rice or slices of rustic bread.

Don't prick your sausages. The meat will cook better with the fat and the sausages will stay juicy.

MAMA'S CURRY

We met Anjie Mosher in Blackpool and she shared some of her mum's great recipes with us. This curry is one of her favourites and she told us that she used to invite her friends round for a curry – cooked by her mum Renee – on her birthday. Her friends always thought Anjie cooked the curry herself but now the secret's out! Sadly, Anjie's mum passed away four years ago, but Anjie says that when she cooks this recipe the smell makes her feel like she's just had a big hug from her mum.

SERVES 4

120ml ghee or vegetable oil
400g braising steak, diced
1 medium onion, diced
2 garlic cloves, finely chopped
1 tsp ground cumin
1 tsp ground coriander
1 tsp ground turmeric
1 tsp black pepper
1 tsp chilli powder
½ tsp ground ginger
3 cloves
3 cardamom pods (optional)
½ tsp ground cinnamon
200g canned tomatoes
125ml natural yoghurt
1 tbsp vinegar
1 tsp salt
pinch of sugar

Heat a frying pan and add the ghee or oil. Brown the meat until sealed on all sides, then take it out of the pan and set aside.

Add the onion and garlic to the pan and fry until soft but not browned. Add all the spices and fry for 1 minute, no longer.

Put the beef back in the pan with the tomatoes and bring to the boil. Take the pan off the heat and stir in the yoghurt and vinegar, then season with the salt and sugar. Place back on the heat, bring back to the boil and simmer for at least 1½ hours until the meat is tender.

Alternatively, if you prefer, you can cook the curry in the oven. Pile it into an ovenproof dish and cook in a preheated oven at 190°C/Gas 5 for at least 2 hours.

SPICED CAULIFLOWER

You have been warned – this recipe is very hot! If you want something milder Anjie
says to halve the amount of spices used.

SERVES 4

60ml ghee or vegetable oil
2 tsp chilli powder
2 tsp ground cumin
2 tsp ground coriander
2 tsp turmeric
2 tsp black pepper
1 cauliflower, divided into florets
25g tamarind paste (optional)
1 tbsp vinegar
1 tsp salt

Heat a frying pan and add the oil. Add the spices and fry them over a medium heat for 2 minutes. Add the cauliflower and stir so all the florets are well coated with spice.

If you're using the tamarind paste, stir it into 250ml of boiling water and add this to the pan. If you don't have any tamarind just add 250ml of boiling water. Add the vinegar and salt and cook until the cauliflower is tender.

SWEET & SOUR POTATOES

Anjie told us how her mum always made these on her legendary curry nights and they are to die for.
Great on their own or as a side dish with Mama's curry and the spiced cauliflower ... yum!

SERVES 4

60ml oil
1 tsp black mustard seeds
1 tsp cumin seeds
6 medium potatoes, peeled and cubed
2 tsp ground coriander
2 tsp salt
1 tsp turmeric
1 tsp chilli powder
4 tsp brown sugar
250ml water
75g tomato purée
3 tbsp vinegar

Heat a frying pan and add the oil. Throw in the mustard and cumin seeds and fry them until they pop, then turn the heat down a little and add the potatoes. Add the remaining ingredients, pour in 250ml of water, then stir everything together well.

Cover the pan and cook over a low heat until the potatoes are tender. Take the lid off the pan and cook until the sauce has thickened.

REALLY RICH OXTAIL STEW

Your butcher will be able to get hold of a whole oxtail and cut it into portions for you. You should end up with at least 5 large pieces, a couple of slightly smaller joints and the little bits from the end of the tail. Cook the little pieces with the rest as they will add lots of flavour to the stew. Oxtails tend to be very fatty, so you'll need to trim your meat before you start cooking.

SERVES 5–6

1 whole oxtail (about 1.3kg),
cut into chunky pieces
3 tbsp plain flour
3–4 tbsp sunflower oil
2 medium onions, sliced
2 garlic cloves, finely chopped
2 medium carrots, peeled and diced
2 celery sticks, de-stringed and diced
4–5 bushy sprigs of fresh thyme
or ½ tsp dried thyme
2 bay leaves
300ml red wine
500ml beef stock
2 tbsp tomato purée
1 tbsp chopped fresh parsley leaves,
to garnish (optional)
sea salt flakes
freshly ground black pepper

Wash the oxtail pieces and pat them dry with kitchen paper. Trim off as much excess fat as possible. Put the flour in a freezer bag and season well with salt and pepper. Drop half the oxtail pieces into the seasoned flour, toss well to coat, then put them on a plate. Do the same with the remaining oxtail pieces.

Heat 2 tablespoons of the oil in a large non-stick frying pan. Brown the oxtail over a medium heat for about 10 minutes until deeply coloured, turning every now and then. You may need to add extra oil or cook the oxtail in batches depending on the size of your pan. Put the oxtail into a flameproof casserole dish.

Return the frying pan to the hob and add the onions, garlic, carrots and celery, with a little extra oil if necessary. Cook gently for 10 minutes until softened and lightly browned, stirring occasionally. Preheat the oven to 150°C/Gas 2.

Tip the vegetables on top of the beef and add the thyme and bay leaves. Stir in the wine, beef stock and tomato purée. Season with salt and pepper and bring to a gentle simmer. Cover the casserole dish with a lid and cook in the centre of the oven for 3 hours or longer, stirring and turning the oxtail halfway through the cooking time. The meat should be falling off the bones and the sauce should be rich and thick.

Remove the casserole dish from the oven and transfer the oxtail pieces to a plate. Using an oven glove, hold the dish up slightly at one side, allowing the sauce to run to the opposite side. Skim off the fat that has pooled on the urface and discard it.

Divide the oxtail pieces between six warmed plates and spoon over the sauce. Sprinkle with chopped parsley and serve with mash and fresh vegetables.

HOME-MADE FISH FINGERS

We know you've got a packet of fish fingers in the freezer, but try our home-made version. We guarantee they'll be the best you've ever tasted. And if you've had a hard day at work or school, put some between a couple of slices of bread, add some ketchup and all your troubles will melt away.

SERVES 4

500g thick skinless fillet of salmon or cod, haddock or other white fish
3 tbsp plain flour
1 large egg
50g golden breadcrumbs or
30g fresh white breadcrumbs, mixed with 20g easy-cook polenta
3 tbsp sunflower oil
sea salt flakes
freshly ground black pepper
bread, butter and ketchup, to serve

Cut the fish fillets into thick fingers – 4 really fat ones or 8 smaller ones, as you like. Don't worry if they're slightly strange shapes. They'll look all the better for it!

Put the flour in a strong freezer bag and season with a good pinch of salt and plenty of black pepper. Break the egg into a shallow dish and beat lightly. Put the breadcrumbs or breadcrumbs and polenta mix in a separate dish.

One at a time, gently toss the fish fingers in the seasoned flour until evenly coated. Next, turn them in the beaten egg until well covered, then dunk them in the breadcrumbs. Put them on a plate, ready to cook.

Pour the oil into a large non-stick frying pan and set over a medium-high heat. Add the fish fingers and fry for 5–6 minutes, turning occasionally until golden brown and crisp on all sides. Don't leave the pan of hot oil unattended.

Remove with a spatula and drain on kitchen paper. Serve in slices of freshly buttered bread with a good dollop of ketchup.

RUTH'S SHEPHERD'S PIE

Ruth Sutcliffe's family have lived in West Yorkshire for generations. They're upland sheep farmers and they need good comforting food to keep out the cold. Ruth still cooks from her Grandma Lassie's handwritten recipe book and she showed us some of her favourites. Grandma always added a handful of oats to thicken the meat stew and Ruth has continued that tradition – useful tip we thought.

SERVES 4–6

2 tbsp vegetable oil
1 large onion, chopped
2 carrots, finely chopped
2 celery sticks, finely chopped
450g minced steak
1 Oxo cube
2 tbsp porridge oats
150ml hot water
700g floury potatoes
butter and milk for the mash
salt and pepper

Heat the oil in a frying pan and fry the onion, carrot and celery until softened. Add the minced steak and fry until browned.

Crumble in the Oxo cube, season and continue to fry for about 10 minutes. Stir in the porridge oats and hot water.

Meanwhile, peel the potatoes, cut them into wedges and boil in salted water until tender. Mash with plenty of butter, milk and seasoning.

Preheat the oven to 180°C/Gas 4. Pile the meat mixture into an oven dish, top with the mash and cook in the oven until bubbling hot and brown on top – about 20 minutes.

GRANDMA SINDY'S GINGER SPONGE

Ruth's mum's mum – Grandma Sindy, also known as Nina – was an excellent baker
and Ruth has many happy memories of Sunday tea at her house.

MAKES ABOUT 12 SQUARES

200g self-raising flour
200g sugar
1 tsp ground ginger
1 tsp bicarbonate of soda
55g margarine
1 egg, beaten
2 tbsp golden syrup
240ml hot water

Line a 28 x 18cm baking tin with baking parchment.
Preheat the oven to 180°C/Gas 4.

Mix the flour, sugar, ground ginger and bicarbonate
together in a bowl. Rub in the marge with your fingers,
then add the beaten egg, syrup and hot water. Mix
everything together well with a wooden spoon.

Pour the mixture into the prepared tin and bake in the
oven for 35–40 minutes. Leave to cool in the tin and
cut into squares when cold.

NINA'S ALMOND & COCONUT SLICE

Nina's tea table was always groaning with buns, cakes and sweet treats. It was all
washed down with a proper cup of tea, made in a tea pot with tea leaves, of course.

SERVES AT LEAST 8

BASE
75g margarine
120g caster sugar
2 egg yolks
2 tbsp milk
1 tsp vanilla extract
170g self-raising flour

TOPPING
2 egg whites
120g caster sugar
55g desiccated coconut
10 glace cherries, chopped
55g flaked almonds

Grease a 28 x 18cm baking tin and line it with baking
parchment. Preheat the oven to 160°C/Gas 3.

Cream the margarine and sugar together until light and
fluffy. Beat in the egg yolks, milk and vanilla, then fold
in the flour. Spread the mixture into the lined tin – it
will be very thick so you might need to use your hands.

To make the topping, whisk the egg whites until they form
stiff peaks, then fold in the sugar and coconut. Spread this
mixture over the base and sprinkle the cherries and almonds
over the top. Bake in the preheated oven for 45 minutes,
then leave to cool in the tin. Cut into slices when cold.

BAKED EGG CUSTARD
& CUSTARD TART

Eat this delicious baked custard as it is or put it into a
crisp pastry case to make a lip-smacklingly rich custard tart.

SERVES 4

butter, for greasing
3 large eggs
2 large egg yolks
100g caster sugar
300ml double cream
300ml whole milk
½ tsp vanilla extract
½ whole nutmeg

PASTRY
200g plain flour
125g butter, cut into cubes
1 medium free-range egg, beaten

Preheat the oven to 150°C/Gas 2. Butter a 1.2 litre ovenproof
dish and set it in a small roasting tin. Bring a kettle of water to
the boil. Mix the eggs, egg yolks and sugar in a heatproof bowl
with a wooden spoon until smooth.

Put the cream and milk together with the vanilla extract in a
medium saucepan. Finely grate half the nutmeg over the mixture
and heat until hot but not boiling, stirring occasionally. Slowly
pour onto the eggs, stirring well. Pour the custard into the
prepared dish and grate the remaining nutmeg over the top.

Pour the just-boiled water into the roasting tin, until it rises no
more than a centimetre or so up the outside of the dish. Bake in
the oven for 25–30 minutes or until only just set. The custard
should be fairly wobbly in the centre, as it will continue to set
as it cools. Remove the tin from the oven, lift the dish from the
water and leave to cool. Chill for 2–3 hours before serving.

CUSTARD TART
To make the pastry, put the flour and the butter in a food processor
and pulse until the mixture resembles fine breadcrumbs. With
the motor running, gradually add the beaten egg and blend
until the mixture forms a ball.

Tip the pastry onto a floured board and roll to around 5mm
thick, turning the pastry and flouring the surface regularly.
Use to a line a 20cm loose-based cake tin. Trim the edges
neatly, prick the base lightly with a fork and chill the pastry
for 30 minutes. Preheat the oven to 200°C/Gas 6.

Put the tin on a baking sheet and cover the pastry with crumpled
baking parchment. Fill with baking beans. Bake the pastry blind
for 15 minutes, then remove the paper and beans. Return the
pastry to the oven for 3–4 minutes, then remove and reduce
the temperature to 160°C/Gas 3. Pour the custard into the pastry
shell, sprinkle with nutmeg and bake for 25–30 minutes until
set. Leave to cool, then slice and serve.

When mixing the eggs
and egg yolks, use a
wooden spoon rather than
a whisk, as you don't
want to incorporate bubbles
into the mixture.

HARGREAVES'S MEAT & POTATO PIE

What could be more comforting than the biggest pie in the world? That's what Dee Briggs of Wakefield says, and she showed us how to make her dad's version of Denby Dale Pie, which he learned from his dad. Amazing! Her dad's recipe for special seasoning is lost, but Dee uses the mixture below. You need a big pie dish – 28 x 38cm – this is a crowd pleaser.

SERVES 12

2.75kg braising steak, diced
3 medium onions, chopped
30g salt
2.75kg potatoes, peeled and cut into chunks
5 tbsp special seasoning, made with
1 tbsp Bovril and 4 tbsp Bisto powder

PASTRY
1.5kg plain flour
30g salt
375g margarine
375g lard
beaten egg

Mix the diced beef and onions with the salt and place in a large pan. Pour in enough water to cover and bring to the boil. Put a lid on the pan and simmer for 2½–3 hours, or until the meat is really tender.

To make the pastry, put the flour and salt into a bowl. Dice the margarine and lard and add them to the flour. Process in a food processor or mix by hand until the mixture has the texture of breadcrumbs. Add 340ml of water and mix until the pastry forms a ball – add more water if needed. Leave the pastry in the fridge for 2 hours while the meat is cooking.

When the meat has been cooking for a couple of hours, cook the potatoes in salted water until tender. Drain and set aside, reserving the cooking water to make extra gravy.

Once the meat is cooked, remove the pan from the heat. Ladle some of the broth from the meat into a jug to cool. Once the broth has cooled, gradually add some of the gravy paste, mixing thoroughly all the time. Pour this gravy back into the meat and place the pan over a gentle heat. Once the meat is simmering, take the pan off the heat again.

Preheat the oven to 200C/Gas 6. Cut off a small amount of pastry and roll it out. Cut enough 4cm wide strips to edge the rim of the pie tin. Strain the meat and onions, reserving the gravy, then place in the tin in an even layer. Put the potatoes on top of the meat. Pour enough gravy over the filling in the pie tin to come to just under the potatoes – usually about 3 ladlefuls. Save the rest to make extra gravy to serve with the pie, thickening it with the rest of the gravy paste if necessary.

Roll out the rest of the pastry to the size of the tin. Brush the strips of pastry on the tin with beaten egg and place the pastry lid on top. Crimp the edges and brush the pie with beaten egg. Make a few slits in the top with a knife to allow the steam to escape. Cook in the preheated oven for 50–60 minutes.

Make the gravy paste, using 5 tablespoons of special seasoning mixed with 140ml of cold water (or potato cooking water). Stir until thoroughly mixed, then leave to infuse.

STEAMED SYRUP SPONGE PUDDING

This pud is comfort food heaven just as it is or you can vary the basic recipe by adding some cocoa, choc chips and orange zest to make a chocolate orange steamed pudding. Or try adding stem ginger and using honey instead of golden syrup.

SERVES 6

100g golden syrup, plus an extra
4–5 tbsp for serving
175g softened butter,
plus extra for greasing
125g golden caster sugar
grated zest of 1 lemon
3 medium eggs, lightly beaten
175g self-raising flour

Using golden syrup in the sponge batter as well as on top gives this pudding a more syrupy flavour and a light, open texture.

Generously butter the inside of a 1.2 litre pudding basin. Place the basin on a set of scales and spoon 50g of the golden syrup into the base. Set this aside. Put a large mixing bowl on the scales and add the remaining 50g of golden syrup, then the butter, sugar and lemon zest. Beat with an electric whisk until light and fluffy.

Whisk half the beaten eggs into the creamed mixture. Whisk in half the flour, then the remaining eggs and finally the rest of the flour. Spoon into the basin and smooth the surface.

Cover the dish with a large circle of baking parchment, with a pleat in the middle to allow for expansion. Cover the parchment with a circle of foil, again with a pleat. Tie both tightly in place with string. Create a carrying handle by tying the excess string across the top of the basin – this will help you lift the pudding out of the pan once it's cooked.

Place on an upturned heatproof saucer or small trivet in a large, deep saucepan and add enough just-boiled water to come halfway up the sides of the basin. (Alternatively, cook in a hob-top steamer.) Cover the pan with a tight-fitting lid and place over a low heat. Allow to steam in gently simmering water for about 1 hour and 45 minutes, adding more water if necessary.

When the pudding is done, turn off the heat and carefully lift the basin from the water. Leave to stand for 5 minutes. Cut the string from the basin and discard the foil and paper. Loosen the sides of the pudding with a round-ended knife and invert onto a deep plate.

Spoon over the extra syrup, which will warm up on contact with the sponge and run slowly down the sides of the pudding. Serve in generous wedges with custard.

VEGGIE TABLE @ BATH PLACE COMMUNITY VENTURE

These recipes are from the Veggie Table Café, which is part of the Bath Place Community Venture in Leamington Spa. The Venture was established in 1974 and provides a wonderful centre for people in the area, with access to all kinds of facilities, support, information and education. There are workshops, classes, fun nights out as well as places where you can meet and talk – something for everyone. These dishes are regulars on the café menu.

MUSHROOM SOUP

This tasty mushroom soup is easy to prepare and makes a lovely comforting lunch, served with some warm crusty bread.

SERVES 4

25g butter
1 large onion, finely chopped
1 green pepper, finely chopped
1 medium leek, finely chopped
1–2 garlic cloves, crushed
300g mushrooms, grated
2 tbsp plain flour
450ml vegetable stock
450ml milk
1 tbsp chopped parsley
sea salt flakes and black pepper

Melt the butter in a pan and fry the onion, pepper, leek and garlic until they start to soften. Add the mushrooms and continue frying until they are cooked.

Stir in the flour, then add the stock. Bring to the boil and allow the soup to simmer for a few minutes. Pour in the milk and bring back up to simmer. Season, stir in the chopped parsley and serve with crusty bread.

If you want a smoother consistency, blitz the soup in a blender after adding the milk.

MUSHROOM & SPINACH TAGLIATELLE

SERVES 4

1 tbsp olive oil
1 bunch of spring onions, finely chopped
2 garlic cloves, finely chopped
10 button or chestnut mushrooms, sliced
200g spinach, washed
1 tbsp plain flour
1 x 200ml tub of crème fraîche
300g tagliatelle
sea salt flakes and black pepper

Heat the oil in a pan and fry the spring onions and garlic for a few minutes. Add the mushrooms and fry for another 10 minutes. Add the spinach and allow to wilt, then continue cooking over a medium heat until most of the water has evaporated.

Sprinkle the flour over the mixture and stir it in well, then stir in the crème fraîche. Season, bring to the boil, then simmer for a few minutes.

Meanwhile, cook the pasta in plenty of boiling salted water according to the instructions on the packet. Drain, toss with the mushroom and spinach sauce and serve immediately.

Al fresco

LIL'S CHICKEN KIEV
WITH CUCUMBER & SPRING ONION SALAD

This is a recipe from Lil, Dave's missus, and it's one of her favourites. It's best if the chicken breasts aren't too large, so go for free-range ones, which tend to be smaller – and tastier.

SERVES 4

4 free-range chicken breasts, skin removed
150g butter, room temperature
1 bunch of fresh parsley, finely chopped
3 garlic cloves, crushed
2 spring onions, finely chopped
50g Cheddar cheese,
or any hard cheese in the fridge, grated
2 eggs, beaten
3 tbsp plain flour
3 tbsp golden breadcrumbs
sunflower oil, for deep-frying
sea salt flakes
freshly ground black pepper

CUCUMBER & SPRING ONION SALAD
2 cucumbers, peeled and cored
2 spring onions, chopped
50ml soured cream
1 tbsp mayonnaise
large pinch of paprika
2 hard-boiled eggs, sliced

Slit each chicken breast down one side and cut through almost to the other side so you can open the breast out like a book. Place it between 2 pieces of clingfilm and flatten with a rolling pin, then sprinkle with salt and pepper. Repeat with the other breasts and set them aside.

In a bowl, mix the butter, parsley, garlic, spring onions and grated cheese. Divide this stuffing into 4 and form each portion of stuffing into a baguette shape. Put the beaten eggs in a bowl and spread the flour and breadcrumbs on separate plates.

Next, prepare the salad. Using a vegetable peeler, cut the cucumbers into ribbons and mix with the spring onions, soured cream, mayonnaise and paprika. Garnish with the slices of hard-boiled egg.

Lay a chicken breast flat on a chopping board and place a portion of stuffing in the middle. Roll up the chicken very tightly around the stuffing and roll in the flour. Dip in the beaten egg, then roll in the breadcrumbs. Repeat with the remaining chicken breasts and stuffing.

Heat the oil in a deep-fat fryer to 160°C – you don't want the temperature too hot or the outside of the chicken will burn before the inside is cooked. Cook for about 15 minutes until the coating is golden and crispy and the chicken is cooked through. Serve with the salad.

TORTILLA

We met Rebecca Simpson-Hargreaves near Stockport where she lives, but she was born in Spain and still loves to cook the wonderful Spanish dishes she learned from her mum and her gran. This is her family's way of making tortillas.

SERVES 6
AS PART OF A TAPAS SELECTION

2 tbsp olive oil
1 large onion, sliced
vegetable oil for deep-frying
4 large potatoes, cut into thin slices
2 free-range eggs
½ tbsp salt

Heat the olive oil in a small frying pan and gently fry the onions until they are soft but not overly coloured. Transfer the onions to a bowl, then discard as much of the oil as possible.

Half fill a deep pan with vegetable oil and heat to 170°C or use a deep-fat fryer. When the oil is hot, add the sliced potatoes and cook until a fork goes through them easily – don't let them go crisp and brown. Put the cooked potatoes in the bowl with the onions and set aside. Beat the eggs for a few minutes until well mixed, then add the salt and beat again. Add the eggs to the potatoes and onions and gently mix with a fork to break up the potato slices.

Using the frying pan that you cooked the onions in, pour in the potato mixture and flatten it down. Leave to cook over a gentle heat for about 5 minutes. Once the tortilla is done, slide it onto a plate, cooked side down. Take your pan, place it over the non-cooked side, then gently turn everything over so the tortilla is back in the pan, cooked side up. Place the pan back on the heat and cook as before. When it's light brown underneath, take it off the heat. Tortilla is nice warm but best served cold.

TIO ROBERTO'S GAMBAS AL AJILLO

SERVES 6
AS PART OF A TAPAS SELECTION

4 tbsp extra virgin olive oil
3 garlic cloves, chopped
2 chillies (as hot or as mild as you like), deseeded and chopped
1 tbsp spicy paprika
½ onion, finely chopped
large bag of frozen prawns, defrosted, or a large handful of peeled fresh prawns

Heat the oil over a gentle heat and add the garlic, chillies, paprika and onion. Cook until the onions are soft, but don't let them brown.

Wash the prawns and add them to the oil for 5 minutes to cook through and add their flavour to the mixture. If you are using fresh prawns, cook them until each one turns dark pink – about 5–10 minutes. Rebecca likes to cook them for at least 10 minutes which gives the sauce a great flavour. Serve with crusty bread.

BOOMER'S ALBONDIGAS

Rebecca's brothers called their grandma Boomer – her real name was Mercedes.
She was a real character, apparently, and a great cook, but she didn't trust male chefs!

SERVES 6
AS PART OF A TAPAS SELECTION

500g minced beef or pork,
or a mixture of both
1 onion, finely chopped
4 garlic cloves, chopped
4 tbsp dried parsley (do not use fresh)
1 slice of bread, made into fresh breadcrumbs
1 free-range egg, beaten
plain flour
olive oil
2 carrots, quartered
and sliced into small triangles
1 tbsp paprika
generous pinch of saffron
½ tbsp salt

Put the minced meat in a bowl with half the chopped onion, 1 of the garlic cloves, 2 spoonfuls of parsley and breadcrumbs and mix with your hands. Squash everything together until well combined. Add the beaten egg and mix well to bind. Shape the mixture into small balls.

Sprinkle some plain flour round the edge of the mixing bowl and roll the meatballs in the flour until they are well coated. Heat a good glug of olive oil in a frying pan and add the meatballs, a batch at a time. Fry gently until crispy on the outside, then drain on kitchen towel. Continue until all the meatballs are cooked, topping up the oil as needed.

In the same pan, cook the carrots with the rest of the onions and garlic until the onions are soft and lightly coloured. Pour everything, including the oil, into a saucepan and place over a medium heat. Add the rest of the parsley, then the paprika, saffron and salt, and pour in a cup of water – about 300ml. Add the meatballs and warm through before serving.

PATATAS BRAVAS

SERVES 6
AS PART OF A TAPAS SELECTION

3 large potatoes, chopped into chunks
2 onions, chopped
olive oil
salt
1 tbsp sugar
1 garlic clove, chopped
6 ripe tomatoes, sliced
2 chillies, deseeded and chopped
spicy paprika

Parboil the potatoes until just cooked, drain and set aside to cool. Next make the sauce. Gently fry the onions in about a tablespoon of olive oil until soft, then season with salt and add the sugar. Add the garlic and tomatoes and simmer for about an hour. As the tomatoes are cooking, mash them from time to time with a potato masher or a spoon to break them down. When they're very soft, take them off the heat and press them through a sieve. Pour the sieved sauce back into the pan.

Add the chillies and a tablespoon of spicy paprika. If you like really spicy food, add more paprika and chillies to taste. Warm over a moderate heat for about 5 minutes. Fry the potatoes in olive oil until crispy, then drain on kitchen paper and put them into a bowl. Cover with the spicy bravas sauce and serve.

If you're short of time, you can cheat by buying some tomato frito sauce from the supermarket and adding paprika and chilli.

SPICED POTTED BEEF

A traditional potted beef recipe that's perfect for a picnic – delicious spread thickly onto fresh, crusty bread. There's a picture of the potted beef with the potted salmon over the page.

SERVES 4–6

100g butter
1 tsp freshly grated nutmeg
½ tsp ground ginger
½ tsp sea salt flakes
good pinch of cayenne pepper
2 garlic cloves, peeled
300g braising steak
freshly ground black pepper

PEPPERCORN TOPPING
25g butter
4 tsp green peppercorns in brine, drained

Preheat the oven to 150°C/Gas 2. Put the butter in a small saucepan and sprinkle over the nutmeg, ginger, salt, cayenne and garlic cloves. Season with lots of freshly ground black pepper and place over a low heat. Leave the butter to melt slowly, stirring occasionally.

Put the beef on a chopping board and trim off any hard fat or sinew. Cut the beef into 4 or 5 large chunks and place them in a small ovenproof dish. Pour the melted butter, spices and garlic over the top so that the beef is almost completely covered.

Place the dish on a baking tray and cover it with a tight-fitting piece of foil or a lid. Cook in the centre of the preheated oven for 3¼–3½ hours or until the beef is very soft. About halfway through the cooking time, remove the dish from the oven and turn the beef pieces over. Cover again and return to the oven for the remaining time.

At the end of the cooking time, take the beef out of the oven and remove the foil or lid. Press a chunk of the meat with a table knife – it should offer very little resistance. If the beef still feels a little firm, return to the oven for a further 20–30 minutes or so. Leave to cool for 30 minutes.

Tip the beef into a bowl with the garlic and buttery juices and mash until the mixture is as smooth as possible. Transfer to a small preserving jar or a ceramic bowl and spread evenly.

Melt the butter for the topping slowly in a small pan over a low heat. Spoon off any white foam that rises to the surface, then carefully pour the clarified butter onto the potted beef, leaving any sediment at the bottom of the pan. Scatter the peppercorns on top. Cover the jar or bowl and chill. Use the beef within 3 days.

POTTED SALMON

**The inspiration for this and the potted beef on the previous page came from those dinky little jars
of potted beef and salmon spread we remember from our youth. These are grown-up versions!**

SERVES 6

2 x 150g skinless salmon fillets
1 small unwaxed lemon
1 bay leaf
50g butter
100g smoked salmon slices
100g full-fat soft cheese
small bunch of fresh dill, feathery leaves
stripped from the stalks
freshly ground black pepper
tiny bay leaves, snipped chives or dill sprigs,
to garnish

Put one of the salmon fillets in a small saucepan and pour over
enough water to cover. Peel a wide strip of lemon zest using a
vegetable peeler and add it to the pan. Drop the bay leaf into the
pan and bring the water to a gentle simmer. Cover with a lid and
cook for 6 minutes. Drain the salmon, transfer it to a plate and
leave to cool.

Cut the second salmon fillet into small cubes, each roughly
1.5cm square – about the size of a dice. Put the cubes in a clean
pan with the butter and set over a low heat. When the butter has
melted, cook the salmon cubes for 2–3 minutes or until just
cooked through, turning once. Remove from the heat and set aside.

Flake the poached salmon into chunky pieces and put in a food
processor with the smoked salmon, soft cheese and dill sprigs.
Finely grate the zest of half the lemon onto a board and scrape
it into the food processor. Add plenty of black pepper.

Blend the fish mixture until almost smooth, removing the lid
and pushing down once or twice with a rubber spatula. Transfer
the mixture to a bowl. Using a slotted spoon, add the cooked
salmon cubes, reserving the melted butter, and fold them in
very gently.

Spoon the salmon mixture into a preserving jar or small ceramic
dish. Pour over the melted butter (used to cook the salmon
cubes), leaving any sediment at the bottom of the pan. Garnish
with tiny bay leaves, snipped chives or sprigs of dill, cover and
leave to set in the fridge. Eat within 2 days.

*Make our quick melba toast
to go with this. Just toast
some white sliced bread and
split the slices in two.*

STUFFED CABBAGE

Marika Gallimore and her brother Karl are from Hungary, although they were born in Britain, and they like to keep their Hungarian heritage alive through food. They took us on a camping trip and showed us how to cook some traditional Hungarian dishes over the camp fire. Wonderful stuff!

SERVES 10

1 large white cabbage
40g lard
1 large onion, chopped
2 tbsp paprika
1.4kg minced pork
450g long-grain rice
1 x 400g can of tomatoes
soured cream, to serve
salt and pepper

Put the cabbage in large pan, add hot water and boil until the leaves fall off the cabbage. Put the leaves on a plate to drain and cool.

Melt the lard in a frying pan, then add the chopped onion and fry until soft. Take the pan off the heat, tip the onions into a bowl and stir in the paprika, adding more or less as required. Add the minced pork and the rice, then season to taste and mix well.

Take a cabbage leaf and cut away a little of the stalk so that it is easy to roll. Add a spoonful of the mincemeat mixture to the stalk end of the leaf, then roll the cabbage into a sausage shape, tucking in the ends. Try to roll the leaf as firmly as possible, so that it doesn't unroll during cooking. Continue until you have used all the stuffing mixture.

Shred any leftover cabbage and use it to line the bottom of a large pan – this prevents the stuffed cabbage leaves from burning. Place the stuffed leaves in the pan as snugly as possible, then cover with some more shredded cabbage.

Add boiling water to cover, bring to the boil, and then add the tomatoes and more seasoning. Allow the cabbage to simmer for 1–1½ hours, until the pork is cooked.

Serve the stuffed cabbage drizzled with the juices of the cabbage and topped with soured cream. Good with some crusty bread too.

PÖRKHÖLT

Pörkölt is an Hungarian meat stew, also known as Perka. Shepherds used to make this in a cauldron over an open fire when they were out on the plains and many Hungarians still like to cook it this way. The stew can be made with beef, veal or chicken as well as pork.

SERVES 8–10

40g lard
1 large onion, thinly sliced
2–3 tbsp paprika
1.8kg pork steak, diced
1 tsp tomato purée
1 green pepper, thinly sliced
3 medium tomatoes, sliced
1 tbsp cornflour
salt and pepper

Heat the lard in a frying pan and fry the onion until soft. Take the pan off the heat and stir in the paprika, adding more or less to suit your taste.

Add the pork steak and a little boiled water to keep the meat moist as the juices release. Simmer over a low heat for about 5 minutes to seal in the flavour. Add enough boiled water to cover the meat, bring back to the boil and add the tomato purée, green pepper, sliced tomatoes and seasoning. Cover with a lid to keep the moisture in and simmer for about 1 hour until the pork is tender.

To thicken the sauce, add the cornflour to cold water and mix to form a paste, then stir this into the stew. Bring to the boil again to thicken. Serve with creamy mashed potatoes or macaroni and a side dish of finely sliced cucumber in white wine vinegar and sugar.

SALMON & DILL FISHCAKES
WITH HOLLANDAISE SAUCE

These fish cakes are the best, full of juicy flakes of salmon. The mash needs to be really dry,
so place the pan over a low heat while you mash the potatoes but make sure they don't burn.

MAKES 8

800g skinless salmon fillets
2 bay leaves
small bunch of dill,
stalks and fronds separated
500ml whole milk
600g Maris Piper potatoes, peeled and
chopped into even-sized pieces
grated zest of 1 lemon
4 tbsp mayonnaise
1 tsp Dijon mustard
1 tsp paprika
4 tbsp salted capers, rinsed and dried
plain flour, for dusting your hands
handful of parsley, chopped
100g breadcrumbs
1 egg
vegetable oil, for shallow frying
white pepper
sea salt to taste

HOLLANDAISE SAUCE
225g butter
4 tbsp white wine vinegar
1 small shallot or ½ banana shallot,
finely chopped
10 black peppercorns
1 bay leaf
3 large egg yolks
pinch of sea salt
pinch of caster sugar

Put the salmon fillets in a frying pan with the bay leaves and dill
stalks. Pour over enough milk to cover the fish. Bring the milk
to the boil, then lower the heat to a gentle simmer and leave the
fish to poach for 4 minutes. Turn off the heat and leave the fish
to continue cooking in the poaching liquid for a couple of minutes
longer. Lift the salmon out onto a plate. Flake into large pieces
with a fork, then leave to cool.

Boil the potatoes in salted water until tender. Drain well, then
leave to cool for a couple of minutes before putting them back
into the pan and mashing them. Stir in the zest, dill fronds,
mayonnaise, mustard, paprika and capers. Season to taste.

Pat away any liquid from the fish with kitchen paper, then gently
fold the fish into the mash with your hands until roughly combined.
Try not to break up the flakes. Dust your hands with flour and
shape a handful of the mix into a cake, about 2.5cm thick.
Repeat until you've used up all the mix.

Mix the parsley and breadcrumbs in a bowl and beat the egg in
a separate bowl. Dip the cakes into the egg, then press into the
breadcrumbs and parsley mix, making sure they are well covered.
Heat the oil in a frying pan and fry a few of the fishcakes for
5 minutes on each side until golden. Remove and keep them
warm while you fry the rest.

HOLLANDAISE SAUCE
Melt the butter slowly in a pan over a low heat, stirring
occasionally. Remove from the heat and pour into a jug. Put
the vinegar, shallot, peppercorns and bay leaf in a small pan
over a high heat and bring to the boil. Cook for 1–2 minutes
until the liquid has reduced to about 2 tablespoons.

Put the egg yolks in a heatproof bowl and place over a pan of
simmering water. Whisk the egg yolks with the salt and sugar
until pale. Pour the vinegar reduction through a fine sieve onto
the yolks and continue whisking until thoroughly combined.
Gradually, add the hot butter in a steady stream, whisking
constantly until the sauce is thick and shiny.

MINCED BEEF PINWHEELS

Another triumph with ready-made puff pastry – these help a small amount of meat go a long way. Fun to make with the kids.

MAKES 12

1 tbsp sunflower oil
½ medium onion, peeled and very finely chopped
1 garlic clove, peeled and crushed
500g lean minced beef
1 tsp dried mixed herbs (preferably freeze-dried)
1 tbsp tomato purée
1 tbsp plain flour, plus extra for rolling
500g block of ready-made puff pastry
50g mature Cheddar cheese, finely grated (optional)
1 medium egg, beaten
sea salt flakes
freshly ground black pepper

Preheat the oven to 200°C/Gas 6. Line a large baking tray or 2 smaller baking trays with baking parchment. Heat the oil in a small frying pan and gently fry the onion and garlic for 2–3 minutes until soft, stirring regularly. Tip the mixture into a large heatproof bowl and leave to cool for few minutes.

Add the minced beef, dried herbs, tomato purée and a tablespoon of flour to the bowl with the onion and season well with salt and pepper. Mix with your clean hands until thoroughly combined.

Roll out the pastry on a lightly floured surface into a roughly 34 x 34cm square. Spread the mince mixture over the pastry, leaving a 2cm border around the edges. Sprinkle on the grated cheese, if using, and brush the pastry edges with a little of the beaten egg. Roll up smoothly and firmly, like a Swiss roll.

Cut the roll into 12 slices using a serrated knife – a bread knife is ideal. Place the pinwheels on the baking tray (or trays), spaced well apart to allow for rising. Flatten slightly with the palm of your hand. Brush the pastry sides with more beaten egg to glaze. Bake for 15 minutes or until well risen and golden brown. Best served warm.

You can also make a chicken, sage and onion filling or even use left-over bolognese sauce.

MUM'S PLUM SUMMER PUDDING

We met Jayne Rawlings in Lincoln. She gave us this recipe, which is a Victorian dinner party classic and has been handed down through four generations of her family. Jayne enjoys walking and likes to use wild fruits and other goodies she finds in her cooking.

SERVES 8

750g dark red or black plums
120g sugar
2 tbsp sloe gin, damson vodka or cassis (optional)
½ – ¾ medium white sliced loaf, crusts removed

Remove the stones from the plums and cut them into quarters. Place the plums in a large pan with about 5 tablespoons of water and add the sugar. Heat to dissolve the sugar, shaking the pan frequently so that the fruit doesn't stick to the bottom and burn. Continue to cook the plums, uncovered, until they are soft and have released lots of juice. Taste and add more sugar if necessary and the liquor if using.

Cut the corners off one slice of bread to make a rough circle. Dip it in the plum juice and place it, wet side down, at the bottom of a pudding basin. Cut some more slices of bread in half, dip each one in the juice and place them up the sides of the basin – wet sides outwards. Now cut a second circle of bread and place it on top of the other base piece to keep the sides in place.

Pour the fruit and juice into the bread-lined basin, filling it right to the top. Take 4 more slices of bread and cut an arc on one side of each to fit the curve of the basin rim. Place these shaped slices on top of the fruit. Cover tightly with clingfilm and invert onto a plate, then place in the fridge for at least a day.

When ready to serve, turn the basin right side up again and remove the clingfilm. Run a knife around the edge of the pudding and then invert the basin to turn the pudding out onto a deep wide dish. The pudding will sag with the weight of fruit, but don't worry. Cut into wedges and serve with crème fraîche.

If you make this pudding with little wild plums, you'll find it easiest to cook them whole, then pick out the stones. You can also use other seasonal fruits, such as apples, strawberries, gooseberries and blackcurrants.

MUD PIE

This is an amazing pudding recipe that Jayne's mum used to cook for her family and Jayne still makes today. The family called it mud pie because ... well, it looked like mud! It's an original and Jayne says she has never seen anything like it in any cookbook.

SERVES 6

200g dark chocolate, at least 70 per cent cocoa solids
100ml strong coffee, cooled, or Camp coffee essence
600ml double cream
4 tbsp milk
200g marshmallows

BISCUIT BASE
200g digestive biscuits
75g butter

First make the biscuit base. Put the biscuits in a freezer bag and crush them with a rolling pin. Gently melt the butter in a pan, add the crushed biscuits and mix together. Tip the mixture into a 25cm flan dish and press down well. Set aside to cool.

Break the chocolate up into chunks and place them in a bowl. set over a pan of simmering water. Make sure the bowl doesn't touch the water. Allow the chocolate to melt, then stir in the coffee or coffee essence. In a separate bowl, whip the cream to soft peaks, taking care not to whip it too much.

Put the milk in a pan and add the marshmallows. Stir continuously over a very low heat until the marshmallows Remove from the heat and stir in the melted chocolate, a tablespoon at a time, mixing well. Beat in the cream, using a balloon whisk to remove any lumps. Pour the mixture onto the biscuit base and leave it in the fridge for about 8 hours to set.

To jazz this recipe up for special occasions, you can add 3 tablespooons of dark rum with the coffee essence.

HOME-MADE LEMONADE

MAKES A LARGE JUGFUL

10 organic lemons, well scrubbed
100g citric acid
2.25kg caster sugar

Slice the lemons thinly, removing any pips. Place the slices in a large heatproof jug and add the citric acid. Tip in the caster sugar, then pour in 1.2 litres of boiling water. Leave to cool, then sieve. Chill and dilute with water or soda to triple quantities or to taste. Serve with ice and some fresh lemon slices if you like.

CINDER TOFFEE

A bonfire night treat for all the family. Watch the cooking times and temperature closely to be sure you end up with light, bubbly cinder toffee (honeycomb) that holds its shape as it cools. A sugar thermometer is a big help and remember to take great care – molten toffee can cause nasty burns.

MAKES ABOUT 20 CHUNKY PIECES

softened butter, for greasing the tin
2 tsp bicarbonate of soda
350g caster sugar
200g golden syrup
75g butter
2 tbsp white wine vinegar
200g dark or milk chocolate,
broken into squares

If you don't have a sugar thermometer, have a large mug of very cold water beside the hob. Drip a little hot toffee from a long-handled spoon into the water. If it's ready, it will form thin brittle threads that harden immediately.

If you use milk chocolate, you'll find it easier to dip the pieces of toffee into the chocolate, as milk chocolate doesn't run as freely as the dark chocolate.

Butter a 25cm square loose-based brownie tin, or cake tin, and line it with baking parchment. Make sure you take the parchment paper right up the sides, so the edges of the toffee can't stick. Set aside. Measure the bicarbonate of soda into a small bowl and have a large metal, balloon whisk standing by.

Put the sugar, golden syrup, butter and vinegar into a large saucepan. Add 200ml of cold water and set the pan over a low heat. (You'll need a large pan because the cinder toffee will bubble up and could overflow.) Stir occasionally until the sugar has completely dissolved.

Place a clip-on sugar thermometer into the pan. The sugar syrup will be heated to an extremely high temperature, so don't be tempted to touch or taste at any stage. Increase the heat under the pan to medium-high and bring the sugar syrup to the boil. Stir once with a wooden spoon, then leave the toffee boiling until it reaches 154°C or the hard crack stage on your thermometer. We found that 158°C gave the best results, so watch carefully.

Taking great care, remove the pan from the heat and place it on a heatproof surface. Sprinkle over the bicarbonate of soda and immediately whisk very lightly with a large metal whisk to combine the soda with the toffee. The toffee will bubble ferociously and rise in the pan. Leave for a few seconds, then while it is still bubbling, pour the mixture gently into the prepared tin, allowing it to flow to all the sides. Leave to cool for 15 minutes. Using a lightly oiled knife, deeply score the cinder toffee into 20 squares. Leave to cool completely.

Melt the chocolate in a heatproof bowl over a pan of gently simmering water, or in the microwave, until smooth. Carefully remove the cinder toffee from the tin and put it on a board. Peel off the baking parchment. Cut the toffee into chunky squares. Place on a wire rack above a plate and spoon over the melted chocolate, allowing it to dribble down the sides.

STUDLEY GROW, COOK & EAT

This lottery-funded arts and health project is based on growing, cooking and eating fresh seasonal fruit and vegetables and was developed by Escape: Community Art in Action, a Warwickshire arts charity. The project enables people to 'feed' their passion for local food and has developed a fantastic community programme of cooking and creative environmental arts.

RICOTTA HOT CAKES
WITH PLUM COMPOTE

Abi Macfarlane, from Studley Grow, Cook and Eat, gave us this recipe. The hot cakes are as light as air and make a delicious brunch, especially when served with a fruity plum compote.

SERVES 10

4 eggs, separated
180ml milk
½ tsp vanilla essence
225g ricotta
2 tbsp caster sugar
140g plain flour
1 tsp baking powder
½ tbsp sunflower oil

PLUM COMPOTE
700g plums, halved and stoned
50g caster sugar
1 cinnamon stick

First make the compote. Cut each plum half into 3 or 4 pieces and put them in a small pan with the sugar and cinnamon stick and a little water. Cook over a moderate heat, stirring occasionally until the plums are soft.

In a bowl, whisk together the egg yolks, milk, vanilla, ricotta and sugar. Mix the flour and baking powder together, then add this to the ricotta mixture. Whisk the egg whites to soft peaks and fold them into the mixture.

Heat the oil in a frying pan. Using a serving spoon, add a few dollops of the ricotta mixture into the pan. When the surface starts to bubble, turn the ricotta cakes and cook on the other side. You should get about 30 hot cakes from this mixture. Serve with plum compote and crème fraîche.

PORT & PLUM SAUCE

This is a lovely versatile sauce recipe from Karen Jones. It can be used to make the plum chocolates opposite or to accompany any sweet dish – truly scrumptious.

MAKES A GOOD BOWLFUL

30g unsalted butter
450g chopped plums
5½ tbsp light brown sugar
125ml ruby port
pinch of freshly grated nutmeg (optional)

Melt the butter over a medium heat. Add the plums and sauté for 2–3 minutes until they begin to soften. Add the sugar and cook for 4–5 minutes until the sugar begins to caramelise. Stir in the port and simmer over a low heat for 3–5 minutes until slightly thickened. Remove from the heat and stir in the nutmeg, if using. The sauce can be prepared and refrigerated for up to 24 hours in advance. Serve at room temperature.

KAREN'S PLUM CHOCOLATES

MAKES 24

DARK PLUM CHOCOLATES
170g dark chocolate
4 tbsp port and plum sauce (see opposite)

RICH PLUM BITES
30g butter
handful of peeled and chopped plums
2 tbsp light brown sugar
170g dark chocolate
4 tbsp port and plum sauce (see opposite)
handful of chopped Brazil nuts (optional)

Melt the chocolate in a bowl over a pan of simmering water. Add the plum and port sauce and mix well. Spoon into small paper chocolate cases and refrigerate until firm.

RICH PLUM BITES
Melt the butter over a medium heat, add the plums and sauté until they begin to soften. Add the sugar and cook until it begins to caramelise, forming a syrup. Remove from the heat.

Prepare the chocolate and port and plum sauce mix as above, then add the caramelised plums. Top with some chopped Brazil nuts, too, if desired. Spoon into small paper chocolate cases and chill before eating.

Taste
of home

SPAGHETTI BOLOGNESE

The long, slow cooking of this sauce tenderises the meat and allows the flavours to bubble through. We know it's not traditional, but we find that adding a touch of flour at the beginning prevents the bolognese sauce looking watery when it's served.

SERVES 5–6

500g lean minced beef
1 medium onion, finely chopped
2 celery sticks, trimmed and finely sliced
2 medium carrots, finely diced
2 garlic cloves, finely chopped
150g small portobello or chestnut mushrooms, wiped and sliced
1 tbsp plain flour
150ml red wine
1 x 400g can of chopped tomatoes
2 tbsp tomato purée
1 beef stock cube
1 tsp caster sugar
1 tsp dried oregano or
1 tsp dried mixed herbs
2 bay leaves
375–450g dried spaghetti
freshly grated Parmesan cheese, for serving
sea salt flakes
freshly ground black pepper

Put the mince in a large non-stick saucepan with the onion, celery, carrots and garlic. Dry fry over a medium heat for 8–10 minutes or until the beef is no longer pink and the vegetables are beginning to brown. Stir the meat with a wooden spoon to break up any large clumps. Add the mushrooms and fry with the mince and vegetables for another 2–3 minutes. Sprinkle over the flour and stir well.

Stir in the wine and add the tomatoes and tomato purée, along with 300ml of cold water. Crumble the stock cube over the top, then add the caster sugar and herbs. Season with a few twists of black pepper, give a good stir and bring to a simmer. When the liquid is bubbling, reduce the heat and simmer very gently for 30–40 minutes, without covering, stirring occasionally.

Half fill a large pan with water and bring to the boil. As soon as the water is boiling, add the spaghetti and push it down with a wooden spoon to encourage the strands to separate. It's important to use lots of water, so the spaghetti can move freely without sticking together. Cook for 10–12 minutes, or according to the packet instructions.

While the spaghetti is cooking, increase the heat under the sauce and simmer for another 10 minutes or until the liquid is well reduced and the sauce looks rich and thick. Stir regularly and adjust the seasoning if necessary.

Drain the spaghetti in a colander and divide between warmed bowls. Spoon the bolognese mixture on top, sprinkle with freshly grated Parmesan cheese and serve immediately. If serving at the table, it's a good idea to toss the spaghetti with a tiny amount of oil before transferring it to a serving dish. This will stop the pasta sticking. Make sure you don't add too much though, or the sauce will slide off the spaghetti.

Mix half a haggis in with the beef to create a spicier sauce that we call hag bog!

MACARONI CHEESE

This is a classic – every home should have one. Don't be pedantic about the cheese and take the opportunity to use up all those little hard scraps in the fridge. They'll taste just as good.

SERVES 4

250g macaroni
50g butter, plus extra for greasing
50g plain flour
500ml whole or semi-skimmed milk
150g mature Cheddar cheese, finely grated
4 medium tomatoes, sliced
sea salt flakes
freshly ground black pepper

Preheat the oven to 200°C/Gas 6. Half fill a large saucepan with water and bring it to the boil. Add the macaroni and return to the boil. Cook for 8–10 minutes, or according to the packet instructions, stirring occasionally.

While the pasta is cooking, prepare the sauce. Melt the butter in a medium non-stick saucepan over a low heat, then stir in the flour and cook for 30 seconds, stirring constantly.

Gradually stir in the milk and bring to a gentle simmer. Cook for 3 minutes until the sauce is thickened and smooth, stirring constantly. Add roughly two-thirds of the cheese and season with salt and ground black pepper. Cook for 2–3 minutes more and keep stirring. Add a little more seasoning if necessary.

Drain the pasta in a large colander and return it to the pan. Gently stir in the hot cheese sauce until thoroughly combined. Tip the macaroni cheese mixture into a large, buttered ovenproof dish – a lasagne dish is ideal – and spread it to all the corners.

Sprinkle with half the remaining cheese and arrange the sliced tomatoes on top, discarding the ends. Sprinkle with the rest of the cheese and add a couple of twists of ground black pepper. Bake for 20–25 minutes until the tomatoes are softened and the cheese is lightly browned. Serve with some lovely fresh bread and butter.

If you like, fry some button mushrooms in a little butter until golden. Stir them into the cooked pasta before adding the sauce. Si likes to add bits of fried bacon too, so give that a try.

SALTFISH & ACKEE
WITH FRIED DUMPLINGS

Julia Titus lives in Reading and her dad is from Jamaica. He came to England in the
1950s but didn't take to English food so taught his family how to cook Jamaican-style.
Julia showed us some great Jamaican classics.

SERVES 4

450g salt cod
1 x 400g can of ackee
olive oil
1 onion, chopped
1 tsp paprika
2 tsp mild curry powder
2 tsp jerk seasoning
1 tsp hot pepper sauce
1 red and 1 yellow pepper, sliced
200g tomatoes, chopped
salt and black pepper

DUMPLINGS
250g self-raising flour
30g vegetable suet
pinch of salt
vegetable oil, for frying

Soak the salt cod overnight, changing the water a couple of times. Drain, then put it in a large pan of fresh water and bring to the boil. Drain, add fresh water and bring to the boil again. Simmer for about 5 minutes until cooked through, then drain and flake the fish into large pieces. Discard any skin or bones.

For the dumplings, mix the flour and suet with a pinch of salt and 250ml water to make a dough. Wrap the mixture in clingfilm and leave in the fridge to rest. Open the can of ackee, drain and rinse, then leave to one side.

Heat a tablespoon of olive oil in a pan and fry the onion until softened. Add the spices, seasoning and pepper sauce, then the sliced peppers and continue to fry until the peppers are tender. Add the chopped tomatoes, then the salt cod and mix together. Lastly stir in the ackee very gently and leave to simmer until ready to serve.

When you're almost ready to eat, heat some vegetable oil in a frying pan and shallow fry the dumplings until golden. Serve with the salt cod stew.

SMASHED-UP CHICKEN
WITH GARLIC & CHILLI PASTA

This is a lovely lemony chicken dish, served with chilli-spiked pasta – perfect Mediterranean-fresh flavours and a real taste of summer. Use whatever pasta shapes you fancy, but we find that fusilli works well. Bashing the chicken is a fantastic way to let out all your pent-up emotions.

SERVES 4–6

2 large chicken breasts, skinned
3 tbsp plain flour
2 tbsp olive oil
150g fresh wild mushrooms, chopped
150ml dry white wine
75ml chicken stock
2 garlic cloves, crushed
1 tbsp chopped fresh tarragon
1 tbsp lemon juice
finely grated zest of 1 lemon
2 tbsp capers (rinsed)
2 tbsp crème fraîche
handful of flat-leaf parsley, chopped
fine sea salt
freshly ground black pepper

GARLIC & CHILLI PASTA
250g pasta, such as fusilli
2 tbsp olive oil
1 tbsp chilli flakes
2 garlic cloves, crushed
Parmesan cheese, to finish

First the fun bit: put a chicken breast between two pieces of clingfilm and beat it with a rolling pin until super thin. We want the chicken all smashed up for this – we don't want schnitzels or escalopes. Remove the top piece of clingfilm and peel off the ribbon-like fragments of chicken. Repeat with the other chicken breast. Season the flour with salt and pepper and roll the chicken bits in the flour.

Heat the oil in the frying pan and cook the chicken until golden and just cooked through. Remove the chicken from the pan and set aside. Fry the mushrooms in the remaining oil, adding a drop more if it looks a bit dry. Set them aside with the cooked chicken.

Pour the wine and stock into the pan and bring to the boil to deglaze all the sticky bits from the bottom of the pan. Cook for a couple of minutes to reduce the liquid, then add the garlic, tarragon, lemon juice and the zest. Cook for 2 minutes, then add the capers.

Remove from the heat and whisk in the crème fraîche, then return the chicken and mushrooms to the pan to warm through. Finish off with the chopped parsley and check the seasoning.

Cook the pasta in plenty of salted boiling water according to the instructions on the packet. Meanwhile, heat a tablespoon of the oil in a frying pan and fry the chilli flakes and garlic. Drain the pasta well, then add the chilli-garlic oil and another tablespoon of oil. Check the seasoning, add the Parmesan cheese and serve with the chicken

Great with a glass of chilled dry white wine and a green salad.

WELSH CAKES

Mary Hamilton lives in Surrey now, but she told us that her heart is still in Wales, where she grew up. Mary learned to cook from her nan and this is one of her favourites – something she and her sons like to enjoy when they're watching Welsh rugby on TV. Apparently, lots of people come round to join them and Mary's not sure if it's the rugby they like or the teatime treats. We think we know!

MAKES 6–8

225g self-raising flour
110g salted butter, diced
85g caster sugar, plus extra for dusting
handful of sultanas
1 egg, beaten
milk, if needed
extra butter, for greasing

Sift the flour into a bowl and add the diced butter. Rub with your fingertips until the mixture has the texture of breadcrumbs. You can do this in a food processor if you prefer.

Add the sugar, dried fruit and beaten egg. Mix well to form a ball of dough, using a splash of milk if needed. Roll the dough out to a thickness of about 5mm. Cut into rounds with a 7.5–10cm plain cutter.

Cook the cakes on a heavy iron griddle or a bakestone. Rub the griddle with butter and wipe away any excess. Heat, then add the Welsh cakes a few at a time and cook for 2–3 minutes on each side, until golden brown. Remove from the griddle and dust with caster sugar while still warm.

LIVER & BACON
WITH ONIONS & GRAVY

A great dish that mums used to cook every week when we were young. This is best made
with lambs' liver, but if you're feeling posh, use calves' liver instead and simmer the onions
with a good slurp of marsala wine instead of making a traditional gravy.

SERVES 4

450g lambs' liver, sliced and
fully thawed if frozen
25g butter
1 tbsp sunflower oil
2 tbsp plain flour
1 onion, peeled,
halved lengthways and sliced
125g rindless streaky bacon rashers,
each cut into 4–5 pieces
1 beef stock cube
500ml just-boiled water
1–2 tsp tomato ketchup
sea salt flakes
freshly ground black pepper

Rinse the liver in a colander under cold water and drain well
on kitchen paper. Melt half the butter with the oil in a large
non-stick frying pan over a high heat.

Put a tablespoon of the flour in a large bowl and season with
plenty of salt and pepper. Add half the liver to the bowl and
toss lightly in the flour to coat. Place each slice carefully in
the hot fat and cook for 1–2 minutes on each side until lightly
browned but not completely cooked through. Transfer to
a plate. Toss the remaining liver in the seasoned flour and
brown in the pan as before. Transfer to the same plate as
the first batch.

Reduce the heat and melt the remaining butter in the same
pan. Add the sliced onion and cook for a minute or so, stirring
to separate the layers. Next, add the bacon and cook together
for 8–10 minutes or until the onion is pale golden brown and
the bacon is beginning to crisp. Stir often.

Sprinkle the rest of the flour over the onion and bacon and stir
it for a minute or so. Dissolve the stock cube in the just-boiled
water and pour slowly into the pan, stirring constantly. Bring
to a simmer and cook over a medium heat until the gravy is
thickened. Add a dash of tomato ketchup and season with
salt and pepper.

Return the liver to the pan with the onion gravy for just
1–2 minutes to warm it through and finish cooking. Serve the
liver and bacon with some mash and freshly cooked greens.

KROKETTEN

Mariken van Dolen is from the Netherlands and she showed us some amazing recipes that are her 'taste of home'. Kroketten are a typical Dutch snack. This recipe is for beef kroketten but you can use any type of meat, fish or vegetables in the filling. Preparing Kroketten is done in three stages. First you make the stock – depending on the type of Kroketten you want to make, you can use chicken, fish, vegetable or beef stock. Next, you prepare the filling or ragout, which must be really thick and firm. Then you make the kroketten.

SERVES 15

STOCK
900g oxtail
100g butter
2 onions, chopped
2 carrots, chopped
1 tbsp salt
2 bay leaves
bouquet garni
6 coriander seeds, crushed (optional)
1 beef stock cube (optional)
salt and pepper

Season the oxtail. Heat the butter in a pan and fry the seasoned oxtail until brown. Add the onions and carrots and continue frying until the onions are nice and brown. Add 2.5–3 litres of water, the tablespoon of salt, bay leaves, bouquet garni and, if using, the crushed coriander seeds. Bring almost to the boil, then turn the gas low, and leave to simmer on the lowest possible heat for a few hours. The longer this cooks, the better – Mariken normally leaves her stock to cook overnight.

Sieve the (hot) stock through a clean tea towel, then transfer the oxtail bones to a plate and leave them to cool. Make sure you remove all the onion and carrot. Check the seasoning of the stock and add salt or a beef stock cube if you like. Remove the meat from the bones when they are cool and throw away the fat.

RAGOUT
6 gelatine leaves
100g butter
150g flour
1 tsp curry powder
few drops of Worcestershire sauce
1 litre beef stock
oxtail meat

Next make the ragout. Place the gelatine leaves in some water to soak. Melt the butter in a saucepan, but don't let it brown. Add the flour, curry powder and Worcestershire sauce and stir until crumbly. Start adding the stock a ladleful at a time, stirring vigorously after each addition. At first, the mixture will form a smooth ball, but gradually it will become a thick sauce – the mixture has to be really firm and thick to make the kroketten. Add the meat and stir. Then squeeze out the gelatine leaves and stir them in well. Taste the ragout and add more salt, Worcestershire sauce or curry powder as you like. Leave the mixture to cool in the fridge until it is really cold.

FINISHING
4 eggs, beaten
golden breadcrumbs
flour
vegetable oil, for frying

Put the beaten eggs in a low, wide bowl and the breadcrumbs and flour in separate bowls. Take a spoonful of ragout and roll it in your hands into a sausage shape. Roll this in the flour, then the egg and lastly the breadcrumbs, making sure both ends of the kroket are well covered. Place on a plate and continue until all the mixture is used up. Then roll the kroketten in egg and breadcrumbs again.

Heat the oil to 180°C in a deep-fat fryer or large saucepan. Fry the kroketten, a few at a time, until deep brown. If the kroketten start to sizzle, take them out of the pan, as this is a signal that the filling is starting to leak. Serve immediately, but take care – they will be very hot.

You can also freeze the kroketten and fry them straight from the freezer without defrosting. Be sure to freeze them separately so they don't stick together. When cooking frozen kroketten, fry them for about 2 minutes, take them out for 2 minutes, then lower them into the fryer for another 2 minutes until they are deep brown.

You can prepare the kroketten earlier in the day and place them in the fridge to cook when you're ready.

DUTCH PEA SOUP

Another recipe from Mariken, this is traditionally served on very cold winter days alongside the canals when everybody is out skating at the so called Koek and Zopie (cookie and drink) stands. The soup warms you up and gives you energy. Many mums also serve this soup on Saturdays with fried bread cubes. It's essential to use meat on the bone for flavour.

SERVES 6–8

1kg dried green peas or split peas
(or half of each)
1kg pork shank or leg (on the bone)
2 pigs' ears (optional)
200g smoked bacon, cut into cubes
2–3 leeks, sliced
5–7 carrots, sliced
1 celeriac, peeled and cut into cubes
1 head of celery
3 bay leaves
1 bunch of flat-leaf parsley, tied with string
1 smoked sausage, sliced
1 tbsp chopped parsley
salt
pepper

Place the dried green peas and/or split peas in water and soak them as directed on the packet.

Put the pork and the pigs' ears, if using, in a large soup pan with the smoked bacon, leeks, carrots, celeriac, celery, bay leaves, bunch of parsley and salt. Pour in water to come up to about 1–2cm below the rim of the pan and gently bring to the boil. Simmer for a few hours – the longer the better.

Add the soaked peas and the slices of sausage to the soup. Bring everything to the boil again and leave to simmer for another 2–3 hours until the peas are soft. If you want a really thick soup, add only half of the peas and boil the rest separately until soft. Then purée them in a food processor and stir this mixture into the soup.

Remove the pork, ears and parsley. Leave the pork and ears to cool, then remove the meat from the bones and put it back in the soup. Add the fresh chopped parsley and season with salt and pepper.

Serve the soup with dark rye bread and cheese or very thin slices of streaky bacon.

ROCKING ROCK CAKES

**These are often the first cakes kids bring home from school cookery class.
They're scones with attitude really. Rock on!**

MAKES ABOUT 8

225g self-raising flour
100g cold butter, cubed
75g caster sugar,
plus extra for dredging
100g mixed dried fruit
1 medium egg
1 tbsp milk

Preheat the oven to 200°C/Gas 6 and line a baking tray with baking parchment. Sift the flour into a mixing bowl and rub in the butter until the mixture resembles fine breadcrumbs. Stir in the sugar and mixed fruit until everything is well mixed together.

Whisk the egg with the milk and add this to the flour mixture. Stir with a wooden spoon until the mixture comes together in a firmish clump.

Drop rough spoonfuls of the mixture on the baking tray, spacing them well apart as they will spread – you should have about 8. Bake in the centre of the oven for 12–15 minutes until risen and pale golden brown. Dredge the cakes with lots of caster sugar and eat while they're still warm to taste them at their best.

BATTENBURG CAKE

This cake is definitely worth the effort it takes to make and is so much nicer than the shop-bought variety. If you want to make life easier, buy a four-compartment battenburg tin. Works a treat.

SERVES 8

175g softened butter, plus extra for greasing
175g golden caster sugar
3 medium eggs
175g self-raising flour
½ tsp vanilla extract
red food colouring paste

COVERING

6 tbsp apricot jam
500g ready-made marzipan
2–3 tbsp icing sugar, for rolling

The cake batter should have a thick dropping consistency, so make sure you don't over-blend it.

Preheat the oven to 190°C/Gas 5. Grease a 20cm square, loose-based cake tin with butter. Take a 30x 20cm wide strip of baking parchment and make a 5cm fold in the centre. This will create a division in the cake so that the two differently coloured sponges can be cooked at the same time. Line the tin with the baking parchment, keeping the division in the centre.

Put the butter, sugar, eggs, flour and vanilla in a food processor and pulse until well combined. Transfer the batter to a bowl set on scales – it will weigh about 700g. Take half the batter and put it in a different bowl. Add a small dab of red food colouring to one bowl, mixing with the batter until it is pink.

Spoon the cake batters into each side of the prepared tin and smooth the surface with the back of a spoon. Bake in the centre of the oven for about 25 minutes or until the cakes have risen. Cool in the tin for 5 minutes, then slide a knife around the outside of each cake and turn them out onto a wire rack. Leave until cold. If the cakes have risen unevenly, press the surface gently until level.

To assemble the cake, first place one sponge on top of the other and trim off the crusty edges so that the cakes are the same size. Cut the cakes in half to make four long rectangles. Warm the apricot jam in a saucepan until soft, then press through a sieve. Brush the long side of one of the cakes with jam and sandwich together with a cake of a contrasting colour. Do the same with the other cakes. Brush the top of the first cakes with jam and place the cakes on top like a checker board. Brush the top and sides with jam.

Place the marzipan on a surface dusted with icing sugar and roll into a rectangle of about 35 x 25cm and large enough to cover the cake. It should be 4–5mm thick. Turn the cake upside down on the marzipan and brush the underside of the sponges with jam. Wrap fully in the marzipan, taking care to keep it smooth, especially where the ends meet. Turn back over with the seam underneath and place on a serving plate.

AFRICAN WOMEN'S GROUP

The African Women's Group, based in Rose Hill, Oxford, is a community group for women from all parts of Africa or with African origins. It aims to provide support and friendship to the women, many of whom are refugees or asylum seekers. The group encourages members and their families to get involved in a range of activities, including cooking. They run an African food event once a month and offer a lunch of hot and cold traditional dishes. Here are two recipes that often feature.

FRIED PLANTAIN

Fried plantain is a simple but delicious African dish. It's easy and quick to prepare, yet very nutritious.

SERVES 4

2 ripe plantains
salt and chilli pepper (optional)
250ml vegetable oil

Peel the plantains and cut them into discs or diagonal slices of about 0.5–1cm thick. Sprinkle with salt and chilli pepper if desired. Heat the oil in a large pan. Add the plantain discs in batches and fry until golden brown. Drain on kitchen paper and serve hot.

JOLLOF RICE

There are lots of versions of this popular African rice dish. The basis is rice, tomato and onion, but you can add other vegetables, chicken or meat if you like.

SERVES 4

1 tbsp olive or vegetable oil
2 large onions, sliced
2 x 400g cans of plum tomatoes
4 fresh tomatoes, chopped
1 red pepper, diced
85g tomato paste
1/4 tsp cayenne pepper or chilli powder
1 tsp curry powder
1 bay leaf
sprig of thyme
1 stock cube
225g long-grain or basmati rice
salt and black pepper

Heat the oil in a large pan and cook the onions over a gentle heat until translucent. Stir in the canned tomatoes, fresh tomatoes, red pepper and tomato paste, then season with salt, black pepper and cayenne or chilli. Add the curry powder, bay leaf and thyme, then pour in 550ml of water and crumble in the stock cube. Cover and bring to the boil, then reduce the heat and simmer for 20–30 minutes.

Rinse the rice well to remove excess starch, then add it to the tomato mixture. Bring to the boil, then reduce the heat to low. Cover and simmer for 25–30 minutes until the rice is cooked. Check the seasoning before serving.

Continued on page 2

Lazy
weekends
∞

BRAISED STEAKS
WITH GRAVY

This is a real weekend treat. It takes a while to cook but it's worth it, we promise. Serve with some crispy home-made chips – everyone loves a bit of gravy with their chips.

SERVES 4

4 braising steaks, each around 200g
3 tbsp sunflower oil
1 medium onion, halved and
cut into 12 wedges
1 garlic clove, crushed
500ml beef stock made with 1 beef stock
cube or a 500ml tub of fresh beef stock
1 tbsp tomato purée
4–5 sprigs of fresh thyme or ½ tsp dried
thyme
1 bay leaf
1 tsp cornflour
½ tsp English mustard powder
sea salt flakes
freshly ground black pepper

Preheat the oven to 160°C/Gas 3. Trim off any hard fat from the beef and season on both sides with salt and lots of freshly ground black pepper. Heat a tablespoon of the oil in a large non-stick frying pan.

Fry the steaks, 2 at a time, over a medium-high heat for a couple of minutes on each side or until nicely browned. Transfer to a large flameproof casserole dish. Add a little more oil to the pan between batches.

Return the pan to the hob and reduce the heat. Add the remaining oil and gently fry the onion for 5 minutes or until softened and lightly browned, stirring regularly. Stir in the garlic for the last minute of the cooking time.

Transfer the onion and garlic to the casserole, pour over the stock and add the tomato purée. Strip the thyme leaves from the stalks and scatter into the pan (or sprinkle over the dried thyme), add the bay leaf and stir well. Bring to the boil then cover the casserole and transfer carefully to the oven. Cook for 1¼ –1½ hours or until the beef is very tender.

Mix the cornflour and mustard powder in a small bowl and stir in a tablespoon of cold water until smooth. Remove the lid from the casserole dish and stir in the cornflour mixture. Place the casserole over a medium-high heat and simmer for 2–3 minutes until the gravy reduces and becomes thickened and glossy, stirring regularly. Divide the steaks between four warmed plates and spoon over the gravy. Serve with chips.

OLD-FASHIONED RABBIT STEW

This is a good old traditional British stew, but give it a pastry top and you've got rabbit pie. Rabbit is a really healthy meat and tastes great too. We reckon we should eat more of it.

SERVES 5–6

3 tbsp plain flour
2 tsp dried thyme (wild if possible) or
2 tbsp finely chopped fresh thyme leaves
1 large farmed rabbit or
2 young wild rabbits, jointed into 8 pieces
15g butter
2–3 tbsp sunflower oil
6 rindless smoked streaky bacon rashers, cut into 2cm squares
2 medium onions, chopped
500ml dry cider
300ml chicken or vegetable stock
2 bay leaves
350g Chantenay carrots or other small, fat carrots, peeled
150g frozen peas
sea salt flakes
freshly ground black pepper

Mix the flour, thyme, a good pinch of salt and plenty of freshly ground black pepper in a large freezer bag. Wash the rabbit pieces and pat them dry with kitchen paper. Melt the butter with 1 tablespoon of the oil in a large frying pan.

Put the rabbit portions in the freezer bag, a few at a time, and shake well until evenly coated in the flour. Fry the rabbit, a few pieces at a time, until golden brown all over. Put all the front and rear leg portions in a large flameproof casserole dish. Put the saddle pieces on a plate, cover loosely and set aside. These will need less cooking time, so can be added later on. Preheat the oven to 170°C/Gas 3½.

Add a little more oil to the pan and cook the bacon, stirring regularly, until the fat is browned and beginning to crisp. Tip into the casserole dish with the rabbit pieces. Add a dash more oil to the frying pan and fry the onion for about 5 minutes until lightly browned and beginning to soften. Add to the casserole. Sprinkle the meat with any flour remaining in the freezer bag and stir well.

Pour about half the cider into the frying pan and stir with a wooden spoon to lift any sediment from the bottom. Simmer for a few seconds, then pour into the casserole. Add the rest of the cider and the stock. Stir the bay leaves into the casserole, cover and cook in the centre of the oven for 45 minutes.

Remove the casserole from the oven and add the reserved saddle pieces and the carrots. Turn all the rabbit portions over, ensuring that as much of the meat is covered by liquid as possible – not all of it will be. Return to the oven for a further 1¼–2 hours, depending on the type of rabbit you are using.

When the rabbit is tender, skim off any fat that may have risen to the top with a large spoon. Put the casserole dish on the hob, bring to a fast simmer and cook for 3–5 minutes until the liquid reduces to a slightly thickened, gravy-like consistency. Stir in the frozen peas and simmer for a further 3 minutes until tender. Season to taste and serve.

The cooking time depends on what type of rabbit you are using – farmed rabbits will become tender more quickly than wild. Once you've added the saddles and cooked them for an hour, keep checking every 30 minutes or so. Poke the leg portions and the saddle pieces with a knife and if it doesn't slide in easily, return the casserole to the oven.

JEAN'S CHICKEN PIE

Elaine Wilson remembers her mum Jean making this pie for family dinners and celebrations when she was a child and says it's the best – she's never met anyone who didn't love it. We certainly did.

SERVES AT LEAST 8

FILLING
1 medium chicken
1 onion, peeled
6 cloves
1 carrot, peeled
2 bay leaves
1 chicken stock cube
6–8 peppercorns

SHORTCRUST PASTRY
450g plain flour
½ tsp salt or to taste
120g butter, cold
120g white vegetable fat, cold
beaten egg, for glazing

SAUCE
250ml whole milk
55g butter
55g plain flour

Rinse the chicken in cold water and place it in a large pan. Stud the onion with cloves and add it to the pan with the carrot, bay leaves, stock cube and peppercorns. Cover with cold water and bring to the boil, then reduce the heat and simmer until the chicken is cooked. This will take 45 minutes –1¼ hours, depending on the size of the chicken.

Meanwhile, make the pastry. Sift the flour and salt together into a large mixing bowl. Dice the cold butter and white fat and rub them into the flour until the mixture resembles fine breadcrumbs. Mix in just enough cold water to form a stiff paste. Turn this out onto a lightly floured surface and knead gently to form a smooth ball of dough. Wrap in clingfilm or place in a plastic bag and chill for at least 30 minutes.

When the chicken is cooked, take the pan off the heat. Remove the chicken and place it on a plate. Put the pan back on the heat and reduce the cooking liquid to about 250ml. Pour it into a jug and leave to cool, then skim off the fat and discard it. Put the stock with the onion – cloves removed – into a blender and blitz. Add milk to make the stock up to 500ml.

When the chicken is cool enough to handle, cut the meat into chunks and discard the skin and bones. Melt the butter in a pan and stir in the flour. Gradually add the stock and milk, then bring to the boil, stirring continuously. Reduce the heat and simmer for a minute or two to cook the flour. Taste and adjust the seasoning, then fold the meat gently into the sauce without breaking up the pieces. Set the mixture aside to cool.

Preheat the oven to 200°C/Gas 7. Roll out two-thirds of the pastry and use it to line a 20–25cm pie plate. Add the cooled chicken mix. Brush the edges of the pastry with beaten egg, roll out the remaining pastry and cover the pie. Trim off any excess and pinch the edges together to seal. Decorate the pie with leaves made from trimmings and brush with beaten egg. Make a hole in the top of the pie to allow the steam to escape. Bake in the preheated oven for about 45 minutes.

DEVILLED KIDNEYS

This makes a great snack or quick supper. It's rich and we find a little goes a long way, but boy it's good.

SERVES 4

375g lambs' kidneys (6 kidneys),
skinned if needed
2 tbsp plain flour
25g butter
1 medium onion, finely sliced
1 tbsp tomato purée
1 tbsp English mustard
1–2 tbsp Worcestershire sauce
4 thick slices of crusty bread
butter for spreading
small bunch of fresh parsley, chopped
(optional)
sea salt flakes
freshly ground pepper

Rinse the kidneys under cold running water and pat them dry with kitchen paper. Using scissors, carefully cut the white cores out of the kidneys and discard them. Put the kidneys on a board and cut them into chunky pieces. Tip the flour into a freezer bag and season well with salt and pepper. Add the kidneys and toss them until well coated with the flour.

Melt the butter in a large non-stick frying pan. Add the onion and fry gently for 3–4 minutes or until soft and slightly golden, stirring regularly. Shake off any excess flour from the kidneys and add them to the pan. Cook them with the onion over a medium-high heat for 2–3 minutes until golden, turning every now and then.

Spoon the tomato purée and mustard into the frying pan, then gradually add 300ml of water, stirring constantly. Bring to the boil, add a tablespoon of the Worcestershire sauce to the pan and season with salt and pepper. Reduce the heat and simmer gently for 15 minutes, or until the kidneys are tender and the sauce is thickened, stirring occasionally. Add a little more Worcestershire sauce to taste if you like.

While the kidneys are cooking, toast the bread on both sides until golden, then spread with butter and put on four small plates. Spoon the kidneys and sauce over the buttered toast and scatter with freshly chopped parsley, if using. Serve immediately while piping hot.

Everything depends on taking the time to core the kidneys properly. Dave uses a pair of hairdressing scissors, but any sharp scissors will do the trick.

CHOLENT

This recipe is from Rosalyn Alexander and this is what she told us. 'Cholent is usually prepared before the Jewish Sabbath, so was cooked overnight on a very low heat and served for lunch and dinner the next day. In the old days, Jewish mothers would take the dish to the local baker and leave the pots to cook in their ovens overnight, then bring them home the next day. My mother often made this dish and I remember waking up on Saturday mornings and inhaling the great scent! Before putting the lid on, mum would cover the ingredients with paper and tie it with string and there seemed to be a ceremony of uncovering the paper and seeing how the dish looked. When I was older and went out on a Saturday night, I would come home, take the pot out of the oven and enjoy the last scrapings of cholent.'

SERVES 6

170g butter beans
280g barley
goose fat or sunflower oil
1.5kg beef (brisket or braising steak)
1.8kg potatoes (King Edward or Maris Piper), peeled and left whole

DUMPLING
280g flour
2 tsp baking powder
1 large onion, cut into small cubes
2 tbsp sunflower oil
salt and pepper

Soak the butter beans in cold water for 24 hours before they are needed. You can use canned beans but dried beans give a much better flavour.

On the evening of cooking the dish, first make the dumpling. Put the flour and baking powder in a bowl and add the onion, oil and seasoning. Add enough water to make a soft dough, then chill in the fridge for at least 30 minutes.

Preheat the oven to 120°C/Gas ½. Wash and drain the barley and drain the soaked butter beans. Grease a large heavy casserole dish or a heavy pot with some goose fat or sunflower oil (not olive oil) and place the beef in the middle of the dish. Position the dumpling, beans, barley and potatoes around the beef, then pour in boiling water to cover everything. Season with salt and pepper and cover with a double sheet of baking parchment. Secure by twisting the paper all round under the rim of the dish. Place on a low shelf in the oven and leave to cook overnight.

In the morning, pull the paper aside carefully and take a peek There's usually enough liquid to leave the dish cooking as it is, but if it looks dry, add a little more. You can eat this dish for lunch or anytime afterwards. It becomes darker coloured the longer it's cooked, but if you want it a darker colour for lunch, you could turn the oven heat up a couple of hours before you eat it.

PLAVA CAKE

This is what Rosalyn told us about this recipe. 'My mother could make, bake and have this cake on the table in under an hour. My mother's plava was famous in our family – no one could make it as well as she did – but over the years, I believe I have perfected the recipe. I still use the tin my mother used. It must be almost as old as me, perhaps older!'

SERVES 8–10

3 large eggs
170g caster sugar, plus an extra tablespoon
1 large tbsp sunflower oil, plus extra for greasing the tin
140g self-raising flour

Grease a 23cm cake tin with oil, then sprinkle it with the tablespoon of caster sugar. Preheat the oven to 180°C/Gas 4.

Beat the eggs with the sugar until very pale and thick, then mix in the sunflower oil. Sift the flour and fold it into the mixture with a large metal spoon. Pour the mixture into the prepared tin and bake for about 35 minutes or until spongy to the touch.

When the plava is done, remove it from the oven and leave it to cool in the tin for about 10 minutes before turning it out onto a wire rack.

Rosalyn always uses a bundt-style tin with a hole in the middle, but don't worry if you don't have one. Use a regular tin and the cake will still taste good.

ROAST BELLY OF PORK
WITH APPLES & SAGE

This recipe is brilliant! Enough said.

SERVES 4–5

1.5kg pork belly, deeply scored
2 tbsp finely chopped fresh thyme leaves
2 tsp sea salt flakes
1 tsp coarsely ground black pepper, plus
extra to season
3 medium apples, peeled, quartered,
cored and cut into thick slices
2 medium onions, sliced
good handful fresh sage leaves
2 tsp plain flour
200ml cider
freshly ground black pepper

Preheat the oven to 240°C/Gas 9. Place the pork on a board and pat the rind dry with kitchen paper if it feels at all damp. Mix the thyme with the salt and pepper and rub this seasoning mixture into the pork rind and the underside of the pork.

Place the pork in a sturdy roasting tin or flameproof baking tray and roast for 25–30 minutes. This will give the rind a chance to bubble and become really crisp. Turn the oven down to 180°C/Gas 4 and continue roasting for another hour.

Toss the apples with the onions, whole sage leaves and a few twists of black pepper. Make a compact pile in the centre of a clean, smallish roasting tin. When ready, remove the pork from the oven and place it on top of the apples and onions, keeping the apple and onion pieces snugly underneath the meat so they don't burn. Keep the first roasting tin to one side because you'll need the cooking juices to make the gravy. Return the pork to the oven and cook for a further hour until the meat is really succulent and tender.

Take the first roasting tin, skim off any fat from the cooking juices and place the tin over a medium heat. Stir in the flour and cook for a minute or so, stirring constantly. Gradually stir in the cider and 100ml of water and bring to a simmer. Cook for 3–4 minutes, while stirring. Strain through a sieve into a small saucepan and season to taste. Set aside.

When the pork is cooked, transfer it to a carving board. Scoop up the apple and onion with a large spoon and place in a warmed serving bowl. Reheat the cider gravy until bubbling and cut the pork into thick slices. Serve the pork and crackling with the apple and sage and the hot gravy.

SPICED TEACAKES

Spiced teacakes before a roaring fire – who could ask for anything more?
And don't forget, teacakes are for life, not just Sundays.

MAKES 6

375g strong white flour,
plus extra for kneading
½ tsp sea salt flakes, lightly crushed
1 x 7g sachet of fast-action dried yeast
1 tsp ground mixed spice
1 tsp ground cinnamon
1 tsp freshly grated nutmeg
finely grated zest of ½ well-scrubbed orange
50g caster sugar
50g butter, cubed
150ml semi-skimmed milk
1 large free-range egg, beaten
125g luxury mixed dried fruit
2 tsp sunflower oil, for greasing
butter, for serving

Mix the flour, salt, yeast, spices, orange zest and sugar in a large bowl. Put the butter and milk in a small saucepan and heat very gently until the butter is melted and the milk is just lukewarm. Remove from the heat and whisk in the egg. Make a well in the centre of the flour mixture and pour in the warm butter, milk and egg. Stir with a wooden spoon until the mixture forms a ball.

Turn out on a very lightly floured surface and knead for 5 minutes to form a smooth, pliable dough. Knead the fruit into the dough for a couple of minutes until evenly distributed. Place the dough in a lightly greased bowl, cover loosely with oiled clingfilm and leave to rise in a warm place for 1½ hours, or until doubled in size and spongy to touch.

Knead the dough lightly and divide into 6 portions. Roll into balls. Using a rolling pin, flatten each ball to a circle around 1cm thick and place on a large baking tray lined with baking parchment. Cover with oiled clingfilm and leave to rise for a further 45 minutes.

Preheat the oven to 190°C/Gas 5. Remove the clingfilm and bake the teacakes in the centre of the oven for 15–18 minutes until well risen and golden brown. Serve warm or leave to cool on a wire rack, then toast. Cut in half when cold using a serrated knife. Grill cut side up until lightly toasted and spread thickly with butter. Eat within 24 hours to enjoy them at their best.

RACLETTE CHEESE & SALADS

Jenny Eigenheer and her Swiss husband both love cooking and this Swiss classic is one of their favourites. The melted cheese is prepared in a raclette machine and served with hot new potatoes and salads and pickled vegetables. Suitable cheeses include raclette, Fontal and Bagnes, available in supermarkets, delis and cheese shops. As a general rule, allow 200g cheese per person.

SERVES 4–6

1kg Raclette cheese or Fontal or Bagnes
black pepper
cayenne pepper

ACCOMPANIMENTS
1kg new potatoes, boiled or steamed in their skins and kept warm
500g carrot salad (see below)
500g celeriac salad (see below)
cornichons
silverskin pickled onions
pickled mushrooms

The preparation of the cheese depends on what sort of machine you have. For round machines with individual trays, cut the cheese into squares of about 6cm. If using a big machine, mount half a cheese into the stand.

Diners should help themselves to a potato and to salads and pickles while they wait for their portion of cheese to melt. Some ham or salami is good, too. Once the cheese is melted, scrape it over the potato and add pepper or cayenne pepper if required. Keep going until you are full!

CARROT SALAD

SERVES 4–6

500g carrots
1 garlic clove, finely chopped
red onion, chopped
1 tbsp chopped flat-leaf parsley

SALAD DRESSING
4 tbsp light olive oil or sunflower oil
1 tbsp wine vinegar
1 tsp Dijon mustard
1 tbsp mayonnaise, cream or crème fraîche
dash of Maggi seasoning (optional)
salt

Peel and grate the carrots and mix with the salad dressing. Add garlic, parsley and as much or little red onion as you like.

To make the dressing, simply mix everything together. You can also add minced garlic or red onion and chopped herbs, such as parsley, chives or coriander, if you like. Jenny suggests making up the basic sauce in a screw-topped jar without the mayo or cream and keeping this in the fridge to use as needed.

CELERIAC SALAD
Use 1 celeriac instead of the carrots. Peel and grate the celeriac and mix it with the salad dressing as above. Add garlic, chopped chives and as much or little red onion as you like.

ROAST CHICKEN
WITH MOREL MUSHROOM SAUCE

Jenny's mother-in-law used to make this dish, and Jenny's husband remembers foraging in the woods for morels when he was a child. It's still a regular for family get-togethers.

SERVES 4

1 x 1kg roasting chicken
50g butter or 2 tbsp olive or sunflower oil
3–4 smoked bacon rashers (optional)
salt and pepper

SAUCE

1 x 20g packet of dried morel
mushrooms, soaked overnight in
500ml whole milk
30g butter
1 tbsp plain flour
100ml dry white wine
100ml double cream
salt and pepper

Don't be tempted to skip soaking the mushrooms – it's really worth it and the flavoured milk makes the sauce taste so good.

Preheat the oven to 180°C/Gas 4. Rub the chicken with butter or oil and season with salt and pepper. Place the bacon rashers over the breast if using. Place the chicken in a roasting tin and roast for 1–1½ hours. The juices should run clear when you prick the bird between the thigh and breast.

About halfway through the cooking time for the chicken, make the sauce. Drain the soaked mushrooms through a sieve lined with muslin or other clean fine-meshed cloth to remove any sand or grit. Set the mushroomy milk aside. Wash the mushrooms carefully to remove any sand or grit and cut them into bite-sized pieces.

Melt the butter in a pan and add the flour, stirring it in well. Gradually add the wine to make a sauce, stirring all the time and taking care not to let the sauce burn. Add the mushroomy milk to the sauce very slowly so it doesn't curdle. Then add the mushrooms and cook for about 20 minutes. Season with salt and pepper to taste, then add the double cream and heat through gently. Taste and adjust the seasoning if necessary. The sauce should have the consistency of custard.

Carve the chicken and place it on a serving platter. Pour over the juices from the roasting pan and serve with the morel sauce. This is good with rice, pasta or French fries and some vegetables or salad.

COFFEE & WALNUT SPONGE

A deliciously moist, old-fashioned coffee and walnut cake is one of our very favourite treats
and we like to make it with Camp chicory and coffee essence. If you can't track this down in your local
stores, use very strong black coffee instead. Make sure the walnuts you use are nice and fresh.

SERVES 12

65g walnut halves
225g softened butter, cubed, plus extra
for greasing
225g caster sugar
4 medium eggs
225g self-raising flour
1 tsp baking powder
2 tbsp Camp chicory and coffee essence

ICING

150g softened butter, cubed
300g icing sugar, sifted
4 tsp Camp chicory and coffee essence
12 walnut halves

Preheat the oven to 190°C/Gas 5. Butter two 20cm loose-based sandwich tins and line the bases with discs of baking parchment. Put the walnut halves in a food processor and blitz them into fairly fine crumbs, but don't worry if there are a few larger pieces remaining. Tip the walnuts into a bowl.

Put the butter, sugar, eggs, flour, baking powder and coffee essence in a food processor and blend on the pulse setting until well combined and creamy. You may need to remove the lid once or twice and push the mixture down with a rubber spatula. Take care not to process for too long or you will end up with a heavy sponge. Add the blitzed walnuts to the batter and mix until just combined. If you don't have a food processor, finely chop the nuts, tip all the ingredients into a large mixing bowl, then beat like hell!

Spoon the mixture evenly into the greased and lined tins and smooth the surface. Bake on the same shelf in the centre of the oven for about 25 minutes or until the sponge is well risen and just beginning to shrink back from the sides of the tin.

Remove the tins from the oven and leave to cool for 5 minutes before running a knife around the edge of the cakes and turning them out onto a wire rack. Peel off the baking parchment and leave to cool completely.

To make the icing, put the butter in a food processor, or mixing bowl, then add the icing sugar and coffee essence. Blend until the icing is smooth and creamy. Add a little more coffee essence to taste if you like.

Place one of the sponges on a plate or cake stand and spread with half the coffee icing. Add the second sponge and spread the remaining icing over the top. Use the back of a spoon or a rubber spatula to create soft swirls and peaks. Decorate with the walnut halves. Leave to stand for at least an hour before serving if possible to allow the icing to become a little firmer.

GROWING TOGETHER

St George's Community Hub, based in Newtown, Birmingham, is in a multicultural neighbourhood with wonderful spicy cooking traditions from the Caribbean, Angola, Somalia and other parts of the world. The Hub's Growing Together project works with local young people and their parents, grandparents and neighbours to grow organic vegetables, herbs and tropical greenhouse crops. Families then take turns to cook their favourite traditional recipes. Centre director Dr Bob Tyler says it has really brought the community together.

PUMPKIN SOUP

This recipe, given to us by the Growing Together project, comes from the tiny island of Carriacou, off the coast of Grenada. It includes classic Caribbean flavours such as local ginger, chillies and coconut milk.

SERVES 4–6

½ large pumpkin (preferably organic)
1 large white onion, chopped
2.5cm piece of root ginger, finely chopped
2 garlic cloves, finely chopped
½ Scotch bonnet chilli, deseeded and chopped
4–5 sprigs of thyme
1 x 400ml can of coconut milk
salt

Cut the pumpkin in half, then into wedges. Peel and deseed each wedge and cut the pumpkin flesh into cubes of about 2.5cm square.

Put the pumpkin cubes in a pan with the onion, ginger, garlic and chilli. Strip the leaves from the thyme and add those in too. Pour in about 400ml of water, bring to the boil and cook until the pumpkin has turned to a pulp.

Pour in the coconut milk and season to taste with salt, then reduce the heat and leave the soup to simmer for another 5–10 minutes. If you like, add chunks of breadfruit or sweet potato towards the end of the cooking process.

High tea

EGG & BACON PIE

We just can't get enough of this, particularly when made with maple-cured streaky bacon.
Add a couple of sliced sausages and you've got an all-day breakfast pie.

SERVES 4

FILLING
1 tbsp sunflower oil
8–10 smoked streaky bacon rashers
9 large eggs
4 tbsp whole milk
sea salt flakes
freshly ground black pepper

PASTRY
300g plain flour, plus extra for dusting
good pinch of sea salt flakes
175g butter, chilled and cubed
1 large egg

To make the filling, heat the oil in a large non-stick frying pan. Cut the bacon rashers in half through the middle and add them to the pan. Fry over a medium heat for 4–5 minutes until the fat is golden and crisp, turning them once. Remove the bacon from the heat and leave to cool. Place a sturdy baking tray in the oven and preheat to 190°C/Gas 5.

For the pastry, put the flour in a food processor and add the salt, crumbling it as you do so. Add the butter and blitz on the pulse setting until the mixture resembles fine breadcrumbs. Whisk the egg with a tablespoon of cold water and pour onto the flour and butter mixture with the motor running. Continue blending until the dough begins to form a ball.

Turn the pastry out onto a lightly floured board. Knead quickly into a ball and cut in half. Roll out one half until it is about 5mm thick and line a 23cm pie plate, leaving any excess pastry overhanging the edge. Scatter the bacon loosely over the pastry case. Gently break 6 of the eggs into the pastry case, spaced evenly apart between the bacon rashers. Beat the remaining eggs with the milk and plenty of salt and pepper.

Slowly pour the beaten eggs into the pastry case, stopping every now and then to allow the beaten egg to find its way between the whole eggs and the bacon. Leave 2–3 tablespoons of the mixture in the bowl for glazing the top of the pie.

Roll out the rest of the pastry to make a lid for the pie. Brush the edge of the pastry case with beaten egg and milk and gently lift the pastry lid over the filling. Press the edges firmly to seal, then trim. Use a fork to help seal the edge all the way around the pie. Brush with the remaining beaten egg to glaze.

Bake the pie on the preheated baking tray for 45–55 minutes until pale golden brown and cooked through. Test by piercing the centre with a sharp knife – the filling should be just set. If it's still runny, put the pie back in the oven for a few minutes. Leave to stand for at least 15 minutes before serving.

This pie needs plenty of salt and pepper so don't skimp on the seasoning. Serve warm or at room temperature to taste it at its best.

CORNED BEEF & ONION PIE

You can make your own shortcrust pastry for this tasty pie or buy a block of ready-made. Our pastry is rich, short and very tasty. If you have problems rolling it, don't worry, just patch up any gaps and carry on. This is great served hot with baked beans or gravy and it's also delicious cold.

SERVES 6

FILLING
15g butter
1 tbsp sunflower oil
1 large onion, sliced or chopped
2 celery sticks, trimmed,
de-stringed and sliced
2 medium carrots,
cut into roughly 1cm dice
300g potatoes, preferably Maris Pipers,
peeled and cut into roughly 1cm dice
good squirt of tomato ketchup
(1–2 tbsp)
1 x 340g can of corned beef
freshly ground black pepper

PASTRY
300g plain flour, plus extra for rolling
175g cold butter, cubed
1 large egg

For the filling, melt the butter with the oil in a large non-stick frying pan. Add the onion, celery, carrots and potatoes. Cook over a low heat for about 15 minutes until the vegetables are softened and beginning to colour, stirring regularly. The carrots should retain a little 'bite'.

Add the ketchup and stir into the vegetables for a few seconds before adding the corned beef. Break the beef into chunky pieces with a wooden spoon and mix with the vegetables. Season with pepper – you shouldn't need salt as the corned beef is fairly salty anyway – and remove from the heat. Leave to cool for about 20 minutes.

Preheat the oven to 190°C/Gas 5. To make the pastry, put the flour and butter in a food processor and blitz on the pulse setting until the mixture resembles breadcrumbs. Lightly whisk the egg with a tablespoon of cold water in a small bowl. Slowly pour all but 1 tablespoon of the egg mixture into the food processor with the motor running and blend until the mixture begins to form a ball.

Turn the pastry out onto a well-floured work surface and bring it together into a ball. Take about a third of the pastry, roll it out and use it to line a 23cm pie plate or 20cm round ceramic quiche dish or deep Victoria sandwich tin. Leave any excess pastry overhanging the edge. Brush the pastry edge lightly with the reserved egg.

Spoon the filling into the pastry base and spread to all the sides. Flour the surface once more and roll out the remaining pastry. Lift the rolled pastry over the rolling pin and place gently over the filling. Press the edges firmly together then trim neatly. Press a fork around the edge to seal.

Brush the top of the pastry with the egg, cut a cross in the centre and place on a baking tray. Bake for about 40 minutes or until the pastry is golden brown and the filling piping hot.

BEEF & HONEY STEW

Polly Findlay and her husband are farmers in Yorkshire and they like to cook with produce from their farm, including their own honey. This is one of Polly's favourite recipes.

SERVES 4

30g plain flour
450g stewing steak, cut into 2.5cm cubes
oil, for frying
1 onion
2 carrots
2 leeks
½ turnip
1 tbsp honey
550ml beef stock
2 large potatoes
salt and pepper to taste

Put the flour in a freezer bag, then add the cubes of meat and shake well to coat. Heat the oil in a large pan and brown the meat a few pieces at a time – adding too much meat at once makes the meat steam rather than brown. Set the meat aside as it is browned.

Cut the vegetables into similar-sized pieces. Fry the onion in the same pan you used for the meat, adding more oil if needed. Once the onion is browned, add all the other ingredients except the potatoes. Put a lid on the pan and simmer the stew for at least 2 hours – the longer it cooks, the better it will be.

Twenty minutes before serving, add the chunks of potato to the stew – adding them at this point means they keep their shape. Season to taste before serving.

WELSH RAREBIT

Cheese on toast, by any other name. When you're cold, tired and hungry, nothing beats it.

SERVES 4

25g butter
25g plain flour
100ml strong, dark beer
50ml whole milk
150g mature Cheddar cheese, grated
1 egg yolk
1 tsp English mustard
4 tsp Worcestershire sauce
good pinch of cayenne pepper
(optional)
4 thick slices of wholemeal or
granary bread
freshly ground black pepper

Melt the butter in a non-stick saucepan and stir in the flour. Cook over a low heat for about half a minute, while stirring. Slowly add the beer, then the milk. Simmer for 2–3 minutes, stirring constantly until the sauce is thick and smooth.

Add the cheese, egg yolk, mustard, Worcestershire sauce and cayenne pepper, if using. Cook until the cheese melts, stirring constantly. Season with lots of freshly ground black pepper and set aside to cool for a couple of minutes. Leaving the sauce to cool a little will help you spread it more thickly on the toast. Preheat the grill until hot.

Place the bread on a baking tray lined with foil and toast on each side until golden. Spread the cheese sauce thickly over the bread, making sure the slices are completely covered so the edges don't burn. Return to the grill for 20–30 seconds longer until lightly browned and bubbling.

MEATBALLS IN GRAVY

These are top-notch. You don't get them like this in a can.

SERVES 4

250g lean minced beef
250g minced pork
1 small onion, very finely chopped
1 garlic clove, finely chopped
25g fresh white breadcrumbs
2 tsp dried mixed herbs
2 tsp sunflower oil
sea salt flakes
freshly ground black pepper

GRAVY
1 tbsp sunflower oil
1 medium onion, finely sliced
1 tbsp plain flour
150ml red wine
300ml beef stock made with
1 beef stock cube
1 tbsp tomato purée

Put the beef and pork mince in a large bowl and add the onion, garlic, breadcrumbs and dried herbs. Mix well with clean hands, then divide the mixture into 20 portions and roll into small, neat balls.

Heat the 2 teaspoons of sunflower oil in a large non-stick frying pan and fry the meatballs for 6–8 minutes, or until nicely browned on all sides. Roll and turn the meatballs around in the pan as they brown to prevent them from becoming flattened on one side. Transfer them to a large saucepan.

To make the gravy, heat the tablespoon of sunflower oil in the same frying pan and fry the onion over a low heat for 5 minutes until softened, stirring regularly. Sprinkle the flour into the pan and stir well.

Slowly add the red wine and then the stock and tomato purée, stirring constantly. Pour the gravy over the meatballs and bring to the boil. Reduce the heat, cover the pan with a lid and leave to simmer gently over a low heat for 30 minutes, stirring occasionally.

Remove the lid and turn up the heat under the pan. Boil the gravy for another 3–5 minutes or until thickened. Adjust the seasoning to taste. Serve the meatballs and gravy with mashed potatoes and peas.

MEAT PATTIES

We met Lisa Hobson in Leeds and she told us how she'd found a book of handwritten recipes that had belonged to her step-mum. The recipes are just ingredients – no methods – so Lisa has had to work them out for herself. We love these little meat patties.

MAKES 10

I small onion, chopped
1 tbsp oil or butter
1 thick slice of bread
120g roast beef or other cooked meat
leftover gravy (or make some up with gravy mix)
salt and pepper

PASTRY
75g fat (half lard and half butter)
170g plain flour
pinch of salt
1 egg, beaten with a drop of milk

First make the pastry. Rub the fat into the flour, add the salt and mix with enough water to form a dough – you can do this in a food processor if you prefer. Wrap the dough in clingfilm and leave it to rest in the fridge while you make the filling.

Fry the onion in the oil or butter until soft, then leave to cool. Put the bread in a food processor and blitz to make breadcrumbs. Add the meat and onion and pulse until coarsely chopped. Tip everything into a bowl and add sufficient gravy to make a soft mixture. Season to taste.

Preheat the oven to 200°C/Gas 6. Roll out the pastry and cut 10 large circles for the bases of the pies and 10 smaller circles for the lids.

Place the larger pastry rounds in patty tins and add a heaped teaspoon of filling to each. Dampen the edges of the patties with water and add the lids, making sure the edges are well sealed. Brush the patties with the beaten egg and pierce a hole in each one to allow the steam to escape.

Bake the patties in the preheated oven for 20–30 minutes until golden.

DIGGERS

Two more recipes from Lisa. You can make this flapjack-style treat as cookies or a traybake. Delicious either way.

MAKES AT LEAST 12 SLICES

120g plain flour
225g caster sugar
100g oats
80g desiccated coconut
120g butter
1 tbsp golden syrup
1 level tsp bicarbonate of soda
2 tbsp boiling water

Preheat the oven to 160°C/Gas 3. Mix the flour, sugar, oats and coconut together in a large mixing bowl. Put the butter in a small pan with the golden syrup and heat gently until melted. Mix the bicarb with 2 tablespoons of boiling water and add this to the butter and syrup mixture. Pour the liquid over the dry ingredients and mix well.

Tip the mixture into a greased square tin and press down. Bake in the preheated oven for 20 minutes or until golden. Alternatively, you can shape the mixture into cookies and place them on a greased baking tray. Cook for 10–15 minutes or until golden.

YORKSHIRE MACAROONS

Lisa's gran used to make these for her family and Lisa loves them too.

MAKES 12–14

2 egg whites
150g caster sugar
225g desiccated coconut
100g good quality milk chocolate
100g good quality dark chocolate

Preheat the oven to 180°C/Gas 4. Line a baking tray with greaseproof paper.

Whisk the egg whites and sugar until frothy, then stir in the coconut and mix well. Use an egg cup to shape the mixture into 'domes' and turn these out onto the greaseproof paper. Repeat until all the mixture is used. Bake in the preheated oven for 15–20 minutes or until light golden brown. Remove from the oven and leave them to cool on the baking tray.

When the macaroons are set, melt the chocolates in separate bowls. Dip the macaroons in the chocolate to coat half of each one and place on greaseproof paper to set. Coat some in milk chocolate and some in dark.

ECCLES CAKES

We used to call these dead fly pies when we were lads. They are scrumptious served warm with a cup of tea, or as a quick pud with a good dollop of cream or ice cream. They keep for a couple of days in an airtight container and also warm up beautifully.

MAKES 10–12

plain flour, for rolling
500g ready-made puff pastry
1 egg white
3–4 tbsp caster sugar

FILLING
40g butter
50g light muscovado sugar
100g currants
35g cut mixed peel
heaped ¼ tsp ground mixed spice
finely grated zest of ½ lemon

To make the filling, gently melt the butter in a saucepan and stir in the sugar, currants, mixed peel, spice and lemon zest. Remove from the heat and set aside to cool. Preheat the oven to 200°C/Gas 6.

Dust the work surface with flour and roll out the pastry until it's about 4mm thick. Using a 10cm biscuit cutter, cut the pastry into 10–12 circles. Place a tablespoon of the filling mixture in the centre of each circle.

Beat the egg white until it is slightly frothy. Brush a little beaten egg white around the edge of each pastry circle. One at a time, bring the pastry up around the filling and press the edges together to form little purses. It doesn't matter if they are a little bit wonky as they will be rolled again.

Turn each cake over onto a floured surface and roll into a roughly 8.5cm circle. Place on a baking tray lined with baking parchment and score the surface of each one 3–4 times with a sharp knife.

Brush the cakes with more beaten egg white and sprinkle about half a teaspoon of caster sugar over each one. Bake in the centre of the oven for 18–20 minutes until the cakes are nicely risen and the tops are crisp and golden brown. Cool for a few minutes, then serve warm.

MOM'S HOCKEY PUCK MEATLOAF

American-born Nancy Davis lives in England now but still loves to cook the food she was brought up on. Her mum used to make meatloaf badly and her dad named it 'Mom's hockey puck', as it was so hard it bounced off the floor when dropped! Nancy's version though is yummy, as is her potato salad.

SERVES 4–6

1kg minced steak
1 large red onion, chopped
2 slices of bread, made into crumbs
3 tbsp tomato ketchup
1 medium egg
2 tbsp brown sauce
1 tsp Worcestershire sauce
50–100g Parmesan cheese, grated
1 tbsp fresh oregano
1 tbsp chopped parsley
1 tbsp milk
salt and pepper

Preheat the oven to 180°C/Gas 4. Mix all the ingredients together until the mixture pulls away from the sides of the bowl and forms a ball. Add more breadcrumbs if you need them. Form the mixture into a loaf shape.

Place the mixture in an ovenproof dish or a loaf tin and bake in the centre of the oven for 50–60 minutes until the centre is firm. Great hot or cold, served with potato salad.

POTATO SALAD

SERVES 8

8–10 medium-sized red potatoes
1 tbsp milk
1–2 tbsp American mustard
a few drops of vinegar
2–3 tsp dill pickle juice
½ tsp sugar
mayonnaise, to taste
chopped dill pickle (optional)
1 hard-boiled egg (optional)

Cut each potato into 8 pieces and boil in salted water until tender. Drain and set the potatoes aside to cool slightly.

Mix the milk, mustard, vinegar, pickle juice and sugar together in a small bowl. When the potatoes have cooled, pour over the mixture so the potatoes are coated but not swimming. Add mayonnaise to taste and the pickle and egg if using. Chill in the fridge for a couple of hours before serving.

HOME-MADE LEMON CURD

A perfect lemon curd with just the right amount of zing. Spread thickly on freshly buttered bread or use as a delicious filling for cakes and biscuits.

MAKES 1 JAR

100g caster sugar
finely grated zest of 2 unwaxed lemons
freshly squeezed juice of 3 lemons
2 large whole eggs
2 large egg yolks
75g unsalted butter,
cut into small cubes

Put the sugar in a largish heatproof bowl and stir in the lemon zest and juice. Whisk in the whole eggs and egg yolks. Drop the butter into the bowl and set over a saucepan of very gently simmering water, making sure the bowl doesn't touch the water itself.

Stir the mixture with a wooden spoon for about 5 minutes until the butter melts. Use a whisk to stir the ingredients and cook for 8–10 minutes more or until the lemon curd is thickened to the consistency of custard and leaves a light trail when the whisk is lifted. It will continue to thicken in the jar, so don't allow to overheat or the eggs could scramble.

Pour the hot lemon curd into a warm, very clean jar and leave to cool. Cover the curd with a disc of waxed paper or baking parchment and seal with the lid. Keep the lemon curd in the fridge and use within 2 weeks.

Warm the jar in a low oven for a few minutes before using.

LUSCIOUS LEMON SWISS ROLL

This teatime lovely features a light-as-a-feather lemon sponge, filled with lemon icing and home-made lemon curd. If you fancy a more traditional Swiss roll, flavour the sponge with half a teaspoon of vanilla extract and simply fill with raspberry jam and butter icing instead.

SERVES 8

butter, for greasing
3 large eggs
115g caster sugar, plus 4 tbsp
finely grated zest of 1 unwaxed lemon
115g plain flour

LEMON BUTTER ICING
200g icing sugar
125g softened butter
2 tsp freshly squeezed lemon juice
home-made lemon curd
(see page 345)

To check the sponge is cooked, touch the centre. It should spring back immediately.

Grease and line a 33 x 23cm Swiss roll tin with buttered baking parchment. Preheat the oven to 200°C/Gas 6. Put the eggs, 115g of sugar and lemon zest in a heatproof bowl and place over a pan of gently simmering water. Whisk with an electric whisk until the mixture is pale, creamy and thick enough to leave a trail when the whisk is lifted.

Carefully remove the bowl from the heat and continue whisking for a further 5 minutes. Sift over half the flour and, using a large metal spoon, lightly fold it into the egg mixture. Sift over the remaining flour and fold in. It's important to use gentle movements to retain as much air as possible in the batter, but you'll need to watch out for pockets of flour.

Pour the mixture slowly into the prepared tin and gently spread with a spatula, so the base of the tin is evenly covered. Bake for 10–12 minutes until well risen, pale golden brown and firm to the touch.

Place a damp tea towel on the work surface and cover with a sheet of baking parchment. Dredge with the 4 tbsp of sugar – this will help stop the outside of the sponge sticking. Working quickly, turn the cake out onto the sugared paper and carefully remove the lining paper. Using a sharp knife, cut off the crusty edges from the 2 long sides. Roll the Swiss roll from one of the short ends, starting with a tight turn to make a good round shape and keeping the sugared paper inside the roll. Set on a wire rack and leave to cool.

To make the icing, put the icing sugar and butter in a bowl and beat until smooth and creamy. Add the lemon juice and beat again. When the cake is cold, gently unroll but do not flatten it or it could crack. Spread the cake with lemon butter icing to within 1cm of the edges. Spoon the lemon curd on top – you'll need about half the jar – and spread it evenly over the icing. Slowly roll the cake up again, enclosing the filling, and place on a plate. Sprinkle with extra sugar if you like.

LIFT COMMUNITY TRUST

This is a voluntary organisation, set up in 2001 to work with disadvantaged people. Based on a housing estate in Birmingham, Lift aims to support the local community and enable people to play a fuller part in society. Cooking is a key activity at the centre and they have set up a café called the Taste of Haven, which provides home-made Caribbean food to eat there or have delivered to your home.

CHICKEN WITH RICE, PEAS & DUMPLINGS

There are countless versions of this Caribbean meal, but this is how they cook it at the Taste of Haven.

SERVES 6

150g plain flour
½ tsp garlic powder
1 tbsp Hot & Spicy Seasoning
1½ tbsp all-purpose seasoning
1 packet of Hot & Spicy Chicken Coating
6 boneless chicken breasts
sunflower oil, for deep-frying

DUMPLINGS
¼ tsp salt
250g self-raising flour
2–3 tbsp oil

SAUCE
1 onion, chopped
½ red, green and yellow pepper, chopped
1 Scotch bonnet, deseeded and chopped
2 tbsp ketchup
1 tbsp gravy browning
2 tbsp sugar
1 tbsp cornflour
black pepper

RICE & PEAS
1 x 400g can of red kidney beans
1 x 400ml can of coconut milk
1 Scotch bonnet, deseeded and chopped
2 spring onions
1 sprig of thyme
400g long-grain rice

Mix the plain flour with the garlic powder, seasonings and chicken coating in a bowl. Dip the chicken breasts into the mixture until well coated.

Heat the oil in a deep-fat fryer to about 170°C. Fry the chicken, a few pieces at a time, until cooked through and golden brown. Serve with dumplings, sauce and rice and peas.

DUMPLINGS
Stir the salt into the flour. Add water to make a dough and knead together well. Shape the mixture into small balls.

Heat the oil in a frying pan and shallow fry the dumplings for 2–4 minutes until golden.

SAUCE
Bring about 250ml of water to the boil. Add the chopped onion, peppers and Scotch bonnet and boil for 3 minutes. Add the ketchup, gravy browning and sugar, then simmer for another 3 minutes. In a small bowl, mix the cornflour with a tablespoon of water, then stir this into the sauce to thicken. Season with black pepper.

RICE & PEAS
Tip the beans into a pan, add 400ml of water and boil for 3 minutes. Add the other ingredients, except the rice, bring to the boil again and cook for at least 4 minutes. Then add the rice and, if necessary, add a little extra boiling water so that the rice is just covered. Put a lid on the pan and cook for 12–15 minutes until the rice is done. Season to taste.

Distant shores

⁓

MULLIGATAWNY SOUP

A delicious curried vegetable soup with rice, mulligatawny can be blended for a smooth soup or left as diced vegetables in a fragrant broth – the choice is yours. If you're planning on blitzing the soup, the vegetables can be cut chunky, but go a bit more delicate for the unblended version. For a more filling meal, add some cooked chicken or mince to the soup and heat through before serving.

SERVES 4–5

25g butter
1 tbsp sunflower oil
1 large onion, chopped fairly small
2 garlic cloves, chopped
2 medium carrots, cut into 1.5cm cubes
2 celery sticks, trimmed, stringed and thinly sliced
1 medium sweet potato, cut into roughly 1.5cm cubes
1 eating apple, peeled, quartered and cut into roughly 1.5cm cubes
1 tbsp medium curry powder
1 litre of stock made with 1 chicken or vegetable stock cube
1 tbsp tomato purée
1 tbsp mango chutney
100g easy-cook long-grain rice
natural yoghurt or soured cream, to serve
fresh coriander or flat-leaf parsley, to garnish (optional)
sea salt flakes
freshly ground black pepper

Melt the butter with the oil in a large saucepan and stir in the onion, garlic, carrots, celery and sweet potato. Cook over a medium heat for 10 minutes, stirring regularly until the vegetables are beginning to soften and lightly brown. Stir in the apple pieces and sprinkle over the curry powder. Cook for 2 minutes more, while stirring.

Pour over the stock and stir in the tomato purée and mango chutney. Bring to the boil, then reduce the heat slightly and leave to simmer for 30 minutes, stirring occasionally until all the vegetables are tender.

While the soup is simmering, half fill a medium pan with water and bring to the boil. Add the rice and return to the boil. Cook for 10 minutes or until tender. Drain the rice in a sieve and rinse under running water until cold.

When the soup is ready, either stir the rice straight into it or allow to cool for a few minutes, then blitz with a stick blender or in a food processor until smooth before stirring in the rice. Add enough water to give a good consistency – 150–200ml should be about right. Heat the rice in the soup for 3–4 minutes until hot and season to taste before serving.

Ladle the soup into deep bowls and top with natural yoghurt or soured cream. Garnish with sprigs of coriander or flat-leaf parsley if you like.

FRESH FRUIT PAVLOVA

This pavlova has a crisp meringue shell around a soft, marshmallowy centre and
is filled with lots of softly whipped cream and heaps of your favourite fresh fruit.
Is it from New Zealand? Is it from Australia? Who cares? It tastes great!

SERVES 6

MERINGUE
4 large egg whites
225g caster sugar
½ tsp vanilla extract
1 tbsp cornflour

FILLING
400ml double cream
400g strawberries, hulled and
halved if large
200g raspberries
150g blueberries
3 passion fruit (optional)
Cape gooseberries (optional)
mint sprigs and sifted icing sugar,
to decorate

Preheat the oven to 150°C/Gas 2. Put the egg whites in a large,
grease-free bowl and whisk with an electric whisk until stiff
but not dry. They are ready when you can turn the bowl
upside down without the eggs sliding out.

Gradually whisk in the sugar, just a tablespoon at a time,
whisking for a few seconds between each addition. Adding
the sugar slowly will help build up volume in the meringue
and make it stiff and shiny. Finally, whisk in the vanilla
extract and cornflour until well combined.

Dab a small amount of the meringue in the corners of a large,
sturdy baking tray or sheet. Place a 25cm dinner plate on a
sheet of baking parchment and draw round it. Turn it over
and place the parchment on the baking tray, holding it in
place with the dabs of meringue. You should be able to see
the circle through the paper.

Spoon the meringue into the circle and shape with the back
of a serving spoon or with a rubber spatula to create a large,
meringue nest, with soft peaks rising on all sides. Place in
the centre of the oven and bake for 1 hour until very lightly
coloured and crisp on the outside. (If the meringue seems to
be becoming too brown, reduce the temperature of the oven.)
Turn the oven off and leave the meringue for a further hour
to cool. Remove from the oven and leave to cool completely.
Serve within 6–8 hours.

Up to 2 hours before serving, carefully transfer the meringue
to a large serving platter or board. Whip the cream until soft
peaks form and spoon into the centre of the meringue. Top
with the berry fruits. Cut the passion fruit in half, if using,
and scrape the pulp over the other fruit. Decorate with sprigs
of mint and dust with sifted icing sugar.

*If you prefer a more
chewy meringue, cook for
around 2 hours, turn the
oven off and leave to cool
for 1 hour in the oven
before cooling completely.*

CHICKEN & CHORIZO PAELLA

Karen Mulholland lives in Northern Ireland, but she fell in love with Spanish cooking when she first visited the country 20 years ago. Since then, she has perfected her repertoire of Spanish classics.

SERVES 6 OR SO

1–2 tbsp oil
12 chicken pieces (leg or thigh) on the bone
1 cured chorizo sausage
1 large onion, finely chopped
3 garlic cloves, crushed
2 red peppers, sliced
2–3 red chillies, deseeded and chopped
(or use dried chillies to taste)
2 tsp smoked paprika
(use mild or dulce if you don't like hot spices!)
about 1.5 litres chicken stock
about 400g Spanish paella rice
handful of flat-leaf parsley
12 cleaned mussels or clams (optional)

Heat the oil in a large ovenproof pan or paella pan and fry the chicken pieces until nicely browned. Remove them from the pan and set aside.

Slice the chorizo into pieces about the size of a pound coin and fry them until they are crisp and the lovely juice is released into the pan. Add the onion and cook until soft, then the garlic and fry for another 2–3 minutes. Then add the red peppers, chillies and smoked paprika and cook for another 2–3 minutes.

Return the chicken pieces to the pan and pour in the stock. Simmer for 20–25 minutes until the chicken is tender. Add the rice to the pan, cover with a lid and place in the oven at 180°C/ Gas 4 for 30 minutes or until all the liquid has been absorbed and the rice is cooked. Alternatively, if using a paella pan, cover it with foil and continue cooking on the stove over a low heat as the pan probably won't fit in the oven! Sprinkle with parsley before bringing the pan to the table and let everyone dig in.

For an even more authentic dish, add a dozen or so cleaned mussels or clams to the pan for the last 20 minutes of the cooking time. Discard any that don't open.

CATALAN TOMATO BREAD

This is gorgeous with dry white wine or Fino sherry as an appetizer! The salt makes you want to drink more though so be careful! If you're not keen on tomatoes, leave them out – it's just as nice without them.

SERVES 6 OR SO

1 sourdough loaf (or similar dense bread)
3–4 garlic cloves, cut in half
2–3 fresh organic tomatoes, cut in half
extra virgin olive oil
sea salt flakes

Slice the bread and toast the slices on both sides. Then rub one side of each with a cut clove of garlic.

Next, rub the cut side of a tomato onto the garlicky side of each piece of toast to give a nice reddish colour. Arrange the toasts on a serving plate, drizzle them with olive oil and sprinkle with sea salt.

CHICKEN CHASSEUR

Throw away those jars of instant chasseur sauce and discover the real thing. This is a simple, classic recipe for chicken chasseur – or hunter's chicken – and makes a tasty supper on a winter's evening.

SERVES 4

3 tbsp plain flour
8 chicken thighs, skin on
3 tbsp mild olive oil or sunflower oil
3 banana (long) shallots, finely chopped,
plus 3 banana (long) shallots, quartered lengthways (6 shallots in total)
3–4 sprigs of fresh thyme or 1 tsp dried thyme
2 bay leaves
2 garlic cloves, finely chopped
300ml dry white wine
500ml chicken stock (fresh or made with a good-quality chicken stock cube)
2 tbsp tomato purée
150g chestnut mushrooms, wiped and halved
sea salt flakes
freshly ground black pepper

Put the flour in a large freezer bag and season it well with sea salt and black pepper. Drop the chicken thighs, 4 at a time, into the seasoned flour and shake them well until they are all lightly coated.

Heat 1 tablespoon of the oil in a large non-stick frying pan. Place the chicken thighs in the pan, skin-side down, and cook them over a medium-high heat for 4–5 minutes until golden brown. Turn over and cook on the other side for a further 2 minutes until golden. Transfer to a large flameproof casserole dish or saucepan.

Using the same frying pan, heat a second tablespoon of the oil and add all the shallots, a few sprigs of thyme, or the dried thyme, and the bay leaves. Fry over a medium heat for 5 minutes until soft, stirring regularly. Add the garlic and fry for a further 2–3 minutes until softened.

Tip the shallots, garlic and herbs into the pan with the chicken. Pour over the white wine and bring to the boil. Simmer for a few seconds, then add the chicken stock, tomato purée and plenty of seasoning and stir lightly. Bring to a gentle simmer and cook uncovered for 20 minutes – spoon off any fat that rises to the surface.

Meanwhile, wipe out the frying pan used to fry the shallots with a wad of kitchen paper. Place over a medium-high heat, add the remaining tablespoon of olive oil and fry the mushrooms for 2–3 minutes until lightly browned. Set them aside.

Once the chicken has been simmering for 20 minutes, stir in the mushrooms. Cook for a further 15 minutes, until the chicken is tender and the sauce is glossy and has reduced enough to lightly coat the back of a spoon. Adjust the seasoning to taste and serve.

Look out for long, banana, shallots as they make all the difference to the appearance of this dish. If you can't get hold of any, use 8 traditional shallots or 4 small onions instead. Chop half of them finely and cut the rest into halves or quarters, depending on size. If you avoid cutting through the root ends, the layers will stay together much better.

ESCABECHE OF PARTRIDGE

Conolly McCausland is a reminder that sometimes dads know best too! Conolly's mum is from Argentina and Conolly likes to cook dishes he has learned from her. In Argentina, the escabeche cooking method is used as a way of preserving meat or fish – escabeche means pickled in Spanish.

SERVES 5

5 partridges, cleaned
2 onions, chopped
4 carrots, cut into fine slices or matchsticks
1 tsp black peppercorns
3 bay leaves
4 garlic cloves, peeled
125ml white wine vinegar
75ml white wine
240ml olive or corn oil
4 slices of lemon
1 tbsp chopped flat-leaf parsley
salt and pepper

Put the partridges in a large, flameproof casserole dish. Add the onions, carrots, peppercorns, bay leaves, garlic, vinegar, wine and oil. Season with a pinch of salt.

Cover the casserole with a lid and simmer gently on top of the stove until the birds are cooked – this should take about 40 minutes. Ten minutes before they are due to be ready, add the slices of lemon.

Remove the pan from the heat, and leave the birds to cool in the liquid. Once the partridges are cold, carve them and serve with the escabeche vegetables, having removed the bay leaves and lemon slices. Sprinkle with parsley and pour over some of cooking liquid. Serve with crusty fresh bread to mop up juices.

EMPANADAS

The perfect portable meal – Argentinian style – and another of Conolly's favourites. If you don't want to make your own pastry, you can buy ready-made empanada wrappers in some delis or from Argentinian food suppliers on the internet. The quantity of pastry here is enough for about 12 empanadas.

MAKES ABOUT 12

EMPANADA PASTRY
450g plain flour
2 tsp baking powder
1 tsp salt
60g butter, diced
60g lard, diced

CRIOLLAS (MEAT FILLING)
2 tbsp olive oil
1 onion, finely chopped
1 green pepper, finely chopped
400g best beef, such as silverside or lean stewing beef, minced
1 tsp paprika
1 tsp chilli powder
30g raisins
12 green olives, pitted and chopped
2 hard-boiled eggs, chopped
1 tsp cumin
good pinch of salt
vegetable oil, for frying
1 tsp caster sugar

CHOCLO (SWEETCORN FILLING)
100g butter
3 spring onions, finely chopped
½ green pepper, finely chopped
1 x 340g can of choclo (sweetcorn)
about 250ml béchamel sauce
handful of chopped parsley
2 tbsp grated Parmesan cheese
pinch of chilli or cayenne pepper

Mix the flour, baking and salt in a bowl. Add the diced butter and lard and rub them into the flour with your fingertips until the mixture has the texture of fine breadcrumbs. Add enough cold water to form a soft dough. Put the dough in the fridge to rest for about an hour.

MEAT FILLING

Heat the oil in a frying pan, add the onion and fry until it is transparent. Add the green pepper and meat and sauté until the meat has browned, then add the paprika and chilli powder. Take the pan off the heat and add the raisins, olives, eggs, cumin and salt.

Roll out the pastry and cut out circles using a coffee saucer or a wine glass, depending on how big you want the empanadas. Put a small spoonful of filling onto one half of a pastry circle – not too much. Wet the edges of the pastry with a little water, fold the pastry over the filling and pleat the edges together or use a fork to mark the edges. Continue until you have used up all the filling.

Heat the oil in a large pan and fry the empanadas until golden. Sprinkle with caster sugar and serve warm.

CHOCLO (SWEETCORN) FILLING

Melt the butter in a frying pan and gently cook the spring onions. Add the green pepper, choclo and enough béchamel sauce to bind everything together, then cook over a medium heat for 3–4 minutes.

Remove the pan from the heat and add the parsley, grated cheese, a pinch of chilli or cayenne and some salt and pepper. Proceed in the same way as for meat empanadas above.

DUCK À L'ORANGE

A perfect supper for two. Traditionally, you use a whole duck, but our version is so much easier.
Use the delicious fat from the duck to make the best sautéed potatoes.

SERVES 2

2 fresh duck breasts
½ smallish onion, sliced into slim wedges
2 small garlic cloves, crushed
4 tbsp brandy
75ml red wine
finely grated zest of 1 large orange
freshly squeezed juice of 3 large oranges (about 175ml)
1 tsp cornflour
sea salt flakes
freshly ground black pepper

Preheat the oven to 180°C/Gas 4. Prick the duck skin a few times all over with a fork to allow the fat to run out while cooking. Season both sides of the duck with salt and pepper.

Heat a large non-stick frying pan over a medium heat. Add the duck breasts, skin-side down, and cook them for 5 minutes until the skin is golden brown. Turn the breasts over and cook on the other side for 3 minutes. Put the duck on a baking tray and finish cooking in the oven for a further 5 minutes.

While the duck is roasting, drain all but a tablespoon of the duck fat from the frying pan into a bowl. Return the pan to the heat and add the onion. Fry gently for 5 minutes, stirring regularly until softened and pale golden brown. Add the garlic for the last 2 minutes of the cooking time.

Remove the duck from the oven and leave to rest for 5 minutes. Pour the brandy into the pan with the softened onion and allow it to bubble for a few seconds. Add the red wine and simmer together for about a minute, stirring to lift any ducky sediment from the bottom of the pan.

Stir in the orange juice and zest, return to the boil and cook for 2–3 minutes or until the liquid has reduced by half. Mix the cornflour with 2 teaspoons of cold water in a small bowl until smooth. Stir into the orange sauce and cook for 1–2 minutes more, stirring regularly until the sauce is thickened and glossy.

Pour any juices that have collected from the resting duck into the sauce and simmer for a few seconds, while stirring. If you prefer a smooth sauce, strain it through a sieve into a jug before serving. Carve the duck into diagonal slices and serve on warmed plates with the sauce and some lovely veg.

Our timing is just right if you like your duck a little pink inside. If you prefer your meat well done, roast for 4 – 5 minutes longer.

CREAMY HADDOCK MORNAY

This recipe makes a great light meal for four people or a small starter for six. Serve just as it is for a starter or add a few new potatoes and some peas for a main course. If you like, you can add some cooked peeled prawns or scallops to the hot sauce. A few tiny lightly cooked broccoli florets or asparagus tips can also make a nice addition and because the gratins are grilled rather than baked, the vegetables should retain their colour.

SERVES 4–6

300ml whole milk
1 small onion, peeled and cut into 6 wedges
1 bay leaf
2 long strips of lemon peel
450g thick fresh haddock fillet (or other decent white fish with skin)
40g butter
25g plain flour
2 tbsp white wine or vermouth (optional)
50g Gruyère cheese, finely grated
½ tsp prepared English mustard
3 tbsp double cream
sea salt flakes
freshly ground black pepper

GRATIN TOPPING
25g fresh white breadcrumbs
15g Gruyère cheese, finely grated
½ tsp dried parsley

If you are preparing these ahead of time, cool, cover and chill before the topping is added. Instead of grilling, sprinkle the topping over the top and cook in a preheated oven at 220°C/Gas 7 for 12–15 minutes until golden brown and bubbling. ⟶

Place 4–6 small, shallow flameproof dishes on a baking tray. To make the gratin topping, mix the breadcrumbs, cheese and parsley and set aside while you make the filling.

Pour the milk into a large, deep frying pan and add the onion, bay leaf and lemon peel. Place the fish skin-side down in the pan and bring to a gentle simmer over a medium heat. Cook for 5–6 minutes, basting the fish occasionally with the milk until only just cooked. Leave to stand for 5 minutes. During the standing time the fish will continue to cook, so it is important not to simmer it for too long first.

Drain the fish in a colander over a large jug. Melt the butter in a large non-stick saucepan and stir in the flour with a wooden spoon until thoroughly combined. Slowly add the warm milk, stirring constantly over a medium heat. Bring the sauce to a simmer and continue stirring until it is smooth and thick. Stir in the wine or vermouth, if using, cheese, mustard and cream. Cook over a low heat for a further 2–3 minutes, while stirring. Season with salt and freshly ground black pepper to taste.

Flake the fish into chunky pieces and discard the skin, onion, bay leaf and lemon peel. Add the fish to the pan and heat very gently in the hot sauce for a couple of minutes to warm it through. Stir once or twice, but try not to break up the lovely chunks of fish too much.

While the fish is warming, preheat the grill to hot and place the baking tray with the shallow dishes under the heat to warm for a few seconds. Carefully remove them from the heat and divide the hot fish mixture between the warm dishes. Sprinkle with the breadcrumb mix and return to the grill for 3–5 minutes or until the tops are nicely browned.

SIMPLE CHICKEN CURRY

Helen Mills learned these recipes from her Guyanese dad, who met and married her mum in Northern Ireland, when he was in the RAF in the 1950s. Helen remembers how difficult it could be at that time to find some of the ingredients needed for her dad's favourite dishes – it's much easier now!

SERVES 4–6

1 medium chicken, jointed into 8 pieces
3 tbsp mild or hot curry powder, according to taste
2–3 tbsp vegetable oil
2 medium onions, sliced
2–3 garlic cloves, finely sliced
2 medium waxy potatoes, chopped
2 red chillies, deseeded and finely chopped
2 tbsp garam masala
600ml chicken stock
3–4 spring onions, to garnish

Rub the skin of the chicken pieces with 2 tablespoons of curry powder and leave them overnight to absorb the flavours.

Heat 2 tablespoons of oil in a pan and fry the chicken until well browned all over. Remove the chicken from the pan and set aside. Add a little more oil if needed, then fry the onions, garlic, potatoes and red chillies until the onions have softened. Put the chicken back in the pan and sprinkle over the remaining curry powder and 2 tablespoons of garam masala, then mix well. Add enough chicken stock to barely cover the ingredients, then bring to the boil. Simmer gently until the potatoes are cooked and the chicken is tender. Sprinkle with chopped spring onions and serve with boiled rice and roti.

ROTI

MAKES 6

225g self-raising flour
½ tsp salt
1 tbsp vegetable oil, plus extra for brushing and cooking the roti

Cooked roti can be frozen and reheated in a frying pan or wrapped in foil and heated in a warm oven for a few minutes.

Put the flour and salt in a large bowl. Sprinkle over the oil and add enough water to make a soft, but not sticky, dough – add more flour if needed. Knead gently and leave to rest for about 30 minutes if you have time.

Divide the dough into 6 pieces and roll each one into a thin circle, about the thickness of a 20 pence coin. Brush the bottom third with oil and fold it towards the middle. Repeat with the top third, then turn the roti a quarter turn clockwise and repeat this process. Leave to rest again if you have time.

Heat a little oil in a heavy-based pan. Roll out a roti thinly and fry on one side until it puffs up and is speckled brown. Turn it over and repeat. Remove from the heat, allow it to cool for a few seconds and clap corner to corner to separate the layers. Fold into 4 and wrap in a tea towel placed in a colander until ready to eat. Cook the rest in the same way and serve warm.

TOFFEE APPLES

To make really good toffee, you'll need a sugar thermometer. You'll need some
wooden lolly sticks too and you can buy these from cookware shops or even hobby shops.
If you like, use treacle instead of syrup to make treacle toffee apples. Yum, yum!

SERVES 6

6 medium apples
350g demerara sugar
100g golden syrup
35g butter
½ tsp ground mixed spice
1 cinnamon stick

Take great care to avoid splashing yourself with any of the molten toffee. It's mind-blowingly hot and it can cause very nasty burns. Best to keep the kids well away from the stove while you're making the toffee.

To prepare the apples for coating in toffee, scrub the skins well in warm water. Pat them dry with kitchen paper and remove the stalks. Push a wooden lolly stick firmly into each apple. Line a baking tray with baking parchment.

Put the sugar, golden syrup, butter, 150ml of water, spice and cinnamon stick into a medium saucepan, over a low heat. Stir occasionally until the sugar has completely dissolved. Place a clip-on sugar thermometer in the pan. The sugar syrup will be heated to an extremely high temperature, so don't be tempted to touch or taste from the pan at any stage.

Increase the heat under the pan to medium-high and bring the sugar syrup to the boil. Continue boiling for about 10 minutes, without stirring, then carefully remove the cinnamon stick with metal tongs. Leave the toffee boiling until it reaches just over 150°C or the hard crack stage on your thermometer.

If you don't have a thermometer, have a large mug of very cold water beside the hob. Drip a little hot toffee from a long-handled spoon into the water and it should form thin, brittle threads that harden immediately.

When the toffee is ready, stir once or twice with a long-handled wooden spoon. Remove from the heat and slightly tilt the pan so that the toffee runs to one side. One by one, turn the apples around in the toffee, making sure they are evenly coated on all sides. Slowly spin the apples above the toffee for a few seconds more until the toffee is no longer dripping. Place the apples on the prepared baking tray and leave them to set. The toffee coating should become hard fairly quickly and when cooled the apples can be wrapped loosely in cellophane and tied with pretty ribbons. Eat these the day you make them.

There is a growing community of Nepalese in Oxford, most of them ex-Gurkha soldiers and their families who have opted to settle in the area after their excellent service in the British Army. The aim of this organisation, established in 2006, is to promote, preserve and share traditional Nepalese culture, customs and values. This is one of the great recipes that the Community brought to our recipe fair.

LAMB CHHOEYLA
(NEPALESE GRILLED LAMB)

This is a classic Nepalese recipe that can also be made with chicken or pork.

SERVES 6

1.3kg boneless lamb chops
2 tbsp mustard oil

MARINADE
1 tbsp cumin powder
1 tsp turmeric
¼ tsp grated nutmeg
½ tsp timur (Szechwan pepper)
2 tbsp lemon juice
1 tbsp chilli paste
1 tbsp garlic paste
1 tbsp ginger paste
pinch of asafoetida
2 tbsp vegetable oil

CHHOEYLA SAUCE
1 tbsp cumin seeds, toasted
5 red chillies, cut into julienne strips
3 garlic cloves, halved
2.5cm piece of root ginger, sliced
pinch of asafoetida
½ tsp turmeric
1 tbsp vegetable oil

GARNISH
2 tbsp vegetable oil
1 tsp fenugreek
10 garlic cloves, thinly sliced
½ bunch of spring onions, chopped

Mix all the marinade ingredients together in a large bowl. Add the lamb chops and mix to coat them thoroughly. Set aside for 2 hours.

To make the sauce, place the cumin seeds, chillies, garlic, ginger, asafoetida and turmeric in a blender. Add the oil and a little salt and pepper, then blitz until you have a smooth paste.

Grill the meat on a barbecue until cooked through, then cut into small cubes.

In a bowl, mix the chhoeyla sauce with the meat. Slowly add the 2 tablespoons of mustard oil and toss well so that all the meat is well coated.

For the garnish, heat the oil in a non-stick pan and add the fenugreek. Fry until it turns dark, then add the garlic slices and fry until light brown. Pour this over the marinated meat, then add the spring onions and toss well. Serve with stir-fried vegetables and rice.

Posh nosh

DOUBLE CHEESE SOUFFLÉS

A punchy mixture of mature Cheddar and Gruyère makes these soufflés hard to beat. They're ideal for a dinner party as they can be prepared a day ahead and baked for 10 minutes just before serving.

SERVES 6

1 small onion, peeled and cut into wedges
275ml whole milk
1 bay leaf
40g butter, plus extra for greasing
40g plain flour
100g mature Cheddar cheese, coarsely grated
1 tsp English mustard or 2 tsp Dijon mustard
freshly grated nutmeg
3 large eggs
1 heaped tbsp chopped chives,
plus extra for garnish
50g Gruyère cheese or mature Cheddar,
finely grated
6 tbsp double cream
sea salt flakes
freshly ground black pepper

Butter 6 x 150ml ovenproof ramekins and line the bases with baking parchment. Place on a baking tray. Put the onion into a pan with the milk and bay leaf. Bring to a gentle simmer over a low heat and cook for 5 minutes. Watch carefully so it doesn't boil over. Take off the heat and set aside for a couple of minutes.

Preheat the oven to 200°C/Gas 6. Melt the butter in a medium non-stick saucepan over a low heat. Stir in the flour with a wooden spoon and cook for a minute or so, while stirring. Take off the heat. Strain the milk through a sieve into a jug and discard the onion and bay leaf. (You'll need around 250ml of infused milk.)

Return the butter and flour paste to the hob and gradually stir in the milk. Cook for 2 minutes, stirring constantly, until the sauce is smooth and thick. Add the Cheddar, mustard and a grating of nutmeg and cook for 1–2 minutes more until the cheese melts. Stir in the chives and season to taste. Transfer the cheese sauce to a heatproof bowl and leave to stand for 5 minutes.

Separate the eggs and, one at a time, stir the yolks into the cheese sauce until thoroughly mixed. Whisk the egg whites until stiff but not dry. Fold roughly a fifth of the egg whites into the cheese mixture with a large metal spoon, then gently fold in the rest. Spoon the soufflé mixture into the ramekins until it almost reaches the top. Bake in the centre of the oven for 20 minutes until very well risen and golden brown on top. Remove the tray from the oven and leave the soufflés to cool in the ramekins.

When the soufflés are cold, line a baking tray with baking parchment. Slide a knife around the edge of each ramekin and carefully turn the soufflés out onto your hand. Tip the right way up again and place on the tray. The soufflés can now be covered with clingfilm and chilled for up to 24 hours before baking.

Fifteen minutes before serving, preheat the oven to 200°C/Gas 6. Uncover the soufflés and sprinkle with the grated Gruyère. Spoon a tablespoon of double cream over each soufflé and allow to run down the sides. Bake for 10 minutes until hot and the cheese topping melts. Serve immediately.

LAMB CUTLETS IN PASTRY
WITH RED WINE GRAVY

A posh dinner that's much easier to make than it looks. Choose lovely British lamb, good-quality puff pastry and decent red wine and you can't go wrong.

SERVES 4

1 well-trimmed rack of lamb
or 8 lamb cutlets
1 tbsp sunflower oil
plain flour, for rolling
500g ready-made puff pastry
4 tsp mint jelly
1 egg, beaten
sea salt flakes
freshly ground black pepper

RED WINE GRAVY
150ml red wine
200ml lamb stock (made with
½ lamb stock cube)
1 tbsp redcurrant jelly
1 tsp cornflour

Put the rack of lamb on a board and cut into 8 cutlets. Season the cutlets all over with salt and pepper. Heat the oil in a large non-stick frying pan. Fry the cutlets in batches over a medium heat for 2 minutes on each side until nicely browned. Transfer to a plate and leave to cool.

To make the gravy, return the frying pan to the heat and pour in the red wine. Stir to lift the sticky sediment from the bottom of the pan. Bubble for 30 seconds or so, then add the lamb stock and redcurrant jelly. Bring to the boil and cook for 2–3 minutes or until the liquid has reduced by half.

Mix the cornflour with 2 teaspoons of cold water in a small bowl until smooth and stir into the frying pan. Stir in any juices from the lamb and cook the gravy for a minute more until thickened and glossy. Season and pour into a small pan. Set aside until you are ready to cook the cutlets.

Line a large baking tray with baking parchment. Sprinkle a light dusting of flour over a work surface and roll out the pastry until roughly 30 x 30cm square and about 3mm thick. Cut 8 squares, each measuring about 10–12cm, from the pastry – depending on the size of the cutlets.

Place half a teaspoon of mint jelly just off centre on each pastry square and put a cutlet on top, towards one of the corners. Brush the pastry edges lightly with the beaten egg and fold the remaining three corners of the pastry over the lamb. Wrap firmly around the meat, leaving the bone bare if possible. Turn the parcels over and place on the lined tray. The parcels can now be put in the fridge for a few hours or even overnight, if you like, until you are ready to bake them.

Preheat the oven to 200°C/Gas 6. Bake the cutlets for 20 minutes until risen and golden brown. Reheat the gravy until bubbling and simmer for a minute or two, while stirring. Check the seasoning and serve with the cutlets.

STUFFED MARROW
(ARABALI BILL MIMLI)

Avis Davies was born and brought up in Wales and has lived there all her life. But this family recipe is based on one that her children's grandmother picked up when living in Malta. Avis says that Arabali bill mimli is the family name for the dish and it was her first taste of Mediterranean ingredients, like garlic and tomato paste. She likes to serve this in summer while marrows are plentiful.

SERVES 4–6

1 medium marrow, cut in half
5 garlic cloves
3 tbsp chopped fresh thyme
3 tbsp olive oil, plus extra for brushing the marrow
2 large onions, roughly chopped
500g beef mince
2 tbsp tomato purée
2 tbsp sundried tomato paste
450g fresh tomatoes, peeled and chopped or 1 x 400g can of tomatoes
3 finely chopped tbsp fresh parsley, plus extra for serving
3 eggs, beaten
75g Parmesan cheese, grated, plus extra for serving
75g Pecorino cheese, grated
salt and black pepper

Bring a pan of lightly salted water to the boil – the pan needs to be large enough to hold the marrow. Scoop out the seeds and stringy pulp from the marrow and discard them. Then scoop out some of the flesh from the sides and reserve that for later – you need about 120g. Place the marrow in the pan of boiled water, then turn off the heat and leave it sitting in the hot water until you are ready to use it.

Crush the garlic and fresh thyme in a pestle and mortar and add salt and pepper. Chop up the reserved flesh from the marrow. Heat the olive oil in a pan, add the onions, garlic and thyme, then fry until soft. Add the mince and cook for about 10 minutes until nicely browned. Add the tomato purée and sundried tomato paste and cook for another 5 minutes. Stir in the tomatoes, chopped marrow and parsley and cook for about 10 minutes, stirring occasionally.

Take the sauce off the heat and let it cool slightly before stirring in the eggs – if the eggs are stirred in too soon they will scramble. Then add half the cheeses, stir well and cook for 5 minutes.

Line a baking tin with foil, allowing enough to wrap around the marrow. Preheat the oven to 180°C/Gas 4. Once the sauce is cooked, carefully take the two halves of marrow out of the hot water and place them in the baking tin. Spoon the sauce mixture into the marrow halves until they are full. Gently put the two halves together and brush the skin with olive oil. Sprinkle the rest of the grated cheeses over the top of the marrow. Wrap the marrow in the foil, leaving a gap at the top.

Bake in the preheated oven for about 45 minutes, then turn the oven up to 200°/Gas 6, open out the foil and cook for another 5 minutes so the cheesy top can crisp and brown – tastes wonderful. Take the marrow out of the oven and leave it for 10 minutes. To serve, cut the marrow into rings full of juicy sauce and sprinkle with extra Parmesan cheese and parsley.

Don't worry if some of the sauce spills over the edges when you're filling the marrow. It adds a lovely flavour to the dish.

BARA BRITH & BUTTER PUDDING
WITH RUM SAUCE

Avis told us that she loves making bara brith, a recipe which was resurrected by her son Dylan and given a rum twist. It's a joy to make in the winter as everything has to be kept warm – the basins, the flour, your hands and the room – and the smell of the loaf baking in the oven is wonderful. You have to start the night before by soaking the fruit in Earl Grey tea and a splash of dark rum. Bara brith makes a great bread and butter pudding and is also delicious served sliced and buttered for tea.

SERVES 6

225g dried fruit
Earl Grey tea
splash of dark rum (optional)
450g strong white flour
75g butter, at room temperature, plus extra for greasing the tin
1 packet of dried yeast
55g sugar
1 tsp of salt
2 tsp mixed spice
1 egg, beaten
500ml milk, warmed
1 tbsp honey, warmed

EXTRAS FOR BARA BRITH AND BUTTER PUDDING

600ml full fat milk
175g double cream
120g caster sugar
6 large eggs, beaten
1 vanilla pod, split and seeds removed
butter, for spreading
100g dried or fresh fruit
lemon zest
2 tbsp demerara sugar

RUM SAUCE

55g butter
55g plain flour
350ml whole milk
120ml double cream
75g caster sugar
3 tbsp rum

The night before making the bara brith, put the dried fruit in a bowl and add enough Earl Grey tea to cover it. Add the rum and soak overnight to make the fruit plump and succulent.

Put all the ingredients out in the kitchen so that they are at room temperature when you make the bara brith. Sift the flour into a warm bowl and rub in the butter with your fingertips until the mixture resembles breadcrumbs. Add the yeast, sugar, salt and spice and mix together.

Add the beaten egg and warmed milk and knead into the dry ingredients to make a dough. The dough should look smooth and come away from the sides of the bowl to form a ball – this should take about 20 minutes. Put the bowl in a warm place, sprinkle the dough with flour and cover with a damp tea towel. Leave for about an hour and a half, by which time the mixture should have doubled in size.

Then knock back the dough – this simply means punching the dough to get all the air out of it – add the dried fruit and mix it into the dough thoroughly. Shape the dough into a loaf and place it in a large buttered loaf tin. Cover again and leave to rise for about 30 minutes. Preheat the oven to 180°C/Gas 4.

Once risen, the dough should fill the loaf tin. Bake it in the preheated oven for 20 minutes. Take it out and brush with honey while still hot. Leave to cool slightly in the tin, then turn out onto a wire rack and glaze again with warm honey.

BARA BRITH AND BUTTER PUDDING

To make the custard, pour the milk, cream and sugar into a pan and heat almost to boiling point. Take the pan off the heat and let the mixture cool before adding the beaten eggs – if the mixture is too hot when you add the eggs, it will split. Stir until the mixture thickens slightly, then add the vanilla seeds.

Slice the bara brith, butter each piece and cut into triangles. Lay the slices in an ovenproof pudding dish. Sprinkle with dried fruit or fresh fruit and a little lemon zest if you like.

Preheat the oven to 180°C/Gas 4. Pour the custard mixture over the bara brith. Sprinkle the top of the pudding with demerara sugar. Bake for about 30 minutes, then serve hot with rum sauce.

To make the rum sauce, melt the butter in a small pan. Add the flour and work it into the butter mixture with a wooden spoon to make a smooth paste. Slowly add in the milk and cream stirring constantly until you have a thick creamy sauce. Stir in the sugar and let this cook into the sauce for about 5 minutes. Take off the heat and leave to cool before adding the rum.

When you pour the custard mixture over the bara brith, don't worry if it looks like a lot – the bara brith will soak it up.

BEEF OLIVES

This is a cracking recipe and it's two for the price of one, really – a bit of steak with a meatloaf filling. Try making Scottish beef olives too, replacing some of the beef and breadcrumbs with oatmeal.

SERVES 4

2½ tbsp sunflower oil
4 rindless smoked streaky bacon rashers, chopped fairly small
1 small onion, finely chopped
4 x 150g slices of topside beef
4 tsp prepared English mustard
250g sausage meat or minced pork
25g fresh white breadcrumbs
½ tsp dried mixed herbs
finely grated zest of ½ lemon
3 tbsp plain flour
15g butter
1 medium onion, finely sliced
200ml red wine
300ml beef stock (made with 1 beef stock cube)
1 tbsp tomato purée
1 bay leaf
sea salt flakes
freshly ground black pepper

Be careful not to tie the beef olives too tightly or the filling will bulge out as they cook.

Heat 1 tablespoon of the oil in a large non-stick frying pan. Add the chopped onion and bacon to the pan and fry gently until the onion is soft, stirring regularly. Remove from the heat, transfer to a bowl and set aside to cool for 15–20 minutes.

Put one of the slices of beef on a chopping board and cover with a sheet of clingfilm. Beat with a rolling pin until roughly the thickness of a £2 coin. Cut in half widthways and spread thinly with mustard. Put to one side. Repeat with the rest of the beef and mustard. Preheat the oven to 170°C/Gas 3.

Mix the onion and bacon with the sausage meat or pork mince, breadcrumbs, herbs and lemon zest and season well. Divide the stuffing between the beef slices, spreading evenly. Roll up each piece of beef, starting at the narrow end, to make 8 beef olives. Secure the rolls by tying each end with string.

Sift the flour onto a plate and season well with salt and pepper. Roll the beef olives in the flour until lightly coated. Melt the butter with a tablespoon of the remaining oil in a non-stick frying pan over a medium heat. Fry the beef olives, 4 at a time, until browned on all sides, turning regularly. Transfer to a flameproof casserole dish as soon as they are browned.

Return the frying pan to the heat and add the rest of the oil. Gently fry the sliced onion until softened and lightly browned, stirring regularly. Tip the onion into the casserole with the beef olives. Pour the wine into the frying pan and bubble for a few seconds, stirring to deglaze any juices and sediment from the bottom. Pour into the casserole and add the beef stock, tomato purée and bay leaf. Stir gently and bring to a simmer.

Cover the casserole with a lid and cook in the centre of the oven for about 1½ hours or until the beef is tender and the sauce is thickened and glossy. Turn the beef olives in the sauce halfway through the cooking time. Serve with potatoes and green vegetables.

ASPARAGUS & LEEK BLINTZES
WITH Y FENNI CHEESE

Ruth Joseph lives in Wales. Her mother, Judith, escaped Nazi Germany at the age of 12 and nostalgically taught Ruth all her recipes, which Ruth still cooks today. Blintzes are a type of pancake and she has given them a modern Welsh twist by using Y Fenni cheese.

SERVES 8–10

FILLING
1 tbsp butter
1 tbsp olive oil
250g leeks, washed and finely chopped
250g fresh asparagus

BLINTZES
400g plain flour
pinch of salt
800ml whole milk
4 organic free-range eggs
50ml olive oil
100g butter, melted
oil, for frying

CHEESE SAUCE
50g butter
50g flour
600ml milk, warm
150g Y Fenni cheese, grated

Start by making the filling. Heat the butter and oil in a pan, add the chopped leeks and cook gently until soft, taking care that they don't brown. Trim the woody ends off the asparagus and lay them on top of the leeks. Pour in 120ml of water, put a lid on the pan and cook the asparagus with the leeks for about 3 minutes.

To make the batter for the blintzes, sift the flour into a bowl and add the salt. Whisk the milk and eggs together, then mix them into the flour. Add the olive oil and melted butter and whisk well. Alternatively, you can put all the ingredients, except the oil for frying, in a food processor and mix. Pour the batter into a jug and leave to stand in the fridge.

To make the cheese sauce, melt the butter in a pan and stir in the flour. Slowly add the warm milk and cook for 10 minutes. Stir in the grated cheese and set aside.

Put a non-stick frying pan over a medium-high heat and brush the pan with oil. Pour a little batter into the pan and swirl around until the base of the pan is covered. Cook for 1–2 minutes, then flip over and cook for about a minute more. Put the pancake on a plate and continue until all the mixture is used up. Put sheets of baking parchment between each pancake so that they don't stick together. Preheat the oven to 180°C/Gas 4.

Now stuff the blintzes. Take one, add a spoonful of filling and a good tablespoon of cheese sauce, then roll it up neatly and place in an ovenproof dish. Continue until all the pancakes and filling are used up, then pour over the rest of the cheese sauce. Bake for 20 minutes until piping hot and golden on top.

ORCHID GATEAU

Ruth explained to us that she evolved this recipe for a yeast-based cake when she baked for the Orchid Room, a select restaurant that was at the top of a department store in Cardiff. When she bakes, Ruth is proud to use her mother's cake tin which she brought with her from Germany.

SERVES 10–12

DOUGH
300ml fresh milk,
1 vanilla pod, split and seeds scraped out
400g strong plain flour, plus extra for sprinkling
3 tsp dried yeast
3 tbsp soft brown sugar
4 large organic eggs, beaten
pinch of salt
grated zest of 1 lemon
grated zest of ½ orange
200g butter, softened, plus extra for greasing
natural pink colouring (optional)

SUGAR SYRUP
400g golden caster sugar
strained juice of 1 orange
good glug of Framboise

DECORATION
home-made strawberry jam or apricot jam with water for glazing
400g fresh strawberries
juice of ½ lemon
4 tbsp icing sugar
500ml whipping cream
fresh rose petals

Warm the milk gently with the vanilla seeds, just to body temperature. Pour it into a bowl and add 6 tablespoons of the flour, the yeast and the sugar. Leave in a warm place until the mixture is bubbling, then add the beaten eggs and the grated lemon and orange zest.

Put the remaining flour in a large mixing bowl with the salt, then pour in the milk and egg mixture. Add the softened butter and a drop of pink colouring and beat well until you have a sticky batter. Leave in a warm place to double in size.

Meanwhile, make the sugar syrup. Heat the sugar with the orange juice and 180ml water. Stir until the sugar is dissolved and add Framboise to taste.

Grease a 23cm cake tin and sprinkle with flour. Preheat the oven to 200°C/Gas 6. Check the cake batter and beat it for another minute, then pour it into the prepared cake tin and cover with a cloth. Leave until it has risen three-quarters of the way up the tin.

Place in the preheated oven and bake for 25–30 minutes until the cake is golden and luscious. Take the tin out of the oven and pour over the syrup, then leave to cool in the tin.

Once the cake is cold, cross your fingers and turn it out onto a plate. Warm a couple of spoonfuls of jam with a spoonful of water and brush this over the top of the cake to glaze. Mix the strawberries with the lemon juice and icing sugar and add them to the middle of the cake. Whip the cream and pipe it on top of the strawberries, then decorate the cake with more strawberries and cream. Sprinkle rose petals over and around the cake. Serve and enjoy!

ROAST LEG OF LAMB
WITH GARLIC, ANCHOVY & ROSEMARY

Britain has the best lamb in the world. There are more breeds than you can shake a crook at and all are great to eat. We always say that a roast leg of lamb makes every Sunday an event.

SERVES 4–6

1 x 2kg leg of lamb
2 fresh rosemary stalks
6–7 canned anchovy fillets in oil, drained (optional)
2 garlic cloves
1 medium onion, sliced
200ml red wine
1 tbsp redcurrant jelly
1 tbsp cornflour
½ lamb stock cube (optional)
sea salt flakes
freshly ground black pepper

If you prefer your lamb well done, cook for an extra 20 minutes and if you like your lamb fairly pink, cook for 20 minutes less.

For slow-roast lamb, wrap the leg in foil and cook at 160°C/Gas 3 for 4–5 hours, until the meat is falling off the bone. Turn the oven up to 200°C/Gas 6, remove the foil and cook the lamb for another 10 minutes to crisp the skin.

Preheat the oven to 190°C/Gas 5. Put the lamb on a board and use the tip of a knife to make 15–20 deep holes all over it. Take sprigs of rosemary off the stalks and cut each anchovy fillet, if using, into 3 pieces. Peel the garlic and cut into slivers. Between your thumb and forefinger, pinch a sprig of rosemary, a sliver of garlic and a piece of anchovy, then push this into one of the holes as far as it will go. Fill all the holes like this.

Put the sliced onion in a roasting tin and place the lamb on top, tucking the onion under the lamb as much as possible. (The onion will add colour and flavour to your gravy.) Season the lamb with salt and pepper. Roast for 1 hour and 15 minutes until the lamb is nicely browned.

Take the lamb out of the oven and, using an oven glove, tilt the pan and spoon off any fat that may have collected beneath it. Try to retain the dark cooking juices that will have seeped out of the lamb as these will be used to make the gravy. Pour the wine into the tin and cover with foil, pinching the foil around the edges of the tin to fully enclose the lamb. Return to the oven for a further 45 minutes for medium lamb. Uncover the lamb and put it on a warmed dish. Cover with the foil and a couple of tea towels and leave to rest for 15–20 minutes.

Spoon off any fat from the roasting tin, then put it on the hob and stir in 200ml water and redcurrant jelly. Bring to the boil, stirring constantly until the jelly melts and any flavoursome sediment is lifted from the bottom of the tin. Remove from the heat and pour though a sieve into a pan. Return the strained gravy to the hob and bring to a simmer. Discard the onion.

Mix the cornflour with 2 tablespoons of cold water in a bowl until smooth. Stir into the gravy, add the crumbled stock cube if using, and simmer for 2 minutes more until the gravy is thick and glossy. Season and keep on a low heat until the lamb has finished resting. Pour any juices that may have collected under the meat into the gravy and simmer for a minute or so more. Carve the lamb into slices and serve with the hot gravy.

BAKED WELSH CAKE CHEESECAKE

Derith Rhisiart likes to cook traditional Welsh dishes that she learned from her grandma, but she puts her own subtle twists on them. Here she makes Welsh cakes with cranberries and white chocolate instead of trad dried fruit and then makes them into an amazing cheesecake.

SERVES 8

WELSH CAKES

450g self-raising flour, plus extra for dusting
pinch of salt
120g lard
120g butter
120g caster sugar, plus extra for sprinkling on cooked cakes
50g white chocolate drops
75g dried cranberries, chopped
2 eggs, beaten
drop of milk, if needed

CHEESECAKE

12–14 digestive biscuits or 15 small shortbreads
50g Welsh butter
½ tsp cinnamon
½ tsp nutmeg
600g cream cheese
2 tbsp plain flour
175g caster sugar
3 drops of vanilla essence
2 eggs, plus 1 yolk
142ml soured cream
12 Welsh cakes, already cooked

Tip the flour into a large bowl and add the pinch of salt. Rub the lard and the butter together with the flour until the mixture resembles breadcrumbs. Stir in the caster sugar, then add the white chocolate and cranberries and mix well.

Add the eggs and mix with your hands until everything comes together – add a dash of milk if needed. Put the mixture on a floured surface and roll it out to a thickness of about 60mm. Cut out circles with a 5cm pastry cutter – this mixture should make about 50.

Grease a heavy frying pan or ideally a bakestone (no need to grease) and heat for 5–10 minutes on the hob. Reduce the heat and place the Welsh cakes into the hot pan and cook for about a minute or until golden brown. Turn over and cook for another minute, again until golden brown. Keep an eye on the heat to ensure that the temperature is not too hot or too cold. If too cold they will spread, if too hot, they will burn and cook on the outside too quickly. Keep repeating the process until they are firm. They will rise considerably. Place the cakes on sugared greaseproof paper and sprinkle with caster sugar.

CHEESECAKE

Preheat the oven to 180°C/Gas 4. Put the biscuits in a freezer bag and crush them with a rolling pin. Melt the butter in pan and mix in the crushed biscuits and spices. Press this mixture into a 23cm springform tin and bake for 5–10 minutes, then set aside to cool.

Whisk the cream cheese with the flour, sugar, vanilla essence, eggs and soured cream. Cut up 4 or 5 Welsh cakes into chunky bits and gently fold them into the mixture. Arrange enough of the rest of the Welsh cakes on the biscuit base until it is covered and then pour the cream mixture on top. Bake for 40 minutes – it should still be slightly wobbly in the centre. Leave to cool for a while in the tin and serve warm or cold.

FILLET STEAKS
STUFFED WITH GOAT'S CHEESE
WITH CANDIED SHALLOTS

We love this dish. The sticky, sweet shallots go really well with the cheesy surprise
at the centre of the steak and the bacon keeps the steaks nice and juicy.

SERVES 4

4 good, thick, centre-cut fillet steaks
150g soft goat's cheese
1 tsp finely chopped rosemary
zest of 1 lemon
1 garlic clove, crushed
4 rindless streaky bacon rashers
2 tbsp olive oil
sea salt flakes
cracked black pepper

CANDIED SHALLOTS

12 shallots
4 tbsp butter
1 tbsp caster sugar
75ml red wine
50ml port
50ml cassis
250ml good beef stock
1 bay leaf
½ tsp dried thyme
zest of half a lemon

Take the steaks out of the fridge an hour or so before cooking
so that they are at room temperature. Crumble the cheese into
a bowl, then add the rosemary, lemon zest and garlic.

Cut a pocket into each steak, taking care not to cut all the way
through. Place a quarter of the cheese stuffing into each pocket.
Close the flap, and wrap a rasher of bacon around the side of
each steak. Secure with a cocktail stick.

Rub olive oil over the steaks, then sprinkle with salt and pepper.
Cook in a hot frying pan until the steak is how you like it.
Brown the bacon on the edges just before you remove the
steaks from the pan. Allow them to rest for 5 minutes before
serving with the candied shallots.

CANDIED SHALLOTS

Bring a pan of water to the boil. Simmer the shallots in the
water for 5 minutes, then drain.

Heat the butter in a frying pan, add the shallots and cook until
brown. Add the sugar and stir until the butter starts to caramelise.

Mix the wine, port, cassis and stock in a jug. Add about a quarter
of this to the pan of shallots, bring to the boil, then add the bay
leaf, thyme and lemon zest. Keep adding the remaining liquid
until the shallots are just covered with a lovely sticky glaze,
then set aside until needed.

SLOW FOOD

Slow Food is an international movement, whose members believe in linking the pleasures of good food with a commitment to the environment. The aim is to encourage people to enjoy local, traditional foods that are produced to environmentally friendly standards – and that taste great. The recipe below is a good example and if you can pick the walnuts and fruit yourself – even better.

PIGEON WITH WALNUTS

This recipe can be varied to suit the season and what you have available. Use hazelnuts or Kent cobs instead of walnuts, or seasonal fruit, such as quince, apples or apricots. Soak these in the wine in the same way as the walnuts. Pigeon is best served pink so be careful not to overcook it.

SERVES 4

small handful of walnuts
sweet wine
4 pigeons
2 tbsp olive oil
sprig of fresh thyme
sea salt flakes
black pepper

The night before you want to cook this dish, put the walnuts in a bowl with sweet wine to cover. Leave to soak overnight.

To prepare the pigeons, place one on a chopping board with the breast uppermost and the head pointing away from you. Feel for the backbone and snip the skin with a pair of scissors. Peel off the skin, taking care to keep the feathers underneath. With a sharp knife, remove the breasts from the ribs, trying not to leave any meat behind. Wash the meat under a cool running tap and place on kitchen paper. The rest of the carcass should be skinned and used to make stock – throw the head and feet away. Prepare the rest of the pigeons in the same way.

Heat the olive oil in a large frying pan and add the thyme. Add the pigeon breasts and cook briefly to seal. Take the breasts out of the pan and cut into slices, taking care not to lose any of the cooking juices. Pour the walnuts and sweet wine into the frying pan, bring to boil and continue to cook until slightly reduced. Season, then add the slices of pigeon and any juices. Turn off the heat but leave on the pan on the stove. Cover the pan with a lid or some foil and leave to rest for 10 minutes.

Serve as a first course with bread for the juices or a main course with game chips.

Family
classics

DEEP-FILLED CHICKEN & MUSHROOM PIE

This classic pie has a shortcust pastry base, creamy chicken and mushroom filling and a light puff pastry crust. It's surprisingly easy to make and will go down a treat with all the family. You'll need a pie dish that will hold around 1.2 litres.

SERVES 6

50g butter
1 small onion, finely chopped
1 garlic clove, finely chopped
250g button mushrooms (ideally chestnut mushrooms), wiped and halved
6 boneless, skinless chicken thighs
1 bay leaf
2 tsp freshly chopped thyme leaves or
½ tsp dried thyme or mixed dried herbs
1 chicken stock cube
200ml just-boiled water
50g plain flour
200ml whole milk
4–5 tbsp double or single cream
(or milk if you don't have any cream handy)
2–3 tbsp white wine (optional)
sea salt flakes
freshly ground black pepper

SHORTCRUST PASTRY

200g plain flour, plus extra for rolling
good pinch of sea salt
125g cold butter, cut into cubes
1 large egg
1 tbsp whole or semi-skimmed milk

PUFF PASTRY

500g ready-made puff pastry
(thawed if frozen)

To make the filling, melt the butter in a large non-stick frying pan over a medium-high heat. Add the onion, garlic and mushrooms and fry for 4–6 minutes, stirring often until the onion and mushrooms are lightly browned. Cut the chicken into small bite-sized pieces, season with pepper and add them to the pan with the bay leaf and thyme leaves. Cook everything for 4–5 minutes until the meat is no longer pink, turning often. Dissolve the stock cube in the 200ml of just-boiled water.

Stir the flour into the chicken mixture and cook for a few seconds before slowly adding the milk. Gradually stir in the stock and bring to a gentle simmer. Cook for 2 minutes until the sauce is smooth and thick. Season to taste, remove from the heat and stir in the cream and wine, if using. Cover the pan with clingfilm to prevent a skin from forming and set aside to cool. Preheat the oven to 190°C/Gas 5.

To make the shortcrust pastry, put the flour in a food processor and add the salt. Drop the cubes of butter on top, then blitz on the pulse setting until the mixture resembles fine breadcrumbs. Whisk the egg with the milk and pour onto the flour and butter mixture with the motor running, reserving 2 tablespoons of the egg mixture for glazing the pastry. Continue blending until the dough begins to come together. Turn out onto a lightly floured board and knead quickly into a ball. Roll out to about 4mm thick and large enough to line your pie dish. Carefully lift the pastry over your pie dish, leaving any excess pastry overhanging the edge. Spoon the cooled chicken filling into the dish and brush the pastry edge with a little of the reserved beaten egg.

Place the puff pastry on a well-floured surface and roll out until it is about 4mm thick and large enough to cover the pie. Place the puff pastry over the pie and press the edges firmly together to seal and trim neatly. Brush the top of the pastry with the beaten egg. Decorate with any pastry trimmings and brush with more beaten egg to glaze. Bake for 40–45 minutes until the crust is puffed up and golden brown and the filling is piping hot.

SAMBHAR (LENTIL SOUP)
WITH VADA (SPICY DOUGHNUTS)

Padmaja is from Andhra Pradesh in southern India and has lived in the UK for 12 years. Before coming here, she says she couldn't cook at all, but being so far from home made her want to make her family recipes. Now she has a food blog and teaches her friends how to cook her recipes!

SERVES 6

SAMBHAR
200g toor dal (yellow lentils)
1 onion, chopped
1 green chilli, chopped
2 tomatoes, chopped
1 tsp chilli powder
¼ tsp turmeric
salt to taste

TEMPERING MIXTURE
1 tbsp sunflower oil
1 tsp black mustard seeds
1 tsp cumin seeds
2 fresh curry leaves
1 tbsp sambhar powder
4–5 tbsp tamarind juice
fresh coriander

VADA
200g black gram lentils
1 tbsp rice
1 onion, finely chopped
1 green chilli, finely chopped
pinch of sodium bicarbonate
450ml sunflower oil, for deep-frying
salt to taste

First make the soup. Rinse the dal and put it in a large pan with the onion, chilli, tomatoes and spices. Add 200ml water, bring to the boil and cook for about 30 minutes until the dal is soft. Add salt to taste and set aside.

To temper the lentils, heat the sunflower oil in a large pan and add the mustard seeds and cumin seeds. When they start spluttering, add the curry leaves and sambhar powder. Fry for a minute and then add the cooked dal mixture and the tamarind juice. Check the seasoning and boil for 5 minutes. Garnish with coriander leaves and serve with the spicy doughnuts.

VADA
Soak the lentils and rice in water for 1 hour, then drain. Put them into a food processor or blender with a tablespoon or so of water and blitz to a thick batter. Add the chopped onion and the chilli, bicarbonate and salt and mix well. Set aside.

Heat the sunflower oil in a deep-fat fryer to about 180°C. To shape the doughnuts, drop about 2 tablespoons of batter onto a piece of plastic that you have moistened with water. Press it down slightly, make a hole in the middle, then carefully drop it into the hot oil. Make and fry the doughnuts a few at a time until all the mixture is used up.

SPICY SOUTH INDIAN CHICKEN CURRY

This is one of Padmaja's dad's recipes. At home, he would cook the meat dishes and her mum would make the veggie ones. We loved this curry and we thought Padmaja's food was some of the most enjoyable we had when filming the 'Mums Know Best' series.

SERVES 4

2.5cm piece of fresh root ginger
3 garlic cloves
1 tbsp sunflower oil
1 onion, finely sliced
1 green chilli, sliced
2 chicken breasts, cut into small pieces
1 tsp chilli powder
¼ tsp turmeric
fresh coriander
salt to taste

MASALA PASTE
2.5cm piece of cinnamon stick
2 cardamom pods
2 cloves
1 tbsp white poppy seeds
2 tbsp coriander seeds
2 tbsp fresh coconut flesh

First make the masala paste. Grind all the ingredients together in a pestle and mortar until you have a fine paste.

Make a ginger and garlic paste by pounding the fresh ginger and garlic cloves in a pestle and mortar or by blitzing them in a small blender.

Heat the sunflower oil in a pan and fry the onion and chilli until softened. Add the masala paste and a tablespoon of the ginger and garlic paste and fry for 2–3 minutes. Now add the chicken pieces, chilli powder, turmeric and salt, cover the pan and cook for 5 minutes. Then add about 120ml of water and cook until the chicken is tender. Garnish with coriander leaves and serve with rice.

CHICKEN IN CREAMY TARRAGON SAUCE

You'll need a lidded frying pan or a wide flameproof casserole dish for making this, as the chicken breasts need to be fried until golden and then gently poached to make them extra succulent. Buy the best chicken you can afford for this dish.

SERVES 4

4 boneless chicken breasts, skin on
25g butter
1 tsp sunflower oil
1 small onion, finely chopped
1 garlic clove, finely chopped
100ml white wine
200ml chicken stock (fresh or made with ½ chicken stock cube)
small bunch (about 15g) of fresh tarragon, plus extra sprigs for garnish
150ml double cream
sea salt flakes
freshly ground black pepper

Season the chicken breasts with a little sea salt and plenty of freshly ground black pepper. Melt the butter with the oil in a large pan and fry the chicken, skin-side down, for 3 minutes over a medium-high heat until golden.

Turn the chicken over, reduce the heat and add the onion and garlic to the pan. Cook for 2–3 minutes, stirring regularly until the onion is softened and beginning to colour.

Pour the wine into the pan and let it bubble furiously for 30 seconds, then stir in the stock and 2 of the tarragon sprigs. Cover the pan with a lid and leave to simmer very gently for 10–12 minutes or until the chicken is just cooked.

Transfer the chicken to a warmed plate to rest and remove the tarragon sprigs from the pan. Turn up the heat and bring the cooking liquor to the boil. Cook for about 5 minutes or until the liquid has reduced by half. Strip the leaves from the remaining tarragon sprigs and chop them fairly small.

Stir the cream and tarragon into the pan and simmer for 2–3 minutes longer, stirring occasionally until the sauce is thick enough to coat the back of a spoon. Return the chicken breasts to the pan and heat through for a minute or so. Serve with green beans and new potatoes, garnished with small sprigs of tarragon if you like.

THE JONES BOYS' FAVOURITE CHICKEN & MUSHROOM CRUMBLE

Victoria Jones learned many of her recipes from her grandma and inherited her treasured cookery books and some of her kitchen equipment. This is a family favourite and a good filling meal, ideal for feeding Victoria's three hungry sons and their friends.

SERVES 6

4 chicken breasts, boned and skinned
4 chicken thighs, boned and skinned
1 tbsp olive oil
1 large onion, finely chopped
2 garlic cloves, crushed
250g chestnut mushrooms, sliced
5 smoked back bacon rashers, chopped
1 can of Batchelors condensed mushroom soup
150ml double or single cream
150ml chicken stock
freshly ground black pepper

CRUMBLE TOPPING
100g cold butter
200g plain flour
50g mature Cheddar cheese, grated
50g porridge oats

Cut the chicken breasts and thighs into bite-sized pieces. Heat the oil in a large pan, then add the onion and cook gently over a low heat until soft and lightly covered – this should take about 8 minutes. Add the crushed garlic and cook for another 2 minutes.

Turn up the heat, then add the mushrooms and bacon and fry until both are cooked through. Add the chicken, followed by the soup, cream and stock. Season with black pepper – the bacon should add enough salt. Stir, put a lid on the pan and simmer for 10–15 minutes or until the chicken is cooked.

Meanwhile, put all the ingredients for the crumble mixture in a food processor and pulse until well mixed. Alternatively, rub the butter into the flour with your fingertips until the mixture resembles breadcrumbs and then stir in the cheese and porridge oats.

Preheat the oven to 190°C/Gas 5. Once the chicken and mushroom mixture is cooked, tip it into an ovenproof dish and spread the crumble mixture over the top. Cook in the preheated oven for about 15 minutes until the crumble is crispy on top and the chicken sauce is bubbling up from underneath.

This recipe can be prepared up to 24 hours ahead and left in the fridge. It should then be cooked for about 30 minutes until the crumble is crispy on top and the sauce is bubbling.

You can also freeze the prepared crumble. Defrost thoroughly and cook in the preheated oven for about 30 minutes as before. Serve with potatoes and green vegetables or salad.

MUM'S EVERYDAY FISH PIE
WITH CHEESY MASH

We've given you the ultimate fish pie, now here's the everyday version, without all the palava – a good, quick family feast.

SERVES 4–5

400ml whole milk
1 small onion, thickly sliced
2 bay leaves
500g skinned thick white fish fillets, such as cod, haddock or pollock
40g butter
40g plain flour
150g frozen peas
200g large North Atlantic prawns, thawed if necessary and peeled
sea salt flakes
freshly ground black pepper

TOPPING

800g medium potatoes, peeled and cut into even-sized pieces
40g butter, cubed
3 tbsp milk
100g mature Cheddar cheese, grated

To make the filling, pour the milk into a large pan and add the sliced onion and bay leaves. Season with salt and pepper. Place the fish fillets in the pan and bring to a very gentle simmer, then cover and cook for 2 minutes. Remove from the heat and leave to stand and infuse for 20 minutes. Drain the fish through a colander into a bowl, then pour the milk into a jug.

Meanwhile, make the mash. Half fill a large saucepan with cold water. Add the potatoes and bring to the boil, then reduce the heat and simmer for 15 minutes or until the potatoes are soft. Drain the potatoes and return them to the pan, then mash with the butter, milk and three-quarters of the grated cheese. Season to taste. Preheat the oven to 200°C/Gas 6.

Now, finish the filling. Melt the butter in a medium saucepan and stir in the flour. Cook for a few seconds, then gradually add the infused milk, stirring over a medium heat for 3–4 minutes until the sauce is smooth and thick. Stir in the peas and season with salt and black pepper.

Spread a third of the sauce into the base of a 1.5 litre ovenproof dish. Scatter half the fish fillets over the sauce, breaking them into chunky pieces as you go and discarding the onion and bay leaves. Drop half the prawns on top and pour over another third of the sauce. Continue with the layers and finish with the final third of sauce.

Spoon the potato over the fish mixture, then fork the surface and sprinkle with the remaining cheese. Place the dish on a baking tray and bake in the centre of the oven for about 25 minutes or until the top is golden and the filling is bubbling.

It's important to layer the fish pie up like this so the fish remains in good chunky pieces.

BASIC PASTA SAUCE

Rosita Minichiello's parents are Italian and Rosita learned her cooking skills from her mum. As a child, she believed her mother had special flavour in her hands and that was why her food tasted good!

MAKES ENOUGH FOR 1.5KG OF PASTA

5 tbsp olive oil
1 medium white onion, peeled
1 celery stick, washed
1 carrot, scrubbed
1 clove of garlic, peeled
500g beef bones (optional)
3 rounded dsrtsp tomato purée
4 x 400g cans of plum tomatoes in rich tomato sauce
1 x 680g jar of tomato passata
2 tsp sea salt flakes
1 bouquet garni (optional)
2 bay leaves (optional)
50ml Marsala wine
splash of balsamic vinegar
15–20 basil leaves, washed and torn
salt and pepper

Heat the oil in a large heavy pan and add the whole onion, celery stick, carrot and garlic clove, with the beef bones, if using. Allow everything to brown. When the bones and vegetables have taken on a good colour, add the tomato purée, canned tomatoes and passata. Fill the tomato cans with water and add that to the pan too. Add salt and the herbs, if using.

Bring to the boil and cover the pan with a heavy lid. Reduce the heat so that the sauce just turns over at a simmer. Leave to cook for at least 2 hours but ideally for 4–5 hours. When the fat on the top of the sauce looks dark, you know it is ready. Stir the sauce occasionally while it cooks and as it reduces, top it up from a kettle of boiling water and allow it to reduce again.

After the final reduction, remove the bones, vegetables, bouquet garni and bay leaves. Add the Marsala, balsamic vinegar and basil leaves. Check the seasoning and add salt and pepper if needed, then the sauce is ready.

EVERYDAY MINESTRA

This is an everyday minestra (veg dish) made by Gerarda, Rosita's mum. She used cabbage, spinach, spring greens, kale – whatever was available – but a favourite was endive, which she called scarole.

SERVES 4

1 large bag of fresh greens
glug of extra virgin olive oil
splash of balsamic vinegar
2 garlic cloves, thinly sliced
salt and pepper

Wash the greens in a couple of changes of water and put them into a large pan with some boiling, salted water. Stir the leaves to get them wilting in the hot water. Cook for a few minutes until ready – endive or spinach will only need a minute or two but cabbage will take longer. Refresh the leaves in cold water to stop them cooking.

In a serving bowl, mix a good glug of good olive oil with a splash of balsamic and the garlic, then season to taste. Drain the greens and then squeeze in handfuls until most of the water is gone. Cut or tear the leaves into smaller pieces. Add the greens to the dressing and mix well, lifting the leaves with a couple of forks. Serve while still just warm.

GERARDA MINICHIELLO'S MEATBALLS

Rosita's mum has never officially given her this recipe. She's had to work it out for herself!

MAKES ABOUT 30

100g sourdough bread
(preferably with no added yeast)
6 sprigs of thyme
12 sage leaves
24 mint leaves
24 flat-leaf parsley leaves
5 garlic cloves, finely chopped
100g pine nuts, toasted in a heavy pan
150g raisins
3 large eggs
Worcestershire sauce (optional)
100g Pecorino cheese, grated
500g minced lamb
500g minced beef
sunflower oil or vegetable oil, for frying
salt and pepper

Soak the sourdough bread in warm water for 2–3 minutes. Remove it and squeeze out as much water as you can, then set aside. Chop all the herbs together and mix with the garlic and toasted pine nuts. Soak the raisins in warm water for 5–10 minutes to plump them up, then drain.

Beat the eggs in a large mixing bowl and add salt and pepper and a good splash of Worcestershire sauce, if using. Add the garlic, herbs, pine nuts and grated cheese and mix well.

Break the soaked bread into small pieces and add this with the raisins to the egg mix. With very clean hands, mix in the meats and work until smooth. Use a dessertspoon to shape the mixture into balls and set these on a plate ready for frying.

Pour the oil into a heavy frying pan to a depth of about 0.5cm. Fry the meatballs, about 10 at a time, until brown, turning them several times to make sure they are browned all over.

As each batch is cooked, add them to the simmering tomato sauce (see opposite), from which the bones and veg have been removed. Once the final batch of meatballs have been added, cook them all in the sauce for another 35 minutes. Remove the meatballs to a warm dish. Serve the sauce poured onto the pasta and the meatballs on the side.

SCAPECE

This is another vegetable dish from Rosita. This was something she says she and her siblings would fight over as children. It was special as it could only be made with the very first, young, courgettes.

SERVES 4

sunflower oil, for frying
6 small to medium courgettes
2 garlic cloves, finely sliced
8 fresh mint leaves (from the garden or double if using supermarket mint), torn
6 tbsp red wine vinegar
sea salt and freshly ground black pepper

Pour the oil into a heavy frying pan to a depth of about 1cm. Cut the courgettes into slices 2–4mm thick and arrange them in a single layer. Cook until they brown, then turn them over to brown the other side. Remove and drain on kitchen paper.

Mix the remaining ingredients in a bowl, then add the cooked courgettes. Stir carefully, then cover with clingfilm. Leave for at least 4 hours or overnight if you can. Serve on good chewy bread drizzled with some olive oil and an extra grinding of salt.

ITALIAN PEAR & CHOCOLATE CAKE

Rosita has a pear tree in her garden and used some of her crop to make us
this amazing cake, traditionally served at Italian birthday parties.

SERVES 8

6 large eggs
2 tsp vanilla extract
(depending on the quality – some
are much stronger than others)
200g caster sugar
200g plain flour (preferably '00')
1 tsp baking powder
pinch of salt
cocoa powder, to serve
icing sugar, to serve

LEMON & CHOCOLATE SAUCES
grated zest and juice of 1 lemon
1 litre milk
125g flour
300g caster sugar
2 tsp vanilla extract
2 large eggs
150g dark chocolate, broken into pieces

POACHED PEARS
3 pears
slice of lemon
200g sugar
3–4 dsrtsp Amaretto
3–4 dsrtsp fresh lemon juice

Preheat the oven to 180°C/Gas 4. Grease and line a 25–30cm
cake tin. Put the eggs, vanilla and sugar in a bowl and place
over a pan of simmering water. Whisk until the mixture is
really thick – almost like a mousse. Remove from the heat.

Mix the flour with the baking powder and salt and sift into the
egg mixture. Using a slotted spoon, fold the flour into the egg.
Pour the mixture into the prepared tin and level the surface. Bake
in the lower part of the preheated oven for 15–20 minutes. It
should not wobble when done. Cool in the tin for 10 minutes, then
carefully transfer to a wire rack to cool completely.

LEMON AND CHOCOLATE SAUCES

Put the grated lemon zest and juice in a pan with 50ml of water.
Bring to the boil and reduce to a few spoonfuls, then pour into
a bowl and set aside.

Heat the milk until it is at the point of boiling. In a separate bowl,
mix the flour, sugar and vanilla with the eggs until creamy. Pour
the hot milk onto the egg mix and whisk. Quickly wash the
milk pan, then pour the milk and egg mixture into the clean
pan and bring to the boil while whisking constantly. Allow to
cook for a minute or two.

Pour half the sauce onto the lemon reduction and mix well. Add
the chocolate to the remaining sauce and mix until the chocolate
is melted by the warmth of the sauce and amalgamated. It is
best to stand the pans of sauce in a sink of cold water to cool –
that way they won't form a skin.

POACHED PEARS

Peel the pears, cut them in half lengthways and remove the seeds
and cores. Pour 500ml of water into a pan and add a slice of
lemon and the sugar. Bring to the boil. Add the pears and cook
gently for about 20 minutes or until slightly translucent – some
pears may take longer than this. Remove the pears and leave
them to cool. Slice thinly.

*Conference or other firm-
fleshed pears that cook
well are best for this cake.*

Remove the lemon slice from the sugar stock and discard. Then divide the stock between two cups. Mix the Amaretto into one cup and the lemon juice into the other.

ASSEMBLING THE CAKE

Cut the cake into 3 layers. Place the bottom layer onto a serving plate. Spoon on enough of the Amaretto stock to moisten the cake but don't let it get soggy. Carefully spread the cooled chocolate sauce on top – you may not need all of it – then add the sliced pears. Cover with another layer of cake, soak with the lemon stock and add the lemon sauce (again, you may not need all of it).

Add the final layer of cake and soak with some more of whichever stock you prefer and some of the remaining sauce. If you finish with the lemon sauce, sift a little cocoa powder on top. If you finish with the chocolate sauce, sift a little icing sugar on top. Pop into the fridge for about 2 hours and then the cake is ready to serve.

JAM ROLY POLY PUDDING

A much-mutilated version of this often appears in school dinners. Just have a go at making your own and you'll realise it's a great classic pud. In Si's house, jam roly poly is known as jam splat.

SERVES 6

softened butter, for greasing
200g self-raising flour, plus extra
for dusting
100g shredded suet
1 tbsp caster sugar
good pinch of fine sea salt
150ml semi-skimmed milk or water
6–7 tbsp raspberry or strawberry jam

If you're feeding vegetarians, make this with vegetable suet.

Preheat the oven to 200°C/Gas 6. Butter a sheet of baking parchment, about 38 x 38cm in size, and set aside. Bring a kettle of water to the boil and set a low rack in a smallish roasting tin.

Put the flour, suet, sugar and salt in a large bowl and mix well. Slowly add the milk or water, stirring constantly with a wooden spoon until the mixture forms a soft, spongy dough. Gather the dough and knead it lightly on a floured surface. Roll the dough out into a rectangle roughly 22 x 32cm.

Drop the jam in large spoonfuls onto the dough, leaving a 1.5cm border all the way round the outside. Gently roll up the dough from one of the short ends and carefully transfer it to the baking parchment, seam-side down. Wrap the roly poly in the parchment, making a long pleat in the parchment to allow the pudding to expand as it cooks.

Twist the ends of the parchment like a Christmas cracker to seal the pudding inside and tie tightly with kitchen string. Do the same with a large sheet of foil, making a pleat and twisting the ends to seal. Place the wrapped pudding on the rack in the roasting tin and pour just-boiled water around it. The water should not rise more than a centimetre up the sides of the pudding. Carry the tin very carefully to the oven and bake for 35 minutes.

Remove the tin and carefully lift the pudding off the rack. Unwrap the foil, then snip the string and unwrap the paper. The pudding should be well risen and lightly browned in places. Don't worry if the jam has made its way through to the outside of the pudding a little – it will taste all the more delicious. Put on a board or serving plate and cut into thick slices. Serve with lots of hot custard (see page 211) or cream.

EVE'S PUDDING

**Adam wouldn't stand a chance if tempted by Eve with this apple delight –
nor would any hungry Hairy Biker. Bring it on!**

SERVES 6

3 medium cooking apples
(roughly 600g unpeeled weight),
peeled, cored and roughly chopped
65g golden caster sugar
½ tsp ground cinnamon
juice and finely grated zest of
1 unwaxed lemon

SPONGE TOPPING

115g softened butter,
plus extra for greasing
115g golden caster sugar, plus 1 tbsp
2 large eggs, lightly beaten
½ tsp vanilla extract
125g self-raising flour
3 tbsp flaked almonds (optional)

VANILLA CUSTARD

2 large free-range egg yolks
2 heaped tsp cornflour
25g caster sugar
1 vanilla pod, split, or
½ tsp vanilla extract
250ml whole milk
250ml double cream

Preheat the oven to 180°C/Gas 4. Butter a 1.2 litre pie dish. Put the apples, sugar, cinnamon, lemon juice and zest in the pie dish and toss everything together well.

To make the topping, put the butter in a bowl with the 115g sugar. Using an electric whisk, cream the butter and sugar until light and fluffy. Gradually add half the beaten eggs, whisking well between each addition. Add the vanilla extract, then half the flour and beat well. Whisk in the rest of the eggs and fold in the remaining flour until smooth.

Spoon the cake batter on top of the apples and spread to the sides of the dish. Sprinkle with the remaining tablespoon of caster sugar and the almonds, if using. Bake the pudding in the centre of the oven for 40–45 minutes until the sponge is well-risen and golden brown. Serve hot with cream or home-made custard, sprinkled with a little extra sugar if you like.

VANILLA CUSTARD

Put the egg yolks in a medium saucepan with the cornflour and sugar. Scrape the vanilla seeds into the pan, or add the vanilla extract, and use a metal whisk to combine all the ingredients. Gradually whisk in the milk and cream.

Put the pan over a low heat and cook gently for 6–8 minutes, whisking constantly until the custard is smooth and thick. Do not allow it to overheat.

FRUITY MILK JELLY

A kids' favourite that was popular with lots of mums in the 1970s. You can either make it with normal whole milk or evaporated milk. Both work well, but the evaporated milk version tastes slightly creamier. Make sure you cool the jelly for a few minutes before stirring in the milk, as it will be less likely to separate.

SERVES 4–6

1 x 135g packet of orange or strawberry flavour jelly
1 x 410g can of fruit cocktail in syrup or juice
400ml whole milk or
1 x 410g can of evaporated milk

Break the jelly into cubes and put it in a measuring jug. Pour over enough just-boiled water to bring the liquid up to the 200ml mark. Stir well with a fork until all the jelly dissolves. Set aside to cool for about 5 minutes.

Drain the fruit cocktail, discard the liquid and put the fruit into a jelly mould. Stir the fresh or evaporated milk into the jelly until well combined – you'll feel it begin to thicken as you stir – then gently pour this on top of the fruit. Put the jelly in the fridge and chill until set. This will take about 4–6 hours.

ZIMWOMEN ASSOCIATION, NORTHAMPTONSHIRE

The Zimwomen Association was formed in 2009 to promote cultural identity and positive images of African women in the UK and to provide advice, social and cultural activities, education and training. The aim is to empower women, young people and children for a better today and tomorrow. Based in Northampton, the group was started by women from Zimbabwe but now includes members from many countries. Here are some favourite recipes from the group.

MANYATI'S VEGGIE CHILLI

SERVES 4

3 tbsp olive oil
1 small onion, chopped
2 carrots, diced
½ red, yellow and green pepper
100g green beans, chopped
2 tomatoes, chopped
3–4 chillies, chopped
salt and pepper

Heat the oil in a large pan and gently fry the onion. Add the carrots, peppers and green beans and fry briefly. Add the tomatoes, stir in the chillies and then simmer until cooked to your liking. Season to taste and serve hot or cold. If you have leftovers, this keeps well in the fridge for up to 3 days.

PEANUT BUTTER VEGETABLES

SERVES 4

¼ small cabbage (or any vegetable in season), thinly cut
1 small onion, chopped
1 tomato, chopped
4 tbsp peanut butter
salt and pepper to taste

Pour about 120ml of water into a pan and bring to the boil. Add the cabbage and cook until softened but still crunchy. Then add the onion and tomato and season to taste. Stir in the peanut butter, adding more water if the mixture seems too thick. Season and serve with sadza (see below).

SADZA

SERVES 4

375g white cornmeal (mealie meal)

Mix 225g of cornmeal with 250ml of water. Bring 750ml of water to the boil in a pan, then turn down the heat and add the cornmeal mixture, stirring all the time. Cook for 5 minutes, then slowly add the rest of the cornmeal until the mixture is thick. Transfer to a bowl or plate and shape into a round with a wooden spoon.

k

kale
> Everyday minestra *412*

Karen's plum chocolates *273*

Kaur, Harjinder *87, 88, 90, 94*

Kedgeree *91*

Key lime pie *169*

kidney beans
> Chilli con carne *19*
>
> Piccalilli *82*
>
> Rice & peas *118, 349*

kidneys
> Devilled kidneys *306*
>
> Steak & kidney pudding *32-3*

King, Rachel *45*

Kirkland, Barry *19*

Kirkland, Maureen *16, 19, 20*

Kochera, Padmaja *403, 404*

Koubebia *128-9*

Kringel *60*
> Cheese kringel *60*

Kroketten *288-9*

l

lamb
> Gerarda Minichiello's meatballs *413*
>
> Lamb chhoeyla (Nepalese grilled lamb) *373*
>
> Lamb cutlets in pastry with red wine gravy *379*
>
> Nargis kebabs *196*
>
> Roast leg of lamb with garlic, anchovy & rosemary *391*
>
> Shepherd's pie *see* Cottage pie
>
> *see also* mutton

Lane, Heather *199, 201*

Langford, Yvonne *136, 139*

leeks

Asparagus & leek blintzes with Y Fenni cheese *386*

Boiled leek & onion pudding (with cold cuts & gravy) *31*

Lemonade, Homemade *269*

lemons
> Home-made lemonade *269*
>
> Home-made lemon curd *345*
>
> Lemon butter icing *346*
>
> Lemon drizzle cake *39*
>
> Lemon, ginger & blueberry flan *48*
>
> Lemon meringue pie *160*
>
> Lemon sauce *416*
>
> Lemon soufflé *54*
>
> Luscious lemon Swiss roll *346*
>
> *see also* Butterfly cakes

lentils
> Rumpy-pumpy soup *20*
>
> Sambhar (lentil soup) with vada (spicy doughnuts) *403*

Lift Community Trust, Birmingham *349*

Lil's chicken Kiev with cucumber & spring onion salad *249*

Lil's pretzels *74*

limes
> Key lime pie *169*

Liver & bacon with onions & gravy *286*

Lobster cocktail *see* Prawn cocktail

Luscious lemon Swiss roll *346*

m

Macaroni cheese *278*

Macaroons, Yorkshire *338*

McCausland, Conolly *360, 362*

Macfarlane, Abi *272*

Mama's curry *226*

Manchester tart *139*

Manyati's veggie chilli *425*

Margaret, Princess *54*

marrow

Roast saddle of venison *176-7*
Victoria sandwich *201*
Vine leaves, Stuffed (Dolmades/Koubebia) *128-9*
Vinson, Julia *162, 165, 166*

walnuts
  Coffee & walnut sponge *321*
  Pigeon with walnuts *396*
Welsh cakes *285, 392*
  Baked Welsh cake cheesecake *392*
Welsh griddle cakes *143*
Welsh rarebit *333*
West African Ghanaian Community Group *76, 77*
Wilson, Elaine *305*
Wilson, Jean *305*
Women's Institute (WI)
  Lemon, ginger & blueberry flan *48*
  Scones *49*
Woodcock, Bridget *205, 206*
Woodcock, Jennie *205, 206*

yam
  Saturday soup *122*
  Yam balls *77*
Yellow split pea & ham soup *20*
yoghurt
  Chana chaat *193*
  Minty yoghurt sauce *87*
  Scones *49*
  Yoghurt boondi *91*
Yorkshire macaroons *338*
Yorkshire pudding *151*
Yummy biscuits *201*

Z

Zimwomen Association, Northamptonshire *425*

Acknowledgments

First and foremost, we'd like to thank the mums, dads and families who appear in the programmes and provided recipes for this book: Aida and Victoria, Anjie, Avis, Bridget, Connie and Charlotte, Conolly, Dee, Derith, Eele, Elaine, Fiona and Sybil, Gameelah, Harjinder, Heather, Helen, Ira, Jayne, Jeni, Jennie and Georgia, Jenny, Julia, Karen, Lisa, Leonie and Susan, Marika, Mariken, Mary, Maureen, Muriel, Nancy, Padmaja, Polly, Rebecca, Rosalyn, Rosita, Ruth Joseph, Ruth Sutcliffe, Susan and Peter, Tessa, Victoria, Yasmeen and Yvonne. Huge thanks to you all for letting us into your homes and hearts and sharing your family culinary secrets.

At the recipe fairs we'd also like to thank the various community groups who fed and supported us – the WI, Chinese Older People's Group, the Gurkhas, the Bradford Curry Project, the West African Ghanaian Community Group, the African and African Caribbean Community Group, the Bath Place Community Venture, Studley Grow, Cook and Eat, the African Women's Group, Growing Together (St George's Community Hub), Lift Community Trust, Nepalese Community Oxfordshire, Slow Food and the Zimwomen Association. Thanks must also go to more than a thousand mums and families who turned up with their treasures at our fairs. Without them none of this would have been possible. And many thanks to our mate Gerard Baker, to Toti Gifford and his magical circus folks, and to Claire Bassano, Rupinda Ashworth, Nikki Morgan and Kylie Morris.

Back at the Mailbox mothership, huge thanks to Nick Patten, head of studio BBC Birmingham, Gill Tierney, our executive producer, and editors Simon Prentice, Dan Wardle, Steve Killick, Andrew McKenzie, James Cole, Louise Pearson, Martin Sage, Ant Smith, Kate Davis and Benedict Peissel.

Special thanks to our old friend and colleague from Hairy Baker days Oliver Clark, series producer, and our directors Duncan Barnes, Becky Pratt, Dan Slee, Joanna Brame and Francois Gandolfi.

On the road, we'd like to thank our production manager Sarah Greene, researchers Stu Small, Leila Finikarides, Joe Barrett, Jean Campbell and Keaton Stone, and production coordinators Sarah Reddi, Rachel Holden, Ella Gutteridge and Alison Davy. Also thanks to our great cameramen Roger Laxon, Will Hutchinson, Craig Jones, Jon Boast, Stu Dunn, Adrian Croome and Tom Slee for making us look presentable, and to our sound men Gary Goodhand, Ryan Patton, Paul Miller, James Baker, Mark Skilton, Paul Scurrell and Andy Morton. Thanks also to Tim Jones, Max Beats, Joe Barrett, Dan Slee, Avone Keene, Andy Darbyshire and Anton Inwood and everyone else involved in making the programmes happen.

Last but not least, we owe a huge debt of gratitude to our home economist and good friend Sammy-Jo Squire.

Thanks, too, to MOTO-GUZZI, Alan Jones, Derek Crutchlow, Phil Read and Mark Hemmingway for help with our lovely bikes.

Nancy

Ruth Sutcliffe

Lisa

Polly

Ruth Joseph

Helen

Mary

Anjie

Padmaja

Rebecca

Karen